JOURNAL

OF

SOVIET AND POST-SOVIET

POLITICS AND SOCIETY

Vol. 4, No. 1 (2018)

Identity Clashes:

Russian and Ukrainian Debates

on Culture, History, and Politics

JSPPS 4:1 (2018)

GENERAL EDITOR AND ISSUE EDITOR-IN-CHIEF:

Julie Fedor, University of Melbourne

GUEST EDITORS:

Andrey Makarychev, University of Tartu

Nina Rozhanovskaya, Kennan Institute, Wilson Center

JSPPS Editorial Team

Julie Fedor, *University of Melbourne* (General Editor)
Andrey Makarychev, *University of Tartu* (Editor)
Andreas Umland, *Institute for Euro-Atlantic Cooperation, Kyiv* (Consulting Editor)
Gergana Dimova, *University of Winchester* (Reviews Editor)

JSPPS Advisory Board

Bibliographic information published by the Deutsche Nationalbibliothek

The Deutsche Nationalbibliothek lists this publication in the Deutsche Nationalbibliografie; detailed bibliographic data are available on the Internet at http://dnb.dnb.de.

Bibliografische Information der Deutschen Nationalbibliothek

Die Deutsche Nationalbibliothek verzeichnet diese Publikation in der Deutschen Nationalbibliografie; detaillierte bibliografische Daten sind im Internet über http://dnb.d-nb.de abrufbar.

Cover picture: Ukrainian and Russian coin displaying Crimea.
Source: Wikimedia Commons. Public Domain.

Journal of Soviet and Post-Soviet Politics and Society Vol. 4, No. 1 (2018)

Stuttgart: *ibidem*-Verlag / *ibidem* Press

Erscheinungsweise: halbjährlich / Frequency: biannual

ISSN 2364-5334

Ordering Information:

PRINT: Subscription (two copies per year): € 58.00 / year (+ S&H: € 4.00 / year within Germany, € 7.00 / year international). The subscription can be canceled at any time.

Single copy or back issue: € 34.00 / copy (+ S&H: € 2.00 within Germany, € 3.50 international).

E-BOOK: Individual copy or back issue: € 19.99 / copy. Available via amazon.com or google.books.
For further information please visit www.jspps.eu

CONTENTS

Introduction

Andrey Makarychev, Nina Rozhanovskaya

The annexation of Crimea and the war in the Donbas, apart from their evident geopolitical and security repercussions, have also led to the almost total disruption of communication between the Russian and Ukrainian societies, including the academic communities of the two countries. Predictably, professional contacts between academics and policy experts have become scarce and sparse in the wake of these events, and this in turn has only widened the political gap between Moscow and Kyiv.

Against this gloomy backdrop, the annual conferences of Ukrainian and Russian (and, since 2017, also American) alumni of the Kennan Institute stand out as an exceptional practice aimed at sustaining the academic dialogue that has been severely damaged by the current crisis.[1] It was within this format of interaction that the idea of this special section was born. During the 2016 Kennan Alumni Conference held at the University of Tartu's Johan Skytte Institute of Political Science, we decided to collect and publish a selection of academic papers that would reflect the attitudes existing among Ukrainian and Russian experts with regard to five specific issues in the two countries: the phenomenon of the Euromaidan (2013–2014); subnational policies; relations with the United States; memory politics; and civil society. These issues reflect some of the hottest points in both domestic and foreign policy debates in the two countries, and illuminate the major sources of identity-ridden conflicts and disagreements between them.

---

[1]   Founded in 1974, the Washington-based Kennan Institute is committed to improving expertise and knowledge about Russia, Ukraine, and other states in the region, and its residential scholarships draw some of the best academics in the humanities and social sciences.

In each of these five areas we give the floor to Russian and Ukrainian authors who offer their perspectives on the issue at hand, thus making possible analytical comparisons between the dominant narratives in the two countries. The juxtaposition of Russian and Ukrainian insights gives good food for thought and helps explain the differences in political discourses across the two neighboring Slavic nations. Our approach also makes it possible to spot significant but often overlooked domestic debates—after all, societal perceptions are never limited to a single narrative or point of view, even if it may sometimes look that way to outside observers. The contributors to this special section are all insiders who use analytical tools to dissect political complexities within their own societies, moving beyond the mainstream media accounts.

The first pair of articles addresses the phenomenon of the Euromaidan. Discussing cultural/performative dimensions of the Kyiv Maidan, NATALIA MOUSSIENKO gives a detailed analysis of rich empirical material drawn from different forms and genres of art: performance, installation, cinema, music, painting, sculpture, and literature. This art was created by professionals and amateurs, famous artists and artistic youth; the Maidan united them all and became a major artistic work in itself—the ultimate public installation. Most of these artists came to the Maidan as protestors, and they took part in both fierce confrontations and everyday activities in a form of direct democracy grounded in historical traditions from the Kyiv Rus' Veche to the Orange Revolution of 2004.

ANDREY MAKARYCHEV and ALEXANDRA YATSYK reflect upon a plethora of artistic and performative representations of the Maidan revolution in Russian popular culture marked by a highly affective and emotional level of negative symbolization of the event. As empirical material they use a number of public shows, with a particular focus on the "Night Wolves" bike club show staged annually in Crimea since 2010. The authors build their research strategy on approaches developed within the schools of popular geopolitics and cultural semiotics, focusing on the political dimensions of the object of study.

Next, we turn to the topic of subnational policies. OLEKSIY KRYSENKO explores the prospects for the regional political regimes in Ukraine after the Euromaidan. He warns about the political and institutional risks that decentralization of political governance in Ukraine may entail. This warning stems from his analysis of the nature of regional neo-patrimonial regimes and their effect on the central government's ability to enact reforms and manage political institutions. He closely examines several regional cases before and after 2014, in order to explore the regional dimension of the Ukrainian political process and identify the likely consequences of decentralization.

SERGEY SUKHANKIN traces the development of the North-Western Federal District from 1991 to 2017, using this case study to analyze center-periphery relations in Russia and outline the problems stemming from Russia's interpretation of regionalism as a political phenomenon. This timeframe, combined with attention to both economic and political developments, enables the author to offer a comprehensive picture of the key trends in this macro-region. Particular focus on the post-2014 period serves as a basis for analysis of the regional impact of the post-Crimea international tensions and changes in the Russian domestic agenda.

Next, we turn to the topic of relations with and attitudes towards the United States. OLEKSANDR POTIEKHIN and MARYNA BESSONOVA analyze the attitudes towards the US in contemporary Ukrainian society. Their research is based on data from a range of sources including public opinion polls, expert surveys, pre-election political campaigns, and mainstream media coverage on the most popular US-related topics. They identify the key factors that have a decisive influence on the image of the US in Ukraine, paying special attention to correlations of that image with attitudes to international institutions, as well as to Russia and Europe/the West. The article discusses the regional distribution and temporal dynamics and trends of pro/anti-Americanism in Ukraine.

VICTORIA ZHURAVLEVA focuses on the evolution of the image of the US in Putin's Russia in correlation with the American context (Barack Obama's legacy and Donald Trump's politics); the Russian context (the dominant socio-cultural and political identity markers that explain the mechanisms through which the American "Other" is represented and used); and the context of Russian-American bilateral relations. The article adheres to the social constructivist (sociocultural) approach that gives an opportunity for better understanding the role of the American "Other" in Russian identity discourse.

ROMAN ABRAMOV tackles the museumification of the Soviet past in today's Russia as a contradictory and complicated phenomenon. He sees the government, the mnemonic communities, amateur and professional historians, public intellectuals, and museum professionals as key groups that influence the state of debates on the communist period in Russian history. He specifically focuses on "folk museums" of the Soviet past initiated by entrepreneurs, designers, and journalists inspired by nostalgia and partly counter-balancing the "official history" and the professional "mnemonic communities."

Next, VALENTYNA KHARKHUN analyzes the memory politics of the Soviet past during twenty-five years of Ukrainian independence, relying on the study of some fifty cases of the Soviet-era museumification and their fate in the post-Soviet period. She focuses on the role of museums in the creation of state, regional, and private memory projects, and their impact on the national memory regime. In the limelight of her analysis are the main mnemonic actors/agents in Ukraine, the different types of museum narrations about the Soviet past, and the mnemonic models dominating in the Ukrainian perception of communism.

Finally, we turn to the topic of civil society in the two countries, which opens two different contexts of and perspectives on non-state actors in Russia and Ukraine. KATERYNA SMAGLIY examines the role of Ukrainian civil society after the 2004 Orange Revolution and after the 2014 Euromaidan, in order to present the quantitative and qualitative changes it has experienced and the problems it has faced. Her identification and analysis of seven key limitations in the civil society development serves as a basis for a set of recommendations on what should be done in order to achieve sustainable results and move forward with much-needed reform. Comparison of today's dynamic with the post-2004 developments offers a chance to draw lessons from the past and ensure the lasting positive effect of the civic activists' efforts.

ANNA ARUTUNYAN explores the state of contemporary Russian civil society, undertaking to evaluate its efficacy and agency and tackle some definitional and measurement problems that tend to accompany such exploration. She outlines the reasons for the civil society's weakness since the fall of the Soviet Union and traces the evolution of civic and political activism in Russia over the past few years. Her vast experience as a journalist and interviews with activists, NGO members, and politicians serve as the foundation for her analysis, which uncovers the symptoms of the civil society's weakness, indecisiveness, and lack of resources, while at the same time highlighting signs of its nascent maturation.

Not all of the authors limit themselves to pure academic analysis. Some draw on their extensive practical experience and supplement conclusions with recommendations. The section is also a multidisciplinary collection with no dominant research field or approach, which is not surprising, given that it was prepared in partnership with the Kennan Institute and eight out of twelve authors come from the diverse pool of its alumni. The five objects of research described above give a panoramic view of multiple discrepancies and disagreements that constitute major points of tension between the two national narratives. And yet, despite what the section title suggests, identities do not necessarily clash in each and every case; in some instances we are dealing with different sets of societal concerns and priorities that do not come into conflict, but instead run parallel without intersecting. However, in all five cases the timeline splits clearly into the periods before and after 2014—the year that has become a turning point for both nations.

We see this section as a contribution to a better understanding of discursive gaps and ruptures between Ukraine and Russia on a variety of political, social, and cultural issues, with perceptions, discourses, and cultural representations at their core. But we also see it as an important academic initiative that can help to mend the rupture between the two scholarly communities by engaging Russian and Ukrainian scholars in productive conversation. We hope that readers will find this conversation insightful and thought-provoking.

The Night Wolves' Anti-Maidan and Cultural Representations of Russian Imperial Nationalism[1]

Andrey Makarychev and Alexandra Yatsyk

Abstract: This article applies approaches grounded in popular geopolitics, critical discourse analysis, and cultural semiotics, to an analysis of artistic and performative representations linked to the anti-Maidan in Russia. We use the term "anti-Maidan" here not only to refer to the eponymous pro-Kremlin public movement that appeared in Russia after the Revolution of Dignity in Ukraine in 2013–2014, but also in a wider sense, approaching the anti-Maidan as a cultural phenomenon grounded in the radical rejection of the Ukrainian experience of regime change, democratic transformation, and Europeanization.

In this article we examine the structural logic of the Russian blend of nationalism and imperialism articulated by the Kremlin-sponsored Night Wolves motorcycle club, through their performative and highly publicized actions. We argue that the Night Wolves' bike shows are aimed at normatively appealing to two supreme sources of veracity and universality: the Orthodox faith, and the heroic feats of the Soviet Union in the Great Patriotic War. Both nodal points are juxtaposed and symbolically appropriated as undeniable "truths" beyond political debate, a confected status that turns even the slightest disagreement with either of them into an act of rebellious contestation of Russia's primordial and sacrosanct identity and therefore as lacking in authenticity and normatively false.

From a practical perspective, our research lens and the methodology we apply can be instrumental in identifying key points in radical national imperialist discourses that, under certain circumstances, can be transformed into justification for policy action.

---

[1]   This work was supported by Institutional Research Funding (IUT20-39) from the Estonian Ministry of Education and Research.

Introduction

This article reflects on a plethora of artistic and performative representations linked to the anti-Maidan in Russia as a reaction to the Maidan revolution in Ukraine. In our analysis we refer to the anti-Maidan not only as a pro-Kremlin public movement that appeared in Russia after the Revolution of Dignity in Ukraine in 2013–2014 but also in a wider sense, as a cultural phenomenon grounded in the radical rejection of the Ukrainian experience of regime change, democratic transformation, and Europeanization.

As empirical material we use eight shows staged by the Night Wolves biker club—a direct recipient of Kremlin-controlled funds aimed at supporting nongovernmental organizations—from 2010 to 2017. In their imagery and narrative, the Night Wolves' productions are perhaps the most impressive political performances in today's Russia. The biker shows are one of the key elements in the process of creating what Brian Whitmore has called "an alternative universe, a meta-narrative to feed to the public [that] has long been a cornerstone of Putin's rule,"[2] and the Night Wolves' anti-Maidan is part of this "alternative universe." In this sense the phenomenon of the anti-Maidan is part of a larger debate over the Russian version of the "post-truth society" and alternative realities masterminded by a propaganda machine that produces both textual and visual messages with strong aesthetic components.[3]

The annual biker shows in Crimea are the largest but not the only performative instruments masterminded by the Night Wolves. The bikers are also known for their annual motorcycle rides to Berlin through several cities of Central Europe that observe Victory Day (9 May) over Nazi Germany in the Great Patriotic War. The leader of the Night Wolves, Aleksandr Zaldostanov, nicknamed "Khirurg" (the Surgeon), in addition to overtly supporting Russia's messianic

---

[2] B. Whitmore, "Russia's Deadly Phantasy Politics," *Radio Free Europe/Radio Liberty* website, 1 July 2015, https://www.rferl.org/a/russias-deadly-fantasy-politics/27104860.html.

[3] See, for example, A. Arkhangel'skii, "Tret'ia real'nost': O sposobakh sozdaniia rossiiskimi SMI iskusstvennoi real'nosti," *Iskusstvo kino*, January 2016, http://kinoart.ru/archive/2016/01/tretya-realnost.

imperialism, has made numerous provocative statements against pro-liberal public figures.

The research question that motivates this article is how the Night Wolves' artistic performances can help us better understand the logic behind Russia's Ukraine policy and the motivations for the Crimean annexation. This is particularly important, since in just a few years the performances evolved from a politically marginal narrative to the hegemonic discourse. We start by sketching some theoretical basics for a political reading of cultural performances, and then explain how the Night Wolves represent and visualize key nodal points in Russia's hegemonic discourse—a mélange of communist nostalgia and Christian sloganeering, with a strong neo-imperial drive. We then analyze the performative representations of evil, along with issues of life and death, that appear to be central in the Night Wolves' imagery. In conclusion, we discuss the popular culture of the Night Wolves' anti-Maidan from the vantage point of a trans-ideology that blends Russian nationalist and imperial identities to the point of indistinction.

Theoretical Frame

To explore the political dimensions of the negative symbolization of the Maidan in Russian popular culture, we draw on approaches developed by cultural semiotics, critical discourse analysis, and popular geopolitics. Cultural semiotics is a relevant source for understanding how mechanisms of meaning making (signification) function. These mechanisms include the process whereby discourse is consolidated and stabilized through a particular emphasis on key concepts or issues.[4] Attempts to stabilize hegemonic narratives also presuppose erasing and excluding certain content from public debate and memories.[5] In addition, a semiotic approach is helpful for comprehending cultural mechanisms of totalization inherent to

---

[4]   See further on this process, L. Hansen, "How Images Make World Politics: International Icons and the Case of Abu Gharaib," *Review of International Studies* 42 (2015): 263–88, at 274.

[5]   M. Ilyvitzky, "Perm-36: Erasing the Gulag," *Dissident*, 30 March 2015, http://blog.victimsofcommunism.org/perm-36-erasing-the-gulags/.

each domain that produces signs and meanings (the semiosphere), which in turn acquire a particularly powerful momentum in the presence of a certain constellation of factors. In this respect, cultural semiotics is a helpful instrument for tracing the genesis and reification of ideas of imperial revival in Russia. The annexation of Crimea as an act of "restoration of historical truth" lies at the core of these processes.

Critical discourse analysis also facilitates understanding the logic of meaning construction. In this article, we borrow from Ernesto Laclau the ideas of *nodal points* (key concepts that play the role of anchors for fragmented discourses) and *chains of equivalences* (sets of concepts logically linked to each other and thus forming semantic groups). We apply these concepts to instances of securitization marked by "the social production of war"[6] through artistic and cultural performances linked to the anti-Maidan. In this sense, critical discourse analysis is instrumental in elucidating and reinterpreting the multiple cultural and historical parallels, analogies, and allusions that are constitutive of the artistic discourse of the Night Wolves and the group's political core.

Popular geopolitics is a constructivism-informed field of study that explains how geographic names can be used in non-academic contexts, and especially in vernacular narratives, as crucial elements of storytelling.[7] The Night Wolves' narratives and imagery are replete with various self-constructed meanings attached to geographic objects. This is particularly the case with respect to cities that have a high value and significance for boosting patriotic feelings and that constitute an imaginary map of Russian imperial resurrection as a cultural phenomenon.

In our analysis, we acknowledge the validity of—yet wish to analytically reach beyond—two more or less established arguments in the existing research in this terrain. One is the importance of the emotive components of public politics, the other is the well-

---

6   J. Tidy, "Visual Regimes and the Politics of War Experience: Rewriting War 'from Above' in 'WiKiLeaks' 'Collateral Murder,'" *Review of International Studies* 43, no. 1 (2016): 95–111.

7   J. Dittmer, *Popular Culture, Geopolitics, and Identity* (Lanham, MD: Rowman and Littlefield, 2010).

researched characterization of Russian patriotic discourse as propagandistic and manipulative in form and nostalgic, revanchist, and lacking due consistency in content.[8] In this article we take a step further in comprehending the structural logic of the Russian blend of nationalism and imperialism articulated by the Night Wolves through their performative and highly publicized actions. We argue that the Night Wolves' concerts are aimed at normatively appealing to two supreme sources of veracity and universality: the Orthodox faith and the heroic feats of the Soviet Union in the Great Patriotic War. Both nodal points are juxtaposed and symbolically appropriated as undeniable "truths" beyond political debate, a confected status that turns even the slightest disagreement with either of them into an act of rebellious contestation of Russia's primordial and sacrosanct identity and which ought therefore to be marked as lacking in authenticity and normatively false.

From a practical perspective, our research lens and the methodology we apply can be instrumental in identifying key points in radical national imperialist discourses that, under certain circumstances, can be transformed into justification for policy action. In one of our previous publications we demonstrated how the opening ceremony of the Sochi Olympics in February 2014 could at least partially serve as an explanatory guide to the logic of the annexation of Crimea, which took place only one month later.[9] The same type of reasoning can be applied to the Night Wolves' performative language: since at least 2010, the narrative of the biker shows has included references to Sebastopol as "a great Russian city," "the city of our strength" and "truth," combined with anticipation of a military conflict (particularly telling in this respect was a song with lyrics that included the politically mobilizing elocution, "I am waiting for the start of a new war," in the 2010 show).[10] The 2013 narrative of the

---

8   E. Gaufman, "Memory, Media and Securitization: Russian Media Framing of the Ukraine Crisis," *Journal of Soviet and Post-Soviet Politics and Society* 1, no. 1 (2015): 141–74.

9   A. Makarychev and A. Yatsyk, "Four Pillars of Russia's Power Narrative," *International Spectator* 49, no. 4 (2014): 62–75.

10 **nwsev**, "Baik Shou 2010, Sevastopol': Kul'minatsiia polnaia versiia," *YouTube*, 22 February 2012, https://www.youtube.com/watch?v=IeOAb9Wb2Pk&t=297s.

bike show held in Volgograd included explicit references to Sebastopol as an inherently Russian city spiritually linked to other places of Russian military glory, among them Stalingrad.[11] Moreover, the Stalingrad/Volgograd–Sebastopol linkage, in a figurative form, symbolically attached Crimea to Russia a year before the annexation.

It is at this point that the political meanings of fantasy become relevant. According to Jacques Lacan, political "subjects constitute themselves around a void that marks the primordial loss, a lack of essence or foundation that would anchor their identity beyond the ultimately unstable and 'foreign' play of signifiers.... The fundamentally inescapable ontological lack is temporarily covered by fantasies, which function as a protecting mechanism that prevents us from being overcome by anxiety."[12] A Lacanian approach seems well-suited to the Night Wolves' attitude towards Crimea. The Crimea appears to function here as a missing "object whose recapturing promises restoration of an imaginary full identity" of the Russian nation.[13] But since any identity is doomed to remain incomplete,[14] the construction of new fantasies—through Laclau's chains of equivalences—becomes an inevitable component of "popular geopolitics" aimed at stabilizing the mainstream worldviews through their dramatic oversimplification. Consequently, the figure of the public enemy—a generalized object of hate that allegedly wishes to prevent the Russian collective self from attaining security and integrity—is an indispensable actor in the imaginary scenery, which is vividly exemplified by the Night Wolves' performances with their clearly articulated anti-Western pathos.

The case of the Night Wolves is exemplary for understanding the complex and many-faceted nature of the Kremlin's performative creatures as hybrid policy tools: the bikers are openly patronized by

---

[11]   **ya777kosmosstars**, "Baik Shou v Volgograde. Polnaia versiia, rtv-34.com," *YouTube*, 24 August 2013, https://www.youtube.com/watch?v=KONQMt6xeOY.

[12]   Quoted in J. Eberle, "Narrative, Desire, Ontological Security, Transgression: Fantasy as a Factor in International Politics," *Journal of International Relations and Development*, 2017, doi:10.1057/s41268-017-0104-2.

[13]   *Ibid.*

[14]   V. Strukov and A. Makarychev, "(In)complete Europe vis-à-vis (In)complete Russia," *PONARS Eurasia* blog, 5 June 2017, http://www.ponarseurasia.org/artic le/incomplete-europe-vis-a-vis-incomplete-russia.

Putin[15] and funded by his administration, yet mimic "civil society organizations"; their performances are mostly aimed at domestic audiences, yet they also wish to have their say in Russia's relations with its neighbors, from Ukraine and Georgia to Germany.[16] But the feature most worthy of attention is the close and direct linkage between performing and acting: the Night Wolves have formed an armed battalion in the separatist region of Donbas where volunteers from Russia were recruited to wage a "holy war" against Ukraine's "junta."[17] A product of the Kremlin's proverbial "political technologies," the Night Wolves demonstrate how short the distance is from staging shows to mobilizing fighters, and how easily the imperial aesthetics of widely consumed cultural fantasies can morph into a network of real military combatants.

Patriotic Postmodernism: A Stalinist–Orthodox Potpourri

Contemporary Russian political culture is marked by two conflicting trends—the ongoing process of the disintegration of post-Soviet imperial structures[18] and Moscow's attempts to reconsolidate its power base by all possible means. These trends go hand in hand, permeating Russia's post-Soviet trajectory with ambiguity. In addition, attempts to reconsolidate Russia's identity are grounded in two seemingly contradictory discourses.

On the one hand, there is a growing tendency toward a religious renaissance and the ensuing politicization of the Russian Orthodox Church. What started in the early 1990s as a revival of faith earlier suppressed by the Communists since the 1917 revolution evolved, in the matter of a decade, into an imposition of the Orthodox moral, cultural, and social norms as interpreted by the Russian

---

[15]   **larasdvatri123,** "Putin, the Bikers and Sevastopol Bike Show," *YouTube* video, 11 April 2014, https://www.youtube.com/watch?v=QOcWN46TUEY.

[16]   "Putin's Bike Gang."

[17]   **larasdvatri123,** "Putin, the Bikers and Sebastopol Bike Show."

[18]   "The Soviet Union Is Gone, But It's Still Collapsing," *Foreign Policy*, 20 December 2016, http://foreignpolicy.com/2016/12/22/the-unlearned-lessons-from-the-collapse-of-the-soviet-union/.

Orthodox Church (Moscow Patriarchate), which led to the creeping revision of the very principle of the secular state.[19]

On the other hand, simultaneously, nostalgia for Soviet times transformed into a political platform with the overt rehabilitation of Stalinist rule as its central tenet. The nostalgia for Soviet times is a complex phenomenon that exists deep within society and represents a meeting point for the cultural acceptance of authoritarian rule[20] and commercial reasoning (including patriotic fashion[21] and "gastronomic nostalgia"[22]). Arguably, an important cultural precondition for the spread and proliferation of nostalgic sentiment since the beginning of the 1990s was a "feeling of the impossibility of returning" to the communist era.[23] Yet today it is exactly this feeling that the performative culture of imperial nationalism endeavors to undo, in conjunction with the practical attempts of some Kremlin-affiliated officials to legally contest the dissolution of the Soviet Union.[24]

Both nostalgia for the "good old times" of an "authentic" pre-revolutionary Russia as an Orthodox state and nostalgia for the Soviet era represent phenomena that were initially cultural, only to later become deeply political. But the problem we are going to tackle is not politicization of culture as such, but rather the paradoxical convergence of two nostalgic cultures: the Orthodox and the Soviet.

---

[19]   Sh. Kakabadze and A. Makarychev, "A Tale of Two Orthodoxies: Europe in Religious Discourses of Russia and Georgia," *Ethnopolitics*, 17 July 2018, https://www.tandfonline.com/doi/abs/10.1080/17449057.2018.1495367?journalCode=reno20.

[20]   D. Okrest, "Inogda oni vozvrashchaiutsia," *Open Democracy* website, 10 November 2015, https://www.opendemocracy.net/od-russia/okrest-inogda-oni-vo zvrashaetsya.

[21]   "Reportazh: Pobednyi pokaz mod ot molodykh yedinorossov," *Medialeaks.ru*, 30 April 2015, http://medialeaks.ru/3003_okrest_moda.

[22]   A. Makarychev and A. Stepanovich, "Depolitizatsiia sovetskogo opyta: kul'tura, sport, kino... i pragmatizm," *Forum noveishei vostochnoevropeiskoi istorii i kul'tury* 1 (2014), http://www1.ku-eichstaett.de/ZIMOS/forum/docs/forumruss21/13Makaryc hev.pdf.

[23]   D. Volchek and A. Ostrovskii, "Konstruktor real'nosti," *Radio Svoboda*, 7 June 2016, https://www.svoboda.org/a/27784428.html.

[24]   "Deputat Gosdumy vnov' poprosil proverit' zakonnost' raspada SSSR," *Gazeta.ru*, 4 November 2015, https://www.gazeta.ru/social/news/2015/11/04/n_7847345.shtml.

The Night Wolves' performative concerts offer abundant evidence of such a merger. The 2013 bike show, for example, delivered a postmodernist potpourri of popular Soviet songs and Orthodox symbols. The patriotic blend of communism and religiosity found its visual rendering in the portrayal of Stalingrad as an icon, a city possessing "a holy might." This synthetic narrative reached its affective peak in representing the 1943 Battle of Stalingrad as "the second advent of Jesus attired in the uniform of the Soviet soldier." Two coats of arms, the Soviet one and the pre-revolutionary one, visually merged into one, followed by a song that started, "We still have not burned everything down."[25]

The same combination of Soviet and Christian motifs was central to the 2015 biker show titled *The Forge of Victory*.[26] In a historical reconstruction of the 1941 German invasion of the Soviet Union, the YouTube video of this production starts with a tableau in which a frightened woman center-stage kisses the Orthodox cross during an air strike. The narrator says that "the Soviet Union was praying all the years of the Great Patriotic War and turned into a huge red monastery ready to sacrifice its lives for the sake of humanity." Then the voiceover asserts that both Stalin and Zhukov prayed before each battle; ultimately, the 1945 victory became an icon, and the Soviet flag over Reichstag in Berlin was tantamount to Gonfalon. Since Russia was blessed by the Virgin Mary, the wine of victory was Jesus's blood, the narrative continues.[27] Predictably, in this context the dissolution of the Soviet Union in 1991 is interpreted as the result of a "demons' conspiracy" that, in the 2017 show, was visualized as a gigantic snake "transgressing Russian space and Russian time," as Khirurg's voice explained offstage.[28]

Religious and Soviet motifs were likewise a major focal point of the 2016 biker show, titled *Ark of Salvation*.[29] The performance offered a peculiar vision of the Soviet past, claiming that "the

---

[25]   ya777kosmosstars, "Baik Shou v Volgograde."
[26]   **Thesavspb**, "Kuznitsa Pobedy 2015. XX Yubileinoe Baik Shou," *YouTube*, 22 August 2015, https://www.youtube.com/watch?v=WrwsJAqo7Jk&t=95s.
[27]   *Ibid.*
[28]   **Thesavspb**, "Kuznitsa Pobedy 2015."
[29]   **nwsev**, "Baik Shou 2010."

Bolsheviks drove Russia to the abyss of world revolution and chaos, but Stalin salvaged the country, transforming it into a complete and aggressive alternative to the West." The religious zeal reached its zenith with mystic claims that "Russian empires from the outset rejected Western reason" and that "Stalin's empire debunked the third law of thermodynamics."[30]

Of course, the Night Wolves' performances are not the only productions to fuse Stalinist nostalgia with a politicized Orthodoxy. The openly pro-Stalinist writer Aleksandr Prokhanov in 2015 symbolically sanctified an icon bearing the likeness of Stalin, and gained the tacit approval of some Orthodox priests.[31] In the same vein, the Russian Orthodox tycoon Konstantin Malofeev suggested in 2015 that there was "nothing wrong with the 'Orthodox Chekists.'"[32]

The uncanny convergence of religious mystique with imperial nationalism leads to an explicitly political assumption of the "unfinished business of the 1941–1945 Great Patriotic War": "a new fight with fascism is inevitable, as is inevitable Stalin's eleventh strike," Khirurg claimed with pathos at the 2014 bike show, alluding to the "ten most successful Soviet military operations against fascist Germany" and extrapolating these historical events to contemporary Russia's confrontation with the West.[33] This discourse stretches far beyond the rhetoric of a vague militaristic mobilization: it de facto legitimizes the public discussion of imminent global war.[34] This marks a radical shift from the "never again" discursive frame, central

---

[30]   *Ibid.*

[31]   I. Azar, "Trepeshchite, iadom pliuite," *Meduza*, 25 February 2016, https://me duza.io/feature/2016/02/25/trepeschite-yadom-plyuyte.

[32]   K. Malofeev, "Ne vizhu nichego plokhogo v pravoslavnom chekizme," *Forbes Life*, 26 June 2015, http://www.forbes.ru/forbeslife/292319-konstantin-malofeev -ne-vizhu-nichego-plokhogo-v-pravoslavnom-chekizme?page=0,1.

[33]   A. Protsko, "Baik Shou 'Sevastopol'—Stalingrad,'" *YouTube*, 23 February 2014, https://www.youtube.com/watch?v=O455zIvjapQ.

[34]   See further A. Kolesnikov, "Predchuvstvie tret'ei mirovoi," *Gazeta.ru*, 18 October 2016, https://www.gazeta.ru/comments/column/kolesnikov/10255583.sht ml?utm_source=gazetafb&utm_medium=social&utm_campaign=andrey-koles nikov-o-tom--pochemu-nastoyascha; Ye. Rykovtseva, "V shage ot bol'shoi voiny," *Radio Svoboda*, 17 February 2016, https://www.svoboda.org/a/27558 062.html; and M. Nemtsev, "Sostoianie voiny," *Gefter.ru*, 5 October 2015, http://gefter.ru/archive/16143.

to the Soviet culture of war commemoration, to the celebratory and aggressive sloganeering ("We can do it again") typical of today's popular geopolitics in Putin's Russia. In other words, it is a victorious festivity that defines the nature of nationalist-cum-imperialist discourse in contemporary Russia.[35]

It seems symptomatic that new efforts to rehabilitate Stalin have proliferated in the aftermath of the annexation of Crimea. This act of imperial nationalism, widely supported in Russian society, reveals, in historian Andrei Zubov's words, the centrality of Stalin for Putin's regime.[36] For professional historians it is clear that the USSR actually entered World War II on 17 September 1939, as an ally of Nazi Germany along with which it divided Eastern Europe in full accordance with the secret protocol annexed to the non-aggression pact of 23 August 1939 which went down in history as the Molotov-Ribbentrop Pact.[37] Not incidentally, the annexation of Crimea instigated intense discursive activity in the imperial flank of Russian nationalists who openly advocate for the rehabilitation of Stalin[38] as a step toward a new division of Europe into spheres of influence[39]—a gloomy scenario that presupposes only limited sovereignty for the Baltic states, and the de facto elimination of Ukraine as an independent nation.

---

[35] D. Volkov, "Mifologizatsiia pobedy," *Intersections*, 9 May 2017, http://intersectionproject.eu/ru/article/society/mifologizaciya-pobedy.

[36] A. Zubov, "Stalin—eto os', vokrug kotoroi vrashchaetsia vsia nyneshniaia vlast'," 17 February 2016, http://ww.aboutru.com/2016/02/24540/.

[37] N. Sokolov, "Forgotten Truth about the Beginning of the War," *Intersections*, 22 June 2016, http://intersectionproject.eu/article/society/forgotten-truth-about-beginning-war.

[38] Veselyi Rodzher, "Sergei Kurochkin: Vernite Stalina" (song), *YouTube*, 29 August 2015, https://www.youtube.com/watch?v=Rao-BWDpQp8.

[39] "Izborsky Club Calls for New Molotov-Ribbentrop Pact to Re-divide Eastern Europe between Moscow and Berlin," *EuroMaidan Press*, 12 May 2017, http://euromaidanpress.com/2017/05/12/izborsky-club-calls-for-new-molotov-ribbentrop-pact-to-re-divide-eastern-europe-between-moscow-and-berlin-euromaidan-press/.

Constructing Chains of Equivalences: The Popular Geopolitics of Empire

An important inspiration for the Night Wolves' performative Russian imperial nationalism comes from popular geopolitics, a sphere of semantically constructed images of geographic places with a high level of political symbolization. The main nodal point in this playful manipulation of geopolitical signs is the reconnection of Crimea in general and Sebastopol in particular with other imperial places.

In 2013, almost a year before the annexation of Crimea, Khirurg vociferously proclaimed: "Better that Europe become an African country than Sebastopol lose its Russian roots."[40] Apart from racist allusions, the narrative of the 2013 show put a premium on symbolically relating Sebastopol to Stalingrad: "Let Sebastopol flaunt over the Volga, and Stalingrad meet its friends in the Black Sea."[41] This pre-emptive reconnection of Crimea to the geographies of past military glory not only charted an imaginary pathway to the annexation, but also—again—placed the name of Stalin at the core of Russia's imperial aggrandizement.

The program of the 2010 show included a Soviet-era song, "My Black Sea," that served as a meaningful addition to the revived imperial narrative of Putin's Russia.[42] The 2015 show was marked by overt rehabilitation of Russia as the "eternal empire," accompanied by the assertion that Russia should neither hide nor regret its unremovable imperial identity.[43] In the 2017 show Crimea was referred to as "the savior" of the Russian imperial tradition, which extends to the war-torn Donbas.[44] This pathos of self-assertive impunity represented a drastic departure from the cultural mainstream of the late Soviet era, symbolized, in particular, by the Georgian film *Repentance* (dir. Tengiz Abuladze, 1984) and making a strong case for

---

40   Protsko, "Baik Shou 'Sevastopol'—Stalingrad.'"
41   *Ibid.*
42   **nwsev**, "Baik Shou 2010."
43   **Thesavspb**, "Kuznitsa Pobedy 2015."
44   RT, "Transliatsiia 360: Baik Shou v Sevastopole," *YouTube*, 18 August 2017, https://www.youtube.com/watch?v=tHOZ776MNuk.

accepting and recognizing the guilt of the past as an indispensable step toward spiritual self-purification.

Within the Putin-era anti-repentance framework, popular geographies of imperial glory play a particularly important role. The 2015 show featured a symbolic parade of cities known for their outstanding contributions to the victory over fascist Germany.[45] All of them, including the Crimean cities of Kerch and Sebastopol, were portrayed as inalienable parts of Russian military history, In a clear politicization of wartime memories, the narrative ascribed to Odesa the disapproval of the "Kyiv junta," while Kyiv itself was compared to "Judas, who fails to notice a noose behind his head."[46] The Maidan was directly referred to as a source of "lies," while the "truth" remained deeply imperial: the "imperial flag of liberty" was called on to reunite expanses from "Baikal to Ukraine."

The 2016 bike show followed the same line, claiming that a "new epoch of the Russian state" was being formed in anticipation of the Fifth Empire to come (the previous four were the Kievan Rus', the Moscow kingdom of Rurik's dynasty, the Romanov empire, and the Soviet Union). This imperial mystique is a replica of the narrative widely propagated by *Zavtra* newspaper and its editor, Aleksandr Prokhanov. Again, popular geopolitics is an organic part of the imperial logic that symbolically aggregates in one chain of equivalence, whereby Narva (conquered by Peter the Great), Donbas, Palmyra, and Karabakh feature as places culturally or linguistically connected, in one way or another, to the *"Russkii mir."* The 2012 show portrayed through the lens of imperial geography cities as different as Warsaw (liberated by the Soviet troops in 1945) and Kandahar (a city in Afghanistan where a Soviet military brigade was stationed[47]). The fact this chain consists of cities located beyond Russia's borders attests to the Russian imperial imagery's detachment from the realities of the international system. With all its absurdity, the proliferation of elements in this self-reproducing imaginary chain seems to

---

45   **Thesavspb,** "Kuznitsa Pobedy 2015."

46   *Ibid.*

47   *Baik-shou 2012, Kul'minatsiia (polnaia versiia HD), YouTube,* 16 June 2013, https://www.youtube.com/watch?v=v36Q-k66Ojo.

be in line with President Putin's provocative statement about Russian borders that "do not end anywhere."[48] In 2017, referring to the first piloted spaceflight, by Yurii Gagarin, Khirurg, echoing the president, claimed that since that time, "the Russian lands have been bounded by the cosmos."[49] This celebratory—if not triumphant—declaration of Russia's "infinity" is metaphorically sustained by the multiple scenes in the biker shows in which motorcyclists ride around in a moving circle,[50] unable to stop without being in danger of falling down and collapsing—an artistic metaphor for the endless movement of Russia.

Another idea behind the geographic chains is to re-signify the peripheral connotations of their elements vis-à-vis Russia's center. The narrative of the 2012 biker show refers to Sebastopol as "the last authentic Russian city" and "God's favorite," counterposed to a Moscow that, in Khirurg's words, "is not a hero anymore"—an allusion to the lack of authenticity in the cosmopolitan capital.[51] In 2014 this argument was strengthened even further, to the point of the group's lyrics referring to Sebastopol as the place where the salvation of Russia would eventually come from.[52] In 2016 this argument was further reiterated by reference to 10 million Russians in so-called Novorossiia who "refused to submit to the global American tyranny" and thus heroically salvaged Russia from "moral slavery."[53] "As long as Sebastopol remains Russian, Russia won't perish," the song went, underlining once again the centrality of Crimea to Russian nationalist geography.[54]

[48] T. Emburg-Dennis, "Putin Says Russia's Borders Do Not End Anywhere," *Independent*, 25 November 2016, http://www.independent.co.uk/news/world/europe/putin-russia-border-do-not-end-anywhere-comments-quote-eu-us-tensions-a7438686.html.
[49] RT, "Transliatsiia 360."
[50] Night Wolves Bike Club, "21e Baik Shou, Sevastopol' 2016," *Motoklub Nochnye Volki*, 28 August 2016, https://www.youtube.com/watch?v=uufxboJCKK.
[51] *Baik-shou 2012.*
[52] Radek Hotovy, "Baik Shou 2014, Sevastopol'," *YouTube*, 8 August 2014, https://www.youtube.com/watch?v=NPnb97ybtiU&t=156s.
[53] Night Wolves Bike Club, "21e Baik Shou, Sevastopol' 2016."
[54] *Ibid.*

Polarizing Binaries and the Name of Evil

In their earlier performances the Night Wolves played with the language of universalism by claiming that Russia's moral revival would ultimately be beneficial for the West and help avoid the collapse of Western civilization. However, the dominant approach articulated in the shows is more binary than universalist: Russia's relations with the West are portrayed as a war of good against evil, a "natural" collision of paradise and hell.

The argument underlying the lambasting of the West in the Night Wolves' performances closely resembles leftist interpretations of globalization as totalitarianism, to be resisted by all means. For example, the 2016 show started with an apocalyptic vision of mankind moving toward the abyss, with dehumanized bodies as visual incarnations of "uncanny ghosts and ugly chimeras" associated with the alleged Western tyranny. The latter featured earlier in 2011 in zoological categories, such as "black ravens" and "jackals."[55] Russia, according to the ensuing narrative, had been forced to temporarily become part of this "anti-humankind," but today it is liberating itself and breaking away from foreign domination.

It is in this context that the United States is represented as the embodiment of global evil: the recognizable national symbols of America are presented as the universal signifiers of domination, control, oppression, and surveillance. One of the performing artists in 2015 wore a t-shirt with the logo "Columbus, un-discover America!" that was later transformed into a song[56]—a clear indication of the rampant anti-Americanism of the whole semantics of the performance. The 2011 show started by portraying the former CIA director Allen Dulles, who, according to the narrative, based in conspiracy theory,[57] in 1948 called for a confrontation with the Soviet Union, which serves as a universal explanation of the reasons behind

---

[55] nwsev, "Baik shou 2011. Novorossiisk. Epilog," *YouTube*, 1 September 2011, https://www.youtube.com/watch?v=jLmGoJaPUSc.

[56] Valentina Gafinets and Gleb Kornilov, "Kolumb, zakroi Ameriku," *YouTube*, 27 September 2015, https://www.youtube.com/watch?v=9hnp6CCtxis.

[57] A. Panchenko, "Teorii zagovora v 21 veke," *Nezavisimaia Gazeta*, 28 February 2017, http://www.ng.ru/stsenarii/2017-02-28/9_6937_zagovor.html.

the Soviet collapse in 1991. In the 2017 show figures representing Mikhail Gorbachev and Boris Yeltsin appeared onstage, accompanied by diabolically spiteful laughter symbolizing America's glee at the fall of the Soviet Union and the subsequent "dull 1990s," a decade reconstructed in the nationalist narrative as destructive and submissive. In the 2014 show the malign West was represented by the voices of Barack Obama and Angela Merkel against the backdrop of the crowd protesting on the Maidan, followed by the voice of Hitler and a swastika made of human bodies.[58] Ukraine in this peculiar interpretation was depicted as a country completely dependent on its sponsors and patrons overseas and a victim of the global Western conspiracy. It is within this discursive frame that neo-fascism is represented as the evil with which Russian imperial nationalists wish to symbolically associate the Maidan. The imagined connection between the Maidan, neo-Nazis, and the United States is presented as a repressive force that only Russia can counterbalance and ultimately defeat. Physical might—celebrated and venerated by long and noisy theatrical shots in the air in 2014—is symbolized as the most effective means of restoring Russia's military potential, which in turn is directly connected to the victory in the Great Patriotic War and Stalin's successful campaigns against Nazi Germany.

Life and Death, Biopolitics and Thanatopolitics

The biker show scenarios can also be interpreted as an intricate combination of biopolitics (the politics of managing people's lives) and thanatopolitics (the politics of death).[59] A key biopolitical metaphor in the shows is the rapture of faceless and similar if not identical bodies of workers, representing the Soviet ideal of disciplinary power. This is reminiscent of the way the Soviet Union was portrayed in the opening ceremony of the Sochi Olympics, as a collective body of people, a biopolitical mass whose individual units are

---

58   Hotovy, "Baik Shou 2014, Sevastopol'."
59   See, for example, S. Murray, "Thanatopolitics: Reading in Agamben, a Rejoinder to Biopolitical Life," *Communication and Critical / Cultural Studies* 5, no. 2 (June 2008): 203–07.

deprived of individuality and agency yet united in sharing a feeling of belonging to a powerful community cemented by its long history, defined above all else by the fight for biological survival. The main politicizing factor at this juncture is the discursively constructed image of dispossession and deprivation, rendered visually in systems of signs and messages and articulated in narratives of victimization. Indicatively, Khirurg started the 2012 show by dedicating it to "my vanished Motherland," that is, the Soviet Union. In biopolitical terms this narrative portrayed Russians as a people without "proper" territorial grounding. This people, according to the narrative of the 2012 show, had been contaminated by traitors: thus, Sebastopol was referred to as a "humiliated city betrayed by grandchildren of the wartime generation" and by "dogs who sold out the country that kept the whole world in fear." Therefore, this people needs "purification" and a rebirth of national spirit. The collective biopolitical "we" on behalf of whom each of the annual stories is told is skillfully constructed by different means, such as by appealing to ethnic Russians as "brothers" (the 2011 show) who are ready to "rise from their knees" and revive their centuries-old belief in "God, love, force and truth" (the narrative of the 2012 show).

It is exactly at this point that this biopolitical imagery reveals its reverse side, which can be viewed through the prism of thanatopolitics as the cult of physical coercion and violence, characterized by the inevitability of sacrificing human lives, with, ultimately, death as a symbol of the great national spirit. "The last mortal combat," heroically proclaimed as an ethical ideal during the revolution and civil war, is now recycled as a thanatopolitical resource and instrument manipulated by the Night Wolves. In this sense it is indicative that the 2016 bike show was replete with fire, a sign semiotically representing the painful and inevitable Real—both in terms of eternal resistance to "devilish forces" (the 2011 show) and in terms of purifying the national self. In the 2012 show one could see multiple references to the forthcoming military conflict with the West: "We'll bring bullets in amounts sufficient to send a clear message to the fascist Maidan.... Actors from NATO will be rehearsing their death": Khirurg set the thanatopolitical tone of the storyline. In a different episode, a voice behind the scenes called out to the audience that they should "be ready for a melée."[60] Constructing the feeling of Sebastopol's submission to a foreign occupation, the narrative continued with direct references to the Great Patriotic War: "Every night here resembles the twenty-second of June, every day here is like the ninth of May.... Soon there will be another 1941, and one more 1945." The appropriation of Victory Day is an important part of the 2017 show as well: "It is impossible to turn aside from the road of the ninth of May," Khirurg declared.

Changing the Tone: Hysterical Overdetermination

The muscular and supremacist language that the Night Wolves speak in their performances is, however, sometimes interrupted by a different narrative. In the 2014 show Ukrainians, represented as slaves of Europe and traitors of a centuries-long tradition of friendship with Russia, became objects of hysterical speech: "How much did you sell the Kievan Rus' to Europe for?" "Who convinced you, Ukraine, that Moscow is your enemy?"[61] In a musical form, this narrative argued that in this part of the world there were different borders that historically had shifted many times, yet now Ukraine preferred to decisively drive to the West, thus abandoning its eastern citizens, who wished to remain in close touch with Russia. The hysterical and highly metaphorical dialogue with Ukraine reached its peak with the frequently reiterated question: "Tell me, Ukraine, why?" In the 2015 show the hysterical appeal to Ukraine continued: 'Who needs you, Ukraine, except Russia, which is of one blood with you?" "Whom do you serve, Ukraine?"[62] the singer Gleb Kornilov rhetorically asks in his composition.

These symbolic appeals to Ukraine only shed light on the numerous discrepancies and inconsistencies in the version of Russian identity shaped by the dominant popular geopolitics. For instance, the reiterated lament "Sebastopol will forever remain Russian" undermines the narrative of Ukraine and Russia as one nation

---

60   **nwsev**, "Baik Shou 2010."

61   Protsko, "Baik Shou 'Sevastopol'—Stalingrad.'"

62   **Thesavspb**, "Kuznitsa Pobedy 2015."

propagated, in particular, by Sergei Ivanov[63] and by and large supported by Putin himself. The Kremlin clearly lacks a single discourse
with respect to Ukraine and thus must vacillate between rhetorical
pragmatism (with Putin's famous phrase, "Let them [Ukrainians] return our money!"[64] at its core) and what might be called "enforced
friendship" or—in even more explicit form—"enforced family relations." The latter model is overtly articulated by Gleb Kornilov, constant participant in the Night Wolves' shows, in his musical reaction
to the Ukrainian poet Anastasiia Daniliuk with the self-explanatory
title, "We'll never be brothers." Kornilov's riposte, marked by a
strongly gender-biased context, portrays Ukraine as a misbehaving
sister that Russia as an elder brother needs to protect and take care
of.[65] This type of attitude, with some conciliatory notes inside it, represents a milder form of Russia's symbolic domination that is still
deeply patronizing, arrogant, and insensitive to Ukraine's political
or cultural subjectivity in its background.

Conclusion

The merger of Orthodox normativity with the centrality of the 1945
victory over fascism for today's memory politics of imperial nationalists has a number of important effects, to which the performative
role of the Night Wolves is essential. First, this mixture of Christi-
anity and imperial rehabilitation of communism gives rise to a pronounced totalizing effect, with a clear shift toward discursive fore-
closure and consequent isolation from the "malign" West. The
speaking position contrived by Khirurg and his scenarists leaves him
with almost free hands in articulating an endless number of the
most pretentious claims: speaking on behalf of the self-contrived
"truth," he feels free to construct and play with equivalences and

---

[63]   Interview with Sergei Ivanov, *TASS News Agency*, 2017, http://tass.ru/opinions/
top-officials/2356242?page=2.

[64]   K. Levchenko, "V. Putin: Pust' den'gi vernut (Video World)," *YouTube*, 12 December 2014, https://www.youtube.com/watch?v=IBchMBob4dg.

[65]   G. Kornilov, "Nikogda my ne budem bratiami (Otvet ukrainke)," *YouTube*, 18
April 2014, https://www.youtube.com/watch?v=ptfn8LX8o1A&list=RDptfn8L
X8o1A.

consequently totalize the discourse to the point of direct explanation of the most repressive of Russia's rulers, from Ivan the Terrible to Stalin. This type of totalization à la Russe might take different forms, including intentional appropriation and the resignification of earlier cultural practices: thus, Viktor Tsoi's famous song "Kukushka" (The Cuckoo), which in the late 1980s was an epitome of youth protest against the Soviet regime, in the 2015 biker show was performed as a declaration of Russia's past and future might, with "my palm turned into a fist" as a metaphor of physical force indispensable to a national imperial revival.[66]

Second, this totalization, with all its inherent indeterminacy, stretches far beyond the aesthetic field of postmodernist irony and is not as harmless or as marginal as it might appear. The juxtaposition of scarcely compatible arguments can be a rather explosive and subversive mix owing to its proclivity to create a fertile ground for manipulations with meanings sustained by culturally appealing techniques. For Laclau, discursive dislocations are tantamount to freedom—but this is only one side of the story.[67] Another side is much less celebratory and has to do with the multiple malicious effects of the dislocated identity grounded in intentionally blurring lines between the national and the imperial, interior and exterior, friend and foe, conservatism and subversion, and—the most consequentially dangerous—between the forceful refutation of fascism and the reproduction of Nazi-like aesthetics and style in artworks.[68] These multiple conflations and overlaps of opposites paradoxically turn Russian imperial nationalism into a rebellious conservatism, purposely crusading against any type of rational knowledge in epistemological sense and revolting against the extant international norms in policy terms. The pathos of emancipatory liberation from the imagined oppression is the reverse side of the well-recorded

---

[66]   **Thesavspb,** "Kuznitsa Pobedy 2015."
[67]   E. Laclau, "Dislocation and Capitalism, Social Imaginary and Democratic Revolution," in *Ernesto Laclau. Post-Marxism, Populism and Critique*, ed. D. Howarth (London and New York: Routledge, 2015), 31.
[68]   I. Malkiel', "Fashizm kak iskusstvo, ili kak estetika tret'ego reikha lozhitsia v osnovu Russkogo mira," *Otkrytaia Rossiia* website, 18 May 2017, https://open russia.org/notes/709612/.

conservative wave in Russian politics, with the overtly retrospective mind-set at its core performed by the Night Wolves.

Ukraine dramatically finds itself at the conflictual intersection of all these dislocations as an object of their external projection: it may be represented as both a brotherly nation and an enemy to the Russian world; as being intrinsically akin to Russia's identity and simultaneously deeply alien to it; as an object of desire and hate. The analysis of the Night Wolves' narrative gives a clear picture of the declared intention to reify the imperial plans of reassembling "the pieces of the Motherland," initially as a series of speech acts and performances, and later in the form of Kremlin policy, supported by a significant part of the society.

Cultural and Performative Dimensions of the Kyiv Maidan (2013–2014)

Natalia Moussienko

Abstract: This article provides an overview of the cultural/performative dimensions of the Kyiv Maidan (2013–14), exploring the special place occupied by art in these revolutionary events. The empirical material attests that the Maidan generated and was reflected in works of art in various genres: performance, installation, cinema, music, painting, sculpture, and literature—in short, across the full range of the creative artistic palette. Professionals and amateurs, famous artists and artistic youth—the Maidan united them all and became the scene for complex collective artistic expression, filled with emotion and creativity. This expression was powerful in form and diverse in content: it was radical and political, philosophical and poetical, and deeply aesthetic.

The cultural and performative dimensions of the Maidan marked a critical pivot away from the old Soviet paradigms. New narratives entered Ukrainian art discourse, ranging from calls for Euro-integration to social mobilization for civil rights and, later, in the work of many artists, the notion of a "battle for the Motherland." The art of the Maidan ranged from witty protest to radical challenge and through to the sacral, and organically drew in elements of the avant-garde, mass culture, and high classicism. These elements dominated differentially across the main phases of the Maidan. The avant-garde tendencies of Maidan art were quickly absorbed by mass culture and applied broadly to easy-to-sell merchandise. This process entailed commodification, but it also offered an efficient way to deliver messages to the public.

Drawing on art data as its primary sources, the article looks first at the interplay of art and politics, placing the Maidan in the broader context of world events and the deeper historical perspective of Ukraine. In the second part it reflects on the Kyiv Maidan in the framework of Bakhtin's carnival theory, analyzing the Maidan in relation to its opposite—the anti-Maidan that supported the ruling regime in the country.

Everything is art. Everything is politics.

Ai Weiwei

Introduction

From the very beginning of the Maidan in November 2013 the artistic aspects of the protest were evident, as was the urgent need to document this extraordinary outburst of revolutionary creativity. In this article, I provide an overview of the cultural and performative dimensions of the Kyiv Maidan (2013–2014).[1] The insights and conclusions are based on the results of fieldwork that I conducted in the winter of 2013–2014. This fieldwork included photographing artistic

---

[1]   My focus here is mainly on the events in Kyiv. It should be noted, however, that "Maidans" were held throughout all of Ukraine and in various cities abroad. The protest started on 21 November 2013, in response to President Viktor Yanukovych's decision not to sign the Association Agreement between Ukraine and the EU. The term "Euromaidan" is often used synonymously with the terms "Revolution of Dignity," "Maidan," "Kyiv Maidan," and "Eurorevolution." However, some argue that the term "Euromaidan" should be used only for the protests' first phase, 21–30 November 2013, when the focus was mainly on European integration. See A. Kyrydon, "Evromaidan/Revolutsiia Hidnosti: Prychyny, kharakter, osnovni etapy," *Istorychna pamiat'* 33 (2015), http://nbuv.gov.ua/UJRN/Ip_2015_33_4; and O. O. Kryvitchenko, "Ievromaidan—maidan iak biopolitychni spilnosti novoho typu, shcho samoorganizuiutsia," *Grani* 6 (June 2014), https://grani.org.ua/index.php/journal/article/viewFile/542/558. More about the Euromaidan can be found in Viktor Stepanenko and Yaroslav Pylynskyi (eds.), *Ukraine after EuroMaidan: Challenges and Hopes* (Bern: Peter Lang, 2015); David R. Marples and Frederick V. Mills (eds.), *Ukraine's Euromaidan: Analyses of a Civil Revolution* (Stuttgart: *ibidem* Verlag, 2015); and Marta Dyczok, *Ukraine's Euromaidan: Broadcasting through Information Wars with Hromadske Radio* (E-International Relations Publishing, 2016).

manifestations on the Maidan, and collecting journalistic pieces on the topic, in particular interviews with artists.[2]

The empirical material attests that the Maidan generated different genres of art: performance, installation, cinema, music, painting, sculpture, literature—in short, the full range of the creative artistic palette. Professionals and amateurs, famous artists and artistic youth: the Maidan united them all and became an artistic event and installation itself. Artists went to the Maidan as protesters and took part in both fierce confrontations and everyday activities. Yet they remained artists, and they began to depict the Maidan in various ways. Indeed, art holds a special place in the Ukrainian revolutionary events of 2013–2014.

Drawing on art data as its primary sources, this article looks first at the interplay of art and politics, placing art at the Maidan in the broader context of the global history of protest and the national history of Ukraine. In the second part I reflect on the Kyiv Maidan in the framework of Bakhtin's carnival theory. I argue that Bakhtin's concept of carnival offers a fruitful line of inquiry for interpreting the Maidan and analyzing it in relation to its opposite—the anti-Maidan, that protested against the protestors, but that proved unable to produce an equivalent of the artistic works created by the Maidan.

---

[2] I have presented the results of this research in a number of public talks. On 30 January 2014, I gave a talk on the artistic elements of the Maidan at the Modern Art Research Institute of the National Academy of Arts of Ukraine in Kyiv. This talk launched the "Art of Maidan" multidisciplinary project, which so far consists of my book, *The Art of Maidan*, trans. Andrii Kulykov (Kyiv: Huss, 2016), and the traveling exhibit, *Revolution of Dignity Art Exhibit: Images from Ukraine's Maidan, 2013–2014*, which has been shown in sixteen locations in Ukraine, the US, the UK, and the Netherlands, exhibiting the work of seventeen Ukrainian artists: Iulia Beliaeva, Oksana Chepelyk, Olena Golub, Anton Hauk, Mar'iana Honcharenko, Irena Khovanets, Mar'ian Luniv, Oleksa Mann, Roman Mykhailiuk, Anastasiia Nekypela, Mariia Pavlenko, Tet'iana Rusetska, Ivan Semesiuk, Andrii Sydorenko, Glib Vysheslavskyi, Andrii Iermolenko, and Nik Zavilinskyi.

Art and Politics: Ukraine

Art has long been understood to be an important tool of social and political change.[3] Boris Groys in *Art Power* (2008) states, "Art is, of course, political. All attempts to define art as autonomous and to situate it above or beyond the political field are utterly naïve."[4] Artists' political engagement varies from the conceptualization and interpretation of social issues to direct political activism, as during the student unrest in Paris in May 1968 or the anti-war protests in Chicago the same year.[5] The artist Olexa Mann argues that the Maidan was launched by artists who wanted to make a European revolution resonating with the events of 1968 and who were able to formulate and convey certain ideas better and more clearly than political scientists and journalists.[6]

In the era of social media, the role of artists in fermenting change has if anything become even more prominent and important.[7] Underscoring art's greatly expanded reach in the digital age, Martha Rosler points to the artistic mode of revolution in her analysis of the Occupy movement, which spread to eighty-seven countries in the form of more than a thousand Occupy events, and

---

3   The French philosopher Michel Dufrenne argued that artistic revolution supplies the impulse for and becomes the detonator of political revolution: Michel Dufrenne, *Art et politique* (Paris: Union Général d'Edition, 1974). Jacques Rancière postulates that an aesthetic regime breaks the barriers between artistic practices and the political sphere; Jacques Rancière, *The Politics of Aesthetics* (New York: Continuum, 2004). For more on the connections between art and politics, see Kemal Salim and Ivan Gaskell (eds.), *Politics and Aesthetics in the Arts* (Cambridge: Cambridge University Press, 2000); and Unmesh Senna Dasthakhir, "The Aesthetization of Politics and the Politicization of Art," *Bodhi Commons* website, 6 December 2013, http://beta.bodhicommons.org/article/the-aesthetization-of-politics-and-the-politicization-of-art.

4   Boris Groys, *Art Power* (Cambridge, MA: MIT Press, 2008).

5   On the Paris unrest, see Julien Besançon, *Les murs ont la parole: Journal mural, Mai 68* (Paris: Tchou, 1968). On the Chicago protests, see Norman Mailer, *Miami and the Siege of Chicago: An Informal History of the Republican and Democratic Conventions of 1968* (New York: New York Review Books Classics, 2008).

6   Cited in A. Babitskyi, A. Borzenko, I. Kaliteevskaia, and P. Ieremenko, "Maidan nam v oshchushcheniiakh," *Esquire*, https://esquire.ru/ukraine.

7   Ben Davis, "This Is the Art That Mattered from the 2016 Presidential Election," *artnet.com*, 7 November 2016, https://news.artnet.com/art-world/election-art-2016-734828.

in its turn drew inspiration from the Arab Spring uprisings in 2011.[8] The Kyiv Maidan, with its significant artistic component, can be understood as linked in spirit to the Occupy movement, which itself echoed the student occupations of the universities in France in 1968.[9] The Maidan can thus be viewed within a broader global and historical context, notably in its reuse of the "Forbidden to Forbid" slogan from 1968 Paris, its appropriation and replacement of the name of the popular Finnish video game "Angry Birds" with the catchphrase "Angry Ukrainians," and its repurposing of the American artist Shepard Fairey's *Obey* poster.[10]

Boris Groys has noted the "ability of art to function as an arena and medium for political protest and social activism."[11] Groys argues that art activism combines art and social action, while at the same differing from the functions traditionally fulfilled by either artists or activists. This thesis can usefully be applied to Maidan art research. The Maidan features art activists, traditional artists, and artists who joined the protests as social and political activists. As Alisa Lozhkina points out, the ranks of artists were populated with leftists, anarchists, and nationalists, each with their own various artistic interventions,[12] though the artists mostly went to the Maidan as citizens, claiming that the instruments of protest could be artistic as well. The artist Mariia Diordiichuk created twelve paintings at the barricades, unifying them under the title "Freedom Colors." The artist

---

[8]   Martha Rosler, "The Artistic Mode of Revolution: From Gentrification to Occupation," *E-flux* 33 (March 2012), http://www.e-flux.com/journal/33/68311/the-artistic-mode-of-revolution-from-gentrification-to-occupation/.

[9]   On the connections between the Maidan and the Occupy movement, see further Nazar Kozak, "Art Embedded into Protest: Staging the Ukrainian Maidan," *Art Journal*, 28 June 2017, http://artjournal.collegeart.org/?p=8682.

[10] See "Angry Ukrainians—nova hra pro Maidan," *Druh chytacha*, 29 January 2014, https://vsiknygy.net.ua/news/33826/.

[11] Boris Groys, "On Art Activism," *E-flux* 56 (June 2014), http://www.e-flux.com/journal/56/60343/on-art-activism/.

[12] A. Lozhkina, "Iskusstvo na barrikadakh: Maidan glazami ukrainskikh khudozhnikov," *Art Ukraine*, 7 February 2014, http://artukraine.com.ua/a/iskusstvo-na-barrikadah-maydan-glazami-ukrainskih-hudozhnikov-ch2#.Whr2jUriblU.

posed the question: "There are military correspondents, so why not create a profession of military artists?"[13]

The diversity of the forms of artistic creativity on display demands that we approach the art of the Kyiv Maidan as a holistic creative phenomenon offering a site for the expression of different artistic modes. In this connection, it is productive to view the Maidan through the frame of Mikhail Bakhtin's concept of carnival, that is, the performative overturning of conventional hierarchies, oppositions, and power relations. The creative interventions on the Maidan, especially during the movement's early stages, appear strikingly consistent with Bakhtin's description, as we shall see below. After the first killings, in January 2014, the carnival mode was seriously undermined, but its traces remained present in the verbal expressions and installations still existing from the previous peaceful period. It is important to emphasize the important ways in which these creative initiatives turned the Maidan into a territory of art and influenced how the Maidan was perceived. At the same time, the artworks provided an artistic contemporaneous documentation of events as they unfolded on the square.

Historically, the artistic factor has always been constitutive for Ukraine. The Cossack Hetman Ivan Mazepa was a composer and poet.[14] When Ukrainians did not have their own state, poets and

---

13   Cited in M. Zahovaiko, "Nedil'ne chtyvo. 'Kol'ory voli': Mystetstvo barykad mandruie Ievropoiu," *Ukrinform*, 29 June 2014, https://www.ukrinform.ua/rubric-other_news/1679294-nedilne_chtivo_kolori_voli_mistetstvo_barikad_mandru e_e_vropoyu_1950638.html.

14   Ivan Mazepa (1639–1709), the Ukrainian statesman, politician, army leader, diplomat, composer, and poet, paid special attention to the development of Ukrainian culture: the arts, sciences, and education flourished on his watch. A patron of the arts, he was depicted as a hero in numerous artworks by famous artists of the nineteenth century: Byron, Victor Hugo, Taras Shevchenko, Alexander Pushkin, Juliusz Słowacki, Franz Liszt, Piotr Tchaikovsky, Michael Balfe, and others. The twentieth and twenty-first centuries saw several cinema portraits of Mazepa, most notably, Iurii Illienko's *A Prayer for Hetman Mazepa* (2001) and Iurii Makarov's *Mazepa: Kohannya, velych, zrada* (2005). Mazepa was also honored in the annual rock festival "Mazepafest" in Poltava (2006–2016) (in 2017 the festival moved to Kolomah, Kharkiv region). For a useful bibliography on Mazepa and the cultural mythology around this figure, see the website for the Harvard University project, "Hetman of Ukraine Ivan Mazepa, 1639-1709

writers became their spiritual leaders: Taras Shevchenko, Lesya Ukrainka, Ivan Franko. This phenomenon is captured in the words of the Ukrainian poet, Yevhen Malaniuk: "If a nation does not have leaders, poets are its leaders." Artists became the leaders of the Ukrainian People's Republic at the beginning of the twentieth century: the writer and historian Mykhailo Hrushevsky was the first Ukrainian president; the dramaturge and writer Volodymyr Vynnychenko was prime minister. Later, Soviet Ukraine went through the so-called "Executed Renaissance,"[15] when the writers and artists of the 1920s to early 1930s were repressed by Stalin's regime; the country also experienced a strong liberal cultural movement in the 1960s that eventually pursued the agenda of Ukrainian independence and later provided the country's politicians.[16]

The active participation of artists in politics was a phenomenon that marked the late Soviet era and the beginning of the post-Soviet period more broadly across the region. Taking seats in the newly elected parliaments in Ukraine, Estonia, Georgia, Russia, and elsewhere were a number of writers, poets, film and theater directors, and actors.[17] The conjunction of art and politics was especially vivid during Estonia's "Singing Revolution" (1986–91), and culminated in the Tartu Pop Music Festival (May 1988) and the massive song festival, "Song of Estonia," staged in the Tallinn Song Festival Arena (11 September 1988). Just a few years later, artists supported the Rose Revolution in Georgia in 2003, urging people to join it.[18] Ukraine witnessed artistic revolutionary culminations of this kind twice over: on the Maidan in 2004, and again in 2013–2014.

The Cultural Legend," available at: https://projects.iq.harvard.edu/huri-maz-epa-exhibit/pages/bibliography.

[15] Iurii Lavrinenko, *Rozstriliane Vidrodzhennia. Antolohiia 1917—1933* (Kyiv: Smoloskyp, 2007).

[16] On the 1960s period, see O. Pakhlovs'ka, "Ukraiins'ki shistdesiatnyky: filosofiia buntu," *Suchasnist'* 4 (2000): 65–84.

[17] I interviewed several artists who became politicians in Ukraine, with the aim of understanding their vision of societal change; see Natalia Moussienko, *Mystetstvo i polityka* (Kyiv: Skarby, 2002).

[18] On the Rose Revolution, see Giorgi Kandelaki, "Georgia's Rose Revolution. A Participant's Perspective," United States Institute of Peace Special Report 167 (July 2006), https://www.usip.org/sites/default/files/sr167.pdf.

In 2004, the Orange Revolution demonstrated the moving force of the arts in Ukraine. A tent, a stage, a microphone, and a TV set became symbols of the revolution. The great variety of artistic expression included art exhibitions, satirical TV series, the weaving of orange carpets, and the practice of dressing in orange attire, with the main component a continuous concert performance by musicians, well-known and otherwise, on Independence Square. The Kyiv Maidan of 2013–2014 further accentuated the close links between political and artistic practices,[19] exhibiting a form of direct democracy that dates back to the Kievan Rus' Viche (Popular Assembly).[20]

By combining aspects of politics and art, posters especially became a principal form of revolutionary creativity at the Kyiv Maidan. Examples ranged from handmade satirical posters to the digital visual posts and memes produced and disseminated by internet communities, often including exhortative calls to action. An important means of expressing civic and political stances, posters appeared at the first large demonstration in Kyiv on 24 November 2013. By the time the "March of a Million" took place on 8 December, their number had grown significantly. It was then that the internet community named "Strike Poster" (Straik Plakat) emerged and quickly gained popularity: "We are convinced that the fate of the country is being decided today[!] We call on all creative people to join the all-

---

[19]   Natalia Usenko, "Political Issues in Contemporary Art of Ukraine," *Journal of Education, Culture and Society* 2 (2014).

[20]   Sociological studies of the protests that provide a portrait of the participants are important for understanding Maidan creativity. See *Maidan-2013: Chto stoit, chomy i za shcho?*, Democratic Initiatives Foundation website, http://dif.org.ua /article/maydan-2013-khto-stoit-chomu-i-za-shcho; Olga Onuch, "The Puzzle of Mass Mobilization: Conducting Protest Research in Ukraine, 2004–2014," *Council for European Studies* website, 2014, http://councilforeuropeanstud-ies.org/critcom/the-puzzle-of-mass-mobilization-conducting-protest-re-search-in-ukraine-2004-2014/; Viktor Stepanenko, *Gromadianske suspil'stvo: Dyskursy ta praktyky* (Kyiv: Instytut Sotsiolohii NAN Ukrainy, 2015), http://i-soc.com.ua/uploads/Stepanenko.pdf; and Vladimir Volkovskii, "Maidan i Anti-maidan: Simvoly i anti-simvoly," *Religiia v Ukraini*, 2014, http://www.reli-gion.in.ua/main/25640-majdan-i-antimajdan-simvoly-i-antisimvoly.html.

Ukrainian strike and create strike posters or any other material."[21] The artists worked anonymously. Journalists have aptly referred to the creators of the "Drop in the Ocean" posters as "creative guerrillas."[22] The artists drew a flag with the message, "I am responsible for what happens tomorrow. I am a drop in the ocean," and made their stance public, inviting everyone "who cannot remain silent anymore" to join them. They produced the posters and collected the posters sent by other artists for immediate release through their web-site and Facebook page. The idea was that anybody could freely download, print and use the posters.

One of the most popular and in the main time one of the most conceptual poster-slogans for the Maidan was "I breathe freely" (see Image 1 below), which appeared at the very beginning of the Maidan.

---

[21]   *Straik Plakat* Facebook page, https://www.facebook.com/strikeposter/info?tab =page_info.

[22]   G. Tytysh, "Tvortsi 'Krapli v okeani': Kreatyvni partyzany," *Ukrains'ka Pravda*, 13 February 2014, http://life.pravda.com.ua/society/2014/02/13/152183/. For the "Drop in the Ocean" poster, see: https://www.facebook.com/strikeposter/pho-tos/a.394488944018312.1073741828.394477144019492/542585115875360/?type=3 &theater.

Image 1. Poster "Ia dykhaiu vil'no" ("I breathe freely"). This poster was situated at the corner of Pushkinska and Prorizna streets, two blocks from Independence Square (Maidan) in Kyiv.[23]

---

23   Image source: https://www.facebook.com/strikeposter/photos/a.39448894401831 2.1073741828.394477144019492/542585072542031/?type=3&theater. To see and download the most popular Maidan posters: "30 naikrashchykh revoliutsiynykh plakativ Maidanu," *Chytomo*, 9 December 2013, http://archive.chytomo.com/new s/30-najkrashhix-revolyucijnix-plakativ-majdanu.

Another poster community, Revplakat, posted a laconic text on Facebook, "A page for posting works on social topics," and the slogan, "I know the strength of a word—it is sharper than a bayonet."[24] Viktor Tryhub, the director of the Museum of Posters of Ukraine (created 2011, and an active supporter of the Maidan from 2013) wrote: "The Revolution goes on. This means there will be new masterpieces! Artists, come out to the Maidan!"[25]

Artists documented the Maidan in different ways. Maksym Vegera did so by painting revolutionary clashes: "Grenades were exploding around, participants in the rally ran around and shouted, and tires were burning.... A guy in a helmet jokingly asked me to paint his portrait: 'Painter, paint! This is our history!'"[26] Glib Vysheslavskyi used in his artworks objects that he collected from the Maidan during the protests—cobblestones, gloves, a bottle for a Molotov cocktail, a gas mask, a yellow-and-blue ribbon, metal wire.[27]

Alongside the painters and musicians,[28] filmmakers recorded the Maidan events. A cinema group, Bimba Production, worked on the project "DNA UA," about the people who were channeling their potential into building a New Ukraine. A civil initiative, "BABYLON'13," shot mini-documentaries. Finally, several cinema sketches were compiled into a full-length film about this period titled

---

[24]   *Revplakat* Facebook page, https://www.facebook.com/revplakat/photos_stream.

[25]   V. Tryhub, "Andrii Iermolenko—shche odyn talant Maidanu," *Narodni blogy*, 8 February 2014, http://narodna.pravda.com.ua/fun/52f647ab8db92/. See also on Maidan posters, "Novi revolyutsiyni plakaty Maidanu: vid klumbu na Hrushevs'koho do amurchika z kokteilem molotova," *Espresso TV*. 14 February 2014, https://espreso.tv/news/2014/02/14/novi_revolyuciyni_plakaty_maydanu _vid_klumby_na_hrushevskoho__do_amurchyka_z_kokteylem_molotova. On the Museum of Posters of Ukraine and its 2014 exhibition "Posters of Maidan," see the Museum's website: https://musplakat.wordpress.com/about/.

[26]   "Hudozhnyk iakii pysav z natury batalii na Hrushevskoho, pokazav gotovu kartynu," *Gazeta.ua*, 31 January 2014, http://gazeta.ua/articles/science-l ife/_hudozhnik-yakij-pisav-z-naturi-bataliyi-na-grushevskogo-pokazav-gotov u-kartinu/539475.

[27]   See the website of Glib Vysheslavskyi, Ukrainian artist, art critic, and art historian, at http://esu.com.ua/search_articles.php?id=34266.

[28]   P. Culshaw, "Rock the Barricades: The Ukrainian Musicians Soundtracking the Unrest," *Guardian*, 29 May 2014, https://www.theguardian.com/music/2014/ may/29/rock-barricades-ukrainian-musicians-soundtracking-unrest.

Euromaidan: Rough Cut.[29] These films afford not only reflections on the Maidan but also precious artistic documentation of the protest, since art documents not only events but also emotions.[30]

The theater community created *The Maidan Diaries*, a performance based on testimony from both sides of the barricades, Maidan and anti-Maidan. In December 2013 the playwright Nataliia Vorozhbyt and Mikhail Ugarov, director of the drama company Teatr.doc,[31] initiated this project to capture what people feel in times of radical uncertainty as to what tomorrow may bring.[32] This resulted in a play written by Vorozhbyt, and produced by the director Andrii Maiem.[33]

The literary critic Oleksandr Boichenko commented in February 2014: "Artists are generally egotistical people.... It is evident that when the situation normalizes we will be at loggerheads again, but for now all the decent people are on this side of the barricades."[34] The message of the mystical writer from Odesa, Max Frei,[35] in that cold winter of 2014 was that the Maidaners in Kyiv were "lifting the

---

29   *Euromaidan: Rough Cut* (ten directors), https://vimeo.com/89969382.
30   The year 2014 saw the films *Black Book of Maidan* (based on thirteen essays by thirteen students), https://www.youtube.com/watch?v=ONGtGOfJ7V8; *The Maidan*, by Serhii Loznytsia, https://www.youtube.com/watch?v=UhDeps KqUoA; and *The Maidan: The Ukrainian Argument*, by Serhii Maslobo-ishchykov, https://www.youtube.com/watch?v=2FOhK1vbH4Q. In 2015, *Winter on Fire: Ukraine's Fight for Freedom*, by Evgeny Afineevsky, was nominated for an Oscar for Best Documentary Feature (see https://www.youtube.com/watch?v=MwWsN7fhgRs).
31   Lucy Ash, "Russia's Most Daring Theatre Company," *BBC News*, 16 April 2015, http://www.bbc.com/news/magazine-32320896.
32   I. Oliinyk, "Shchodennyky Ievromaidanu: Ne mozhesh vplynutu na podii—zafiksyi ikh," *Radio Svoboda*, 4 February 2014, htpp://www.radiosvoboda.org/a/25252295.html.
33   Since February 2014, *The Maidan Diaries* has been performed in Kherson, Moscow, Gdansk, and London. It is in the repertoire of the Ivan Franko National Academic Drama Theater, Kyiv.
34   Cited in M. Antoniuk, "Oleksandr Boichenko: Dali bude te, shcho my sami zrobymo," *Versii*, 7 February 2014, http://versii.cv.ua/new/oleksandr-bojch enko-dali-bude-te-shho-mi-sami-zrobimo/26383.html#comments.
35   Max Frei is a pen name invented by the artists Svetlana Martynchik and Igor Steopin for their comic fantasy series, *Labyrinths of Echo*. Along with these series, Frei also take part in other literary projects; see further: http://www.maxfreibooks.net/.

spell from the Earth"[36]—a proposition that seemed entirely realistic at the time. Poets expressed themselves in verse and song lyrics.[37] Documentaries and diaries appeared soon after the Maidan ended; the novels came later.[38] The Library of the Maidan was set up as a social initiative, founded on the principle that there should be a place for art in any confrontation.[39]

Artists from all over Ukraine flocked to the capital,[40] and the most impressive artistic expressions were found at the Kyiv Maidan. However, L'viv, Kharkiv, Odesa, Dnipro, Vinnytsia, and other cities also had their own Maidans, and these also featured amazing artistic elements. Protestors had the support of well-known personalities in the arts, including the actors Arnold Schwarzenegger and George Clooney, American musician and record producer Quincy Jones, the American punk band Gogol Bordello, and German rock group The Scorpions.[41] Rallies took place in Chicago, Berlin, New York, Paris,

---

[36]   M. Frai, "Tam v Kieve liudi raskoldovyvaiut zemliu," *Telekritika*, http://ua.telek ritika.ua/daidzhest/2014-01-31/89973.

[37]   One of the first was a book of poems by the classic of Ukrainian literature: Dmytro Pavlychko, *Virshi z Maidanu* (Kyiv: Osnovy, 2014).

[38]   Documentaries included Glib Gusev and Tamara Kravchenko (eds.), *#Euromaidan: History in the Making?* (Kyiv: Osnovy, 2014); *94 dni: Ievromaidan ochuma TCN*, euromaidan.tsn.ua/; and Sonia Koshkina, *Maidan: Nerasskazannaia istoriia* (Kyiv: Brait Books, 2015). Diaries included Iulia Orlova, *111 dnei Maidana: Zapiski kievlianki. Time line roman* (Kyiv: Dulibi, 2014); Andrei Kurkov, *Dnevnik Maidana* (Kharkiv: Folio, 2015); and Tet'iana Kovtunovych and Tet'iana Pryvalko (eds.), *Maidan vid pershoi osoby* (Kyiv: Instytut Natsional'noi pamiati, 2016). A notable novel based on these days is Olena Zakharchenko, *Vertep: Roman pro Maidan* (Kyiv: Nora-Druk, 2016).

[39]   The Library of the Maidan hosts a list of the books on the Maidan collected by the Revolution of Dignity Museum, http://www.maidanmuseum.org/galereya/ biblioteka-muzeyu-maydanu.

[40]   O. Balashova, "Khudozhniki i revolutsiia," *Ukrains'ka Pravda*, 4 February 2014, http://life.pravda.com.ua/culture/2014/02/4/151225/.

[41]   See "Arnold Schwarzenegger Sends a Message to the Ukrainian People," *Youtube*, 24 January 2014, https://www.youtube.com/watch?time_continue=10 &v=-zrqcB934Qk; "#Maidan Diary: George Clooney rocks FREE YULIA Tymoshenko tee for press photos and interview," *Voices of Ukraine*, 18 January 2014, https://maidantranslations.com/2014/01/18/maidan-diary-george-clooney-roc ks-free-yulia-tymoshenko-tee-at-press-conference-and-interview/; "Gogol Bordello: Ukraine: Not An Outskirt But A Centre," *Gogol Bordello* website, 20 December 2013, http://www.gogolbordello.com/2013/12/20/ukraine-not-an-out- skirt-but-a-centre/; and "Scorpions i Quincy Jones pidtrymaly Maidan i pryvitay

Warsaw. For the protestors, these artistic demonstrations of solidarity were of great importance, attracting as they did worldwide public and governmental attention to the events playing out in Kyiv. The performance artist Alessandro Rauschmann staged an action of solidarity in Berlin. Symbolizing those who had died in Kyiv, the participants wrapped themselves in thermal foil and lay for several hours on the icy pavement in front of the Brandenburg Gate.[42] On 1 February 2014, all channels of Polish TV simultaneously broadcasted a song, "Give Your Hand to Ukraine," by the band Taraka.[43] Later, Polish artists addressed Ukrainians through video feeds, offering their support.

Revolution and Carnival: Kyiv Maidan

The Maidan came into existence between two eras, one dying, and the other on the cusp of being born. The interregnum was marked by an explosion of creativity, which we might conceptualize as a period of Bakhtinian carnival. Bakhtin's carnival metaphor is related to the philosopher's personal knowledge derived from his experience of living through a period of intense political turbulence. As Michael Holquist notes, "Bakhtin works through his own experience of revolution to provide conceptual categories for the aid of others finding themselves in a similar gap between cosmologies."[44] Exploring Bakhtin's life and legacy, Holquist concludes that "Bakhtin's carnival, surely the most productive concept in this book, is not only not an impediment to revolutionary change, it is revolution itself."[45]

Ukrainu z Novym rokom," *Radio Svoboda* 31 December 2013, https://www.radio svoboda.org/a/25217650.html; and the video published by Partia Udar Vitalia Klychka, *Youtube*, 31 December 2013, https://www.youtube.com/watch?time _continue=3&v=spjPDBt8-r8.

[42]   A. Bazdyreva and M. Churikov, "Alessandro Raushmann: Politicheskii kontekst i demonstratsiia pietà," *ART Ukraine*, 29 January 2014, http://artukraine.com.ua /a/alessandro-raushmann-politicheskiy-kontekst-i-demonstraciya-piet/.

[43]   Taraka, *Podaj Rękę Ukrainie*, https://www.youtube.com/watch?v=vhbl17U RCwE.

[44]   Michael Holquist, "Prologue," in Mikhail Bakhtin, *Rabelais and His World* (Bloomington: Indiana University Press, 1984), xiv.

[45]   *Ibid.*, xix.

In fact, Bakhtin retranslates his vision of revolution through the picture he paints of the carnivalesque world.

Bakhtin's carnival offers a productive lens for interpreting the Maidan. The main features of carnival are all present at the Maidan: the temporary upturning of the social pyramid, familiar and free interactions between people, eccentric behavior, unexpected misalliances, sacrilegious mockery. Following Bakhtin, carnival is not a performance, it is life, where there is no difference between spectator and performer. Those who take part in carnival live it, and the results are also part of real life, leading to the suspension of the usual hierarchy in society.

Carnival finds its opposite in the fixities of officialdom. In Kyiv, this took the form of the so-called anti-Maidan, which took up residence in government quarters near the Ukrainian parliament, in Mariinsky Park. While the creative class occupied the Maidan, the authorities organized a Soviet-style concert at the anti-Maidan, conveying people to the site. According to the logic of Bakhtin's concept, if Maidan is a carnival, the anti-Maidan is an "official feast," or at least an attempt at creating such a feast. As Bakhtin notes, "The official feast asserted all that was stable, unchanging, perennial: the existing hierarchy, the existing religious, political, and moral values, norms, and prohibitions. It was the fête of a truth already established, the dominant truth that had been forwarded as eternal and indisputable."[46] Maidan was a protest against the status quo (the regime). The anti-Maidan was a protest against the protests; it supported the established order.

The film director Valerii Balaian has pointed out the aesthetic polarity of the Maidan and anti-Maidan. He notes that the dividing line had first to run through people's consciousness as, in the words of the philosopher Merab Mamardashvili, they "awoke to life," while other people were stuck in Soviet dreams.[47] The famous composer Valentyn Syl'vestrov likewise remarked, "Ukraine's anthem was sung at the Maidan.... And what happened at the Anti-Maidan?

---

[46]   Bakhtin, *Rabelais and His World*, 9.
[47]   Cited in V. Balaian, "Pesni Maidana i AntiMaidana," *Grani.ru*, 3 February 2014, http://grani.ru/blogs/free/entries/224102.html.

People were silent, listened to some Soviet songs with some stupid words, and did not sing."[48]

Actually, the Orange Revolution in 2004 also saw the Maidan and the Anti-Maidan. The rock music on the Orange stages created a new world with new myths and heroes, while the nostalgic Soviet art of the Anti-Maidan returned people to times past. The new and the old in art were in confrontation, reinforced by a whole range of social, economic, and psychological factors: the acts were broadcast on TV and were seized on for purposes of political bickering.[49]

In keeping with Bakhtin's concept, for the protestors, the carnivalesque Maidan became life itself: they existed in it and participated in it, sharing a universal spirit of freedom. Attendees at the anti-Maidan were, by contrast, spectators of an official show mounted to shore up the strength of the overlords' rule. Bakhtin wrote, "Carnival is the people's second life, organized on the basis of laughter. It is a festive life."[50] Laughter, grotesquery, and satire were important features of Maidan art, especially in posters, songs, performances.[51] Bakhtin points out that feasts sponsored by the state "did not lead the people out of the existing world order and created no second life. On the contrary, they sanctioned the existing pattern of things and reinforced it.... [They] looked back at the past and used the past to consecrate the present."[52] The anti-Maidan aimed to support existing leaders, values, norms, and it was a serious mission, without laughter.

Svetlana Zhabotynskaia, professor and expert in cognitive linguistics, argues that the anti-Maidan often attempted to replicate

48   T. Borodina, "Replika: Valentin Sil'vestrov," *Elegant New York*, 28 March 2014, http://elegantnewyork.com/silvestrov/.

49   The satirical series "Funny Eggs" was extremely popular. See: https://www.yout ube.com/watch?v=VMpfOak4hh4.

50   Bakhtin, *Rabelais and His World*, 9.

51   N. P. Kovtoniuk, "Smyslovy kontsept karnavalu iak prochytannia dyskursu Maidanu," *Movni i kontseptual'ni kartyny svitu*, vyp. 1. (2015), http://nbuv.gov. ua/UJRN/Mikks_2015_1_39.

52   Bakhtin, *Rabelais and His World*, 10.

the Maidan.[53] This attempt was largely unconvincing. It is possible to copy specific material objects—stages, tires, barricades, and sandwiches—but replicating spontaneous outbursts of creativity is not so easy. The Kyiv anti-Maidan lacked the murals and graffiti, the original songs and performances and creative installations of the Maidan. The cartoonist Oleg Smal in February 2014 noted, "for some reason artists do not go to the anti-Maidan. Maybe the smell of Stalin's camps is too strong there."[54]

Andrew Robinson claims that Bakhtin's concept of carnival provides a positive alternative vision, not only a deconstruction of dominant culture but an alternative way of living based on a pattern of play.[55] The Maidan formed its alternative carnivalesque space in and around Kyiv's central square. Henri Lefebvre claims that the production of space is a social process that defines the social behaviour of humans and their perception.[56]

Kyiv Maidan became the territory of art, namely of public art.[57] Spontaneous creative installations together with tents, often decorated with paintings and slogans, filled the carnivalesque space of the Maidan.[58] The artist Petr Pavlenskii draws attention to the

[53]   S. A. Zhabotinskaia, *Maidan-Antimaidan: Slovar'-tezarus leksicheskikh innovatsii. Iazyk kak oruzhie v voine mirovozzrenii*, March 2015, http://uaclip. at.ua/zhabotinskaja-jazyk_kak_oruzhie.pdf.

[54]   K. Avramchuk, "Karykaturyst Oleg Smal': Na Antimaidan mytsi ne idut'. Mabut', tam duzhe tkhne stalinskymy taboramy," *Insider*, 10 February 2014, http://www.theinsider.ua/art/karikaturist-oleg-smal-na-antimaidan-mittsine-idut-mabut-tam-duzhe-tkhne-stalinskimi taborami/.

[55]   A. Robinson, "In Theory Bakhtin: Carnival against Capital, Carnival against Power," *Ceasefire*, 9 September 2011, https://ceasefiremagazine.co.uk/in-theory -bakhtin-2/.

[56]   Henri Lefebvre, "La production de l'espace," in *L'espace social*, ed. Henri Lefebvre (Paris: Anthropos, 1974).

[57]   The art of the Maidan can be analyzed within the framework of public art studies, as "art in the public interest." For more, see Miwon Kwon, "Public Art and Urban Identities," *transversal texts* 1 (2002), http://eipcp.net/transversal/0102/ kwon/en; and Cher Krause Knight, *Public Art: Theory, Practice and Populism* (London: Wiley-Blackwell, 2008).

[58]   Installation art creates artistic environments without a border between art and life, producing a dialogue between artist and space. For more, see Claire Bishop, *Installation Art: A Critical History* (London: Tate Publishing, 2005); and N. A. Kelly, "What Is Installation Art?" *ARROW@DIT*, 2010, http://arrow.dit.ie/cgi/ viewcontent.cgi?article=1006&context=aaschadpcat.

fact that the barricades created a special context for the Maidan and turned it into the ultimate installation, a part of the city that recreated itself and functioned as an art object. Pavlenskii considers the Maidan to have been a great work of art, as a site enabling the process of creation and the emergence of new models of interpersonal communication.[59] The installation-fortification "Artistic Barbican"[60] on Khreshchatyk became a public space for creative intellectuals to hold art events, exhibitions, and literary readings.

The main symbol and central installation was the Euromaidan "Christmas tree."[61] This was a grandiose metal scaffold in the general shape of a tree and covered with protest banners.[62] From the early days, protesters stacked up placards bearing the names of the different cities and villages of Ukraine they came from, as well as districts of Kyiv. The result was a "geographic installation" symbolizing Ukraine's unity. Photographers put together three photo installations jointly known as *Maidan: The Human Factor*, declaring, "We want to tell Ukraine and the world how Ukrainians became a nation."[63] They shot the most striking moments and distributed them on social media, but exhibitions on the Maidan itself also carried the message of their personal involvement. Painters also created their own open-air exhibitions and installations. Graphic artists and cartoonists were the first to show their Maidan works. Wooden

59   M. Lanko and E. German, "Petr Pavlenskii: Maidan dolzhen prisutstvovat' v povsednevnosti kazhdogo, kto ego podderzhivaet," *Ukrains'ka Pravda*, 23 December 2013, http://life.pravda.com.ua/person/2013/12/23/146798/.

60   A barbican is a fortification protecting approaches to city gates. In the late medieval period, such fortifications would meet the first assault of the enemy and give defenders an opportunity to close the gate to the main fortress. See "Artistic Barbican" here: mystetskyi barbakan at https://vimeo.com/88274791.

61   It is now in the Revolution of Dignity Museum.

62   "A New Revolution on Maidan Square," *Economist*, https://www.economist.co om/news/europe/21591217-has-ukrainians-defiance-presidents-european-polic y-split-country-new-revolution; and "Christmas Tree with Protest Banners on Maidan," *Guardian*, https://witness.theguardian.com/assignment/529c5106e4b 0999a297a93b6/704337.

63   *Ukrains'ki fotografy na Khreshchatyku predstavyly instaliatsiiu "Maidan. Ludskii factor,"* http://www.unn.com.ua/uk/news/1286880-ukrayinski-fotografi-na-kh reschatiku-predstavili-instalyatsiyu-maydan-lyudskiy-faktor.

figurines of a "Praying Mother" by an artist from Kolomiia, Yaro-slav,[64] formed an installation not far from the marble sculpture *New Ukraine*, representing a woman emerging from the depths.[65] A French street artist, Roti, presented the Maidan with this allegory of the Ukrainian revolution as a gift symbolizing his solidarity with the protestors.[66]

These installations enlivened the Maidan space and attracted many viewers. They became integral parts of the carnivalesque pattern, along with numerous performances and references to historic Kyiv in the form of catapults, decorated with wooden shields and placed above the artistic barbican. Several artists gave their works the title "The New Middle Ages."[67] Tamara Hundorova argues that the creative sociocultural character of the Maidan extended the carnivalesque formula by transforming this space and place into a cornucopia of opportunities. Ordinary people began writing poetry, singing, painting, and participating in all kinds of performances at the Maidan. Hundorova analyzes the Maidan as a carnivalesque social performance that united politics and aesthetics, and considers this phenomenon to be one of the most significant indicators of the Ukrainian revolution.[68] From this perspective the singing of Ukraine's national anthem on the Maidan deserves special attention: this became one of the most enduring symbols of the Revolution of Dignity. It was sung many times a day, but its singing on New

---

[64] See his story in the film *The Citizen*, by Oleksandr Shkrabak, https://www.you tube.com/watch?v=QrUM1GUy5Xk.

[65] Jaime Rojo and Steven Harrington, "A 'New Ukraine' Sculpture in Kyiv by Street Artist Roti," *Huffington Post*, 29 January 2014, http://www.huffingtonpost.com /jaime-rojo-steven-harrington/street-artist-roti-places_b_4677340.html; see especially the interpolated segment by Alexandra Parrish, "Rotl's 'New Ukraine.'"

[66] This two-meter-high sculpture weighing four tons survived all the tragic events of the Maidan and is now in the Revolution of Dignity Museum.

[67] Some examples are Olexa Mann's painting *New Middle Ages* (2014) and Mariia Pavlenko's photo series *New Middle Ages* (2014). See further Natalia Moussienko, *Mystetstvo Maidanu* (Kyiv: ArtHuss, 2015), 65, 70, http://www.mari.kiev.ua/ sites/default/files/inline-images/pdfs/Moussienko_MAIDAN_ART.pdf.

[68] Tamara Hundorova, "Ukrainian Euromaidan as Social and Cultural Performance," in *Revolution and War in Contemporary Ukraine: The Challenge of Change*, ed. Olga Bertelsen (Stuttgart: *ibidem* Verlag, 2016), 161–79.

Year's Eve in 2013 became an extraordinary performance, when nearly half a million Ukrainians sang the anthem in unison. During this mass singing, participants lit and raised torches.[69]

The art of Maidan covered a wide-ranging territory from witty protest to radical challenge and through to the sacral, and organically drew in elements of the avant-garde, mass culture, and high classicism. These elements dominated differentially across the three main phases of the Maidan. The first phase was focused mainly on Ukraine's place in Europe[70] and was marked by a general mood of carnival. This lasted from 21 November to 30 November 2013, the night of the beating of student protesters. The second phase encompassed 30 November 2013 through to 19 January 2014, when the first dead appeared on the square. During this phase the protests became more numerous and were organized around a dominant theme, the overthrow of criminal power. Satirical and radical art tendencies dominated at this point. This peaceful phase marked the culmination of the carnivalesque phase, with its blossoming of artistic creativity. The third phase, from 19 January until the Maidan's victory at the end of February 2014, turned into an actual battle with live ammunition and snipers operating in Kyiv's downtown, leaving more than a hundred dead.[71] During this phase, sacral[72] and radical art dominated and the playfulness and social inversions of the earlier period fell away. Art born during this third phase already anticipated the war in the Donbas. The avant-garde tendencies of Maidan art in

---

69   "Anthem of Ukraine," *UkrStream.TV*, 2 January 2014, https://www.youtube.com /watch?v=yftjaDXxAGc.

70   Anton Shekhovtsov, "The Ukrainian Revolution Is European and National," *Eurozine*, 13 December 2013, http://www.eurozine.com/the-ukrainian-revolution-is-european-and-national/.

71   "The Heavenly Hundred" was adopted in Ukraine as the collective name for the Maidan dead. It recalls the organization of the army into division into "hundreds," both of the Maidan Self-Defense and the Zaporizhzhia Cossack troops in the seventeenth and eighteenth centuries. The Verkhovna Rada of Ukraine established the Order of the Heavenly Hundred Heroes on 1 July 2014.

72   In the winter of 2014, Valentyn Syl'vestrov dedicated several compositions to the Maidan dead. On 26 February 2014 the National Philharmonic of Ukraine gave a charitable concert, conducted by Roman Kofman, in their memory. The musicians played works by Shostakovich, Grieg, and Beethoven. Admission was free and the concert was broadcast on Ukrainian TV channels.

its installations, performances, and the like were quickly absorbed by mass culture and applied broadly to easy-to-sell merchandise. This process thus entailed a form of commodification, but it also offered an efficient way to deliver messages to the public.

Conclusion

The cultural and performative dimensions of the Kyiv Maidan outlined here lead to the following conclusions. First and foremost, we have shown that the interplay of political and artistic features became one of the main characteristics of the Revolution of Dignity that helped make it comprehensible within a broader world context. The Maidan itself was the scene of complex collective artistic expression, filled with emotion and creativity. This expression was powerful in form and unquestionably diverse in content: it was radical and political, philosophical and poetical, and deeply aesthetic.

As the Ukrainian philosopher and active Maidan participant Vadym Skurativskyi has pointed out, a philosophical understanding of the Maidan and its significance is only now emerging.[73] However, as I have shown in this article, Bakhtin's concept of carnival, with its freedom from quotidian roles and daring renewal of expressive values, offers a fruitful line of inquiry for interpreting the Maidan. As Holquist has argued, Bakhtin's carnival is in the final analysis about "freedom, the courage needed to establish it, the cunning required to maintain it, and—above all—the horrific ease with which it can be lost."[74] A philosopher carnivalizing the present creates hope for the future. Carnival forms, Bakhtin writes, "present the victory of this future over the past.... The birth of the new ... is as indispensable and as inevitable as the death of the old."[75]

For Ukrainians, the cultural and performative dimensions of the Maidan marked a critical pivot away from the old Soviet

---

[73]   Vadym Skurativskyi, interview with Natalia Moussienko, 25 July 2017, personal archives of Natalia Moussienko; "V. Skurativsky: The Art of Maidan," *Ukrainian Week*, 18 November 2016, http://ukrainianweek.com/Society/178789.

[74]   Holquist, "Prologue," xxi.

[75]   Bakhtin, *Rabelais and His World*, 256.

paradigms.[76] New narratives entered Ukrainian art discourse, ranging from calls for Euro-integration to social mobilization for civil rights and, later, the battle for the Motherland, which was highlighted by many artists. Thus, after the Maidan victory, the main challenge to Maidan art appears to be its official status, which threatens to merge that art into what Bakhtin calls "a truth already established, the predominant truth."[77] This is a danger for any revolutionary art. The task facing the artist today has arguably become even more challenging: to avoid the Maidan's "mummification." The Revolution of Dignity Museum faces the most difficult task, for it takes its mission to be not only the collection of Maidan artefacts, remembrance documents, and memorials, but also the creation of a platform for understanding the Ukrainian revolution in the context of modern social and artistic processes.[78]

Three and a half years after Maidan, on 2 September 2017, the last pieces of revolutionary art left in the Kyiv city space, emblematic graffiti known as "Icons of the Revolution," were removed.[79] The existence and subsequent removal of the graffiti, which depicted a trio of historical figures, ignited a wide range of reactions and

---

[76]   Anne Applebaum, "Ukraine Has Finally Removed All 1,320 Lenin Statues. Our Turn," *Washington Post*, 25 August 2017, https://www.washingtonpost.com/opinions/ukraine-has-finally-removed-all-1320-lenin-statues-our-turn/2017/08/25/cd2d5b06-89ae-11e7-961d-2f373b3977ee_story.html?utm_term=.c595dd60c179.

[77]   Bakhtin, *Rabelais and His World*, 9.

[78]   See *Kontseptsiia Natsional'noho Memorial'noho kompleksu Heroiv Nebesnoi Sotni: Muzeiu Revolutsii Hidnosti* (Kyiv: Instytut Natsional'noi pamiati, 2017); and Muzei Maidanu http://www.maidanmuseum.org/uk/storinka/muzey-maydanu.

[79]   In February 2014, next to the barricades on Hrushevskoho Street, the social artist "Sociopath" created a trilogy, "Icons of the Revolution," in which Taras Shevchenko is depicted wearing a bandana; Lesya Ukrainka, a gas mask; and Ivan Franko, a builder's helmet. In this way the most famous writers of Ukraine "joined" the protests. For the author it was "a tribute to heroes, both living and deceased." See more at "Ukrainian Banksy: Street Artist #Sociopath Talks about Social Art," *Ukrainian Week*, 27 May 2014, http://ukrainianweek.com/Culture/115470. The Maidan artifacts are collected in the Revolution of Dignity Museum; see the website: https://www.facebook.com/maidanmuseum.org/.

discussion.[80] The debate around "Icons" brought into sharp focus not only the Maidan art itself and arguments over the destruction versus preservation of contemporary historical memory, but also issues connected to the rule of law, the role of mass media, the function of education, and the nature of vandalism.

Nevertheless, art continues to advance against the backdrop of the difficult reform process in post-Maidan Ukraine. As one observer recently pointed out, "In the wake of the 2014 Maidan Revolution and the breakout of war in the east, the country is undergoing a fast-paced cultural renaissance that recalls the tumultuous 1960s in the United States and Western Europe."[81] Kyiv has been filled with a huge number of murals in different styles, Ukrainian cinema has been re-energized, and artistic life is thriving. Without any question, all of this can be traced to the impact of the Maidan.

---

[80] "Scandal Caused by Destruction of the Maidan Graffiti: How Historical Memory Is Destroyed," Ukrainian Crises Media Centre website, 5 September 2017, http://uacrisis.org/60063-maidan-graffiti-historical-memory-destroyed.

[81] V. Maheshwari, "As Reforms Stall, a Ukrainian Cultural Revolution: 5 Ways in Which Violence, Crisis and Upheaval Are Driving the Country's Arts and Culture," *Politico*, 29 August 2017, http://www.politico.eu/article/ukrainian-cultural-revolution-odessa-as-reforms-stall/?utm_content=buffer2f9fb&utm_medium=social&utm_source=twitter.com&utm_campaign=buffer. For more, see J. d'Orazio, "Why Kiev, Ukraine Is Europe's Next Cool Spot," *Escape*, 6 September 2017, http://www.escape.com.au/world/europe/why-kiev-ukraine-is-europes-next-cool-spot/news-story/598c416e858d5722d8a2dc6b32352ba3.

Regional Political Regimes in Ukraine after the Euromaidan

Oleksiy Krysenko

Abstract: *This article examines the prospects for the formation of regional political regimes in Ukraine after the Euromaidan. The author argues that the current policy of decentralization of political governance in Ukraine against the background of weak state institutions, the Russian occupation of the Crimean peninsula and a significant part of the Donetsk and Lugansk regions, and ongoing military operations, entails serious political and institutional risks in the future as it will lead to the consolidation of neo-patrimonial regional political regimes. The process of decentralization of political governance currently underway in Ukraine with the simultaneous concentration of power in the hands of regional elites threatens to lead not only to a decrease in the manageability of institutional and political infrastructure by the central government in the future, but also to a further consolidation of regional neo-patrimonial regimes which often effectively function as a counterweight to real liberal-democratic reform in Ukraine.*

The article argues that, in the current Ukrainian conditions, decentralization is not an instrument for further political democratization. It rather serves as an instrument for political liberation of destructive political subjects (such as ultra-radical paramilitary organizations, and regional clans). In addition, in the current context, decentralization facilitates actualization of pre-modern forms of political participation, now released from a rigid centralized state system of management and posing a threat to the political stability and territorial integrity of the state. The author concludes that the institutional architecture of the Ukrainian political system, built on the principle of dominance of the informal over the formal sphere, is in urgent need of modernization.

Introduction

At the heart of this article is the question of Ukraine's prospects for further democratic development. According to the Economist Intelligence Unit's Democracy Index (2016 assessments), institutionally, the Ukrainian state can be described as a "hybrid regime," close to a "flawed democracy."[1] The post-Soviet anthropology of Ukrainian political and power institutions does not inspire confidence in the prospects for the further democratic development of Ukraine. The key hypothesis of this article is that the current policy of decentralization of political governance in Ukraine, against a background of weak state institutions, the Russian occupation of the Crimean peninsula and a significant part of Donetsk and Lugansk regions, and ongoing military actions, entails serious political and institutional risks.

Many Ukrainian experts argue that decentralization carries the considerable risk of federalization of the Ukrainian state. The prospect of federalization has been the subject of ongoing scholarly and political debate. There is broad agreement that the federalization of Ukraine is one of the goals pursued by Russia in its efforts to seize control of Ukraine. Under a federative arrangement, the regions of Ukraine would be able to exercise veto power over the foreign policy aspirations of the Ukrainian state. Thus, federation would result in a situation whereby certain regions, such as the Donbas or Crimea (in the event that they are returned to the full control of Ukraine), would be able to block Ukraine's prospects for further European integration.

Most importantly for the purposes of this article, decentralization of political governance also serves to concentrate power in the hands of regional elites rather than local communities, as the Maidan protestors hoped. In this connection decentralization threatens to lead not only to a decrease in the manageability of the institutional and political infrastructure by the central government but also to the further establishment of regional neo-patrimonial

---

[1]   The Economist Intelligence Unit's Democracy Index (2016), https://info graphics.economist.com/2017/DemocracyIndex/.

regimes,[2] which act as a counterweight to real liberal democratic reform in Ukraine. The goal of this article is to describe the character of said regional neo-patrimonial regimes that are being formed and to explain how they inhibit the central government's ability to enact liberal democratic reforms and manage political institutions in Ukraine's regions. In my view, there are two main challenges on the agenda of Ukraine's regional development. First, will the central government be capable of carrying out administrative and territorial decentralization and simultaneously achieving the degree of coordination of regional policies necessary in order to forestall the threat of separatism? Second, will the center succeed in coordinating regional policies and implementing a "new transition" to democracy—the transition from a centralized neo-patrimonial regime with a dominant party through to a way out of post-revolution uncertainty?

The methodological focus of this article is placed on analyses of the regional political process and is an attempt to consider the processes of decentralization through the prism of the formation of regional political regimes. The sources of information are electoral dispositions and informal practices of regional political regimes, including patron-client relations between the central government and regional groups. I use these sources to analyze the conditions for the democratization of the Ukrainian state after the "Revolution of Dignity" in the context of a neo-patrimonial regime.

The general political tenor of Ukrainian regional issues has been well studied. A significant number of works are devoted to regional characteristics,[3] regional integrational political and cultural differences, regional identity, and the civic specifics of local self-

---

2   Neo-patrimonialism (Lat. *patrimonium:* patrimony, personal possession) is a term that characterizes a special type of organization of public political power and relations having to do with power, law, and property, where elements of traditional patrimonial (private, personal) domination are synthesized with modern political and legal practices.

3   See, for example, M. Riabchuk, *Dvi Ukrainy: Real'ni mezhy, virtual'ni viiny* (Kyiv: Krytyka, 2003); and V. Chuzhykov, O. Fedirko, and A. Chuzhykov, "Methodological Background of Post-Soviet Regionalism: The Case of Ukraine," *Baltic Journal of European Studies (Tallinn University of Technology)* 4, no. 1 (2016): 20–33.

government of individual regions.[4] The regional elites (and external actors) sometimes try to use the historical and certain other specific features (cultural, political) of some regions as justification for pursuing a regional development vector that is separate and distinct from the state's development vector—including a forthright separatist vector.[5] However, the problem of the formation of regional political regimes in Ukraine has not yet been adequately addressed theoretically. Indeed, in contrast, for example, to the Russian situation, in which the study of regional political regimes is quite developed,[6] in the Ukrainian situation of unitary political governance it might seem odd, at first glance, even to consider regional political regimes. The eras of the governments of President Leonid Kuchma (1994–2004) and Viktor Yanukovych (2010–2013) were a time of monopolization of the political sphere and excessive centralization of the system of public administration based on regional business and political groupings widely known respectively as the "Dnipropetrovsk" and "Donetsk" camps. The models of government of Leonid Kravchuk (1991–94) and Viktor Yushchenko (2005–2010) (which did not have the support of influential regional groups) could have led to the formation of some constellation of regional political regimes, but those governments turned out to be "weak presidencies" (overseen by presidents who lost the considerable electoral support they

---

4   See, for example, T. Kuzio, "Nationalism, Identity and Civil Society in Ukraine: Understanding the Orange Revolution," *Communist and Post-Communist Studies* 43 (2010): 285–96; and A. Polyakova, "From the Provinces to the Parliament: How the Ukrainian Radical Right Mobilized in Galicia," *Communist and Post-Communist Studies* 47 (2014): 211–25.

5   S. Shulman, "Asymmetrical International Integration and Ukrainian National Disunity," *Political Geography* 18 (1999): 913–39; and R. Clem, "Dynamics of the Ukrainian State-Territory Nexus," *Eurasian Geography and Economics* 55, no. 3 (2014): 219–35.

6   See, for example, V. Gel'man, "Regional'nye rezhimy: Zavershenie transformatsii?" *Svobodnaia mysl'* 9 (1996); V. Gel'man, "Transformatsii i rezhimy. Neopredelennost' i ee posledstviia," in *Rossii regionov: Transformatsiia politicheskikh rezhimov* (Moscow: Ves' mir; Berliner Wissenschaftsverlag, 2000); R. Turovskii, "Regional'nye politicheskie rezhimy v Rossii: K metodologii analiza," *Polis* 2 (2009): 77–95; and Y. Gaivoronskii, "Regional'nye politicheskie rezhimy v Rossii: Kontseptual'nye novatsii i vozmozhnosti izmereniia," *Politeia* 2 (2015): 21–37.

enjoyed at the beginning of their terms), and they had to struggle to hang on to power not in a contest with influential regional business and political elites but merely in order to cohabit with strong prime ministers and their political parties and regional groupings.

Preliminary Conditions for the Current Ukrainian Democratization

The political events of autumn 2013 through winter 2014, known as the Euromaidan or the Revolution of Dignity, engendered a belief in the possibility of destroying the criminal system of power associated with Viktor Yanukovych's regime, as well as a belief in the "democratic character of the new government"—two popular opinions that have almost become clichés. With the subsequent regime change following Yanukovych's departure, the core idea of Ukrainian democratization was formulated by President of Ukraine Petro Poroshenko,[7] entailing decentralization of the system of economic and political governance.[8] In fact, the idea of a "Europe of Regions" had a prolonged life in Ukraine, but unlike the European concept, the Ukrainian concept presupposed not only the creation of a European confederation but also the reconstruction of patron-client verticals in the state government system.

The main problem with the decentralization of political governance in Ukraine, I argue, is that under the conditions that exist in Ukraine today, decentralization has become less an instrument for further political democratization than a tool for the political emancipation of destructive political actors (ultra-radical paramilitary organizations, regional clans) and for the installation of non-

---

[7]   For more detail, see "Detsentralizatsiia trebuet chestnogo razgovora s liud'mi—Prezident," President of Ukraine official website, 9 September 2015, http://www.president.gov.ua/ru/news/decentralizaciya-potrebuye-chesnoyi-rozmovi-z-lyudmi-prezide-35944.

[8]   It should be noted that in carrying out decentralization under current conditions the Ukrainian government faces a difficult trilemma: is it possible to simultaneously implement democratic reforms in the short term, introduce decentralization (and deconcentration) of state governance, and resist external military aggression?

modern forms of political participation (including patriarchal models of elite recruitment and the non-electoral mobilization of public groups), which, once released from a rigid centralized state patrimonial management system, pose a threat to the political stability and territorial integrity of the state. An example can serve to illustrate this point. On 14 October 2017 the chief military prosecutor of Ukraine stated that part of Ukraine's border with Hungary—a 150-kilometer segment in Transcarpathia—was actually privately owned.[9] Ukrainian border and police officers no longer have direct access to this section of the nation's border as the local authorities have given the land that adjoins the border to private entities. Later, this land was captured by regional criminal groups, which use their private access to the border to enable smuggling of drugs and weapons, people-trafficking, and other illegal activities.[10]

The classic assumption is that de-concentration of the public administration system (in some cases, federalization or decentralization)[11] through the devolvement or separation of powers will rein in the neo-patrimonial usurpation of power by the central government and contribute to the overall democratization and liberalization of the architecture of public administration and other components of the political sphere. It is this assumption that has driven the idea of decentralization (regionalization) of the system of political and economic governance in Ukraine (since 2014). Notable in the case of Ukraine, however, was the central government's attempt to refuse subsidizing the regions out of the state budget when the state faced a catastrophic shortage of financial resources after the Russian aggression in 2014.[12] The logic behind decentralization

---

9   112 Ukraine, "Matios soobshchil, chto 150 kilometrov ukrainskoi granitsy s Vengriei iavliaiutsia chastnymi: Reaktsiia GPSU," *YouTube*, 14 October 2017, https://www.youtube.com/watch?v=XonVtnYBM782017.

10   See Dmitrii Gomon, "Chastnaia granitsa Attily. Kak na Zakarpat'e organizowali 5-kilometrovuiu dyru dlia kontrabandy," *Espreso*, 17 November 2017, https://ru.espreso.tv/article/2017/11/17/chastnaya_granyca_attyly_kak_na_zaka rpate_organyzovaly_5_kylometrovuyu_dyru_dlya_kontrabandy.

11   See, for example, D. Elazar, "Sravnitel'nyi federalizm," *Polis* 5 (1995): 106–115.

12   Particularly interesting illustrations, in this case, are the attempts of the Ukrainian government to reform or modernize the health care system, educational system, and road infrastructure. As traditional consumers of state financing and

generally makes sense theoretically, but in reality, if one takes into account the post-Soviet experience of political development, it is easy to conclude together with Russian political scientist Vladimir Nechaev that "the distribution of power from the center to the regions and the introduction of procedures for the democratic legitimization of regional authorities, as a rule, does not lead to the formation of a democratic political regime in the region."[13] Such conclusions are not, of course, axiomatic, but they may suggest the likely outcome of a situation in which "liberalization and democratization" of the public administration in the absence of a system of inclusive institutions (i.e., institutions that guarantee the rule of law and distribute power among a wide range of citizens) in fact reduces access to social and economic benefits for a significant number of people. One of the reasons for the slowing or degradation of liberal democratic reforms in the post-Soviet space is that their intermediate results have not been shared with the majority of the electorate. The Russian economist Sergei Guriev has emphasized this feature very clearly: "If reforms do not bring benefits to everybody, if the benefits of reforms are distributed unjustly and unevenly, these reforms are not legitimate, not sustainable and often reversed."[14]

The Ukrainian political scientist Oleksandr Fisun connects the exceptional features of post-Soviet political development with

---

at the same time symbols of the inefficiency of public administration, these systems were the first to undergo the current version of administrative and territorial reform, aimed at "state decentralization." The central government maintains the pragmatic hope of shifting the burden of financing these areas to the regional budgets (especially with respect to the maintenance and modernization of the road infrastructure). However, the transfer of budget obligations that were traditional for the post-Soviet space to local financing ultimately threatens to reconfigure the entire regional political economy. Thus, local political regimes would have additional financial control over the electoral resources at their disposal; that is, they would be able to expand institutional and financial control over the so-called "local budget workers," or those who are paid out of the local budget, such as teachers, doctors, public service workers—generally, state employees.

[13] V. Nechaev, "Regional'nye politicheskie sistemy v post-sovetskoi Rossii," *Pro et Contra* 5, no. 1 (Winter 2000): 80–95.

[14] S. Guriev, "V Ukraine ne khvatit resursov, chtoby priblizit'sia k Evrope," *YouTube*, 1 December 2016, https://www.youtube.com/watch?v=BcNry-6JgWU.

the neo-patrimonial quality (institutional structure) of both the post-Soviet political systems themselves and their ruling class (the patrimonial elite). He writes, "A specific feature of patrimonialism is, first of all, the appropriation of the sphere of government by the official bearers of political power, as well as the unsegmented public-political and private sphere of society, as a result of which the state is governed as private ownership ('patrimony') of ruling groups that on the basis of the power-property system privatize various public functions and public institutions."[15] The key negative feature of the neo-patrimonial state system is the appropriation of public institutions by influential oligarchic groups, as well as the formation of socio-political relations around the patron-client system in society in general. An acceptance of patronage and client dependence is institutionalized in all areas of social practice without exception— political, economic, legal, cultural, and educational. Post-Soviet neo-patrimonial systems are characterized by the fact that the law loses its universal integrative function, and legal instruments are in demand only in a limited social space, mostly in cases of conflict between influential political and business players, that is, when the pattern of the contractual model of democracy works. In general terms, the justice system departs from the liberal-legal regime of the rule of law and moves toward the political and legal regime of "rule by law."[16] So "legal arbitration" is used separately in the fight against the state or as a legitimate state capture by groups of business interests, with privatization of state property, revision of ownership, job rent, power entrepreneurship, and "selective justice" used as forms of politically inspired legal reprisals against one's opponents. Deformation of the rule of law leads to the blurring of public architecture and the emergence of Ukrainian varieties of regional neo-feudalism, with its institutions of class-based justice.[17] The consequence of such

---

[15]   A. Fisun, *Demokratiia, neopatrimonializm and global'nye transformatsii* (Kharkov: Constant, 2006), 154.

[16]   T. Carothers, "Rule of Law Temptations," *Fletcher Forum of World Affairs* 33, no. 1 (Winter/Spring 2009), http://carnegieendowment.org/files/Rule_of_Law_Te mptations.pdf.

[17]   In the period before the Revolution of Dignity, there were events in the regions that became some of the catalysts of delegitimization of the central

deformation is a systemic failure of legality of the ruling elite, and a situation in which institutions of willful deterrence of the elite are not legal mechanisms, but a factor of affective violence (violent uprising) on the part of the masses. Patronage over local courts—district and regional courts of regional jurisdiction—is one of the key indicators of the formation and reproduction of regional political regimes. The degree of patronage over the courts in cities or megacities by the mayor demonstrates either the degree of inclusion of the mayoral vertical in the national patron-client vertical or the degree of presence of personal control over the local or regional justice system (and/or over certain segments of the law enforcement system in the megacity or region). Unfortunately, Ukraine lacks reliable statistics on the number of court decisions in favor of city halls and their structural units, which could indicate the degree of loyalty of local courts to local political regimes. However, the traditional bias in favor of supporting solutions that are beneficial for local incumbents is very much in evidence.

The "anti-corruption agenda" in the relationship between the central and regional authorities warrants separate investigation. The anti-corruption campaign in Ukraine, which has been conducted (since 2015) at both the central and regional levels, has less to do with corruption, which is a structural component of the post-Soviet order, than with corrupt officials in the context of the struggle between the center and the regions over legitimacy. Kirill Rogov illustrates this post-Soviet situation very well with his concept of a "regime of soft legal restrictions" that develops at both national and regional levels: "Constant *talk about corruption*, discussions of the ubiquity of corruption, almost never lead to the delegitimation of the established social hierarchy and political order but rather strengthen it and serve, as a result, the goals of propaganda and legalization of this order as an irresistible fact of life (while the legal

---

government. For example, the so-called popular rebellion in Vradievka in the summer of 2013 and the case of Anastasia Makar in 2012 highlighted the level of corruption in the state law enforcement system and showed that the central government is incapable of liberal democratic compromises with society on sensitive issues of public justice and relies on cronyism of power and the development of repressive practices.

order begins to be considered an artificial fiction)."[18] Rogov based his conceptualization on the Russian case, but it also reflects well the current Ukrainian situation in general: this is a situation in which the fight against corruption is often replaced by the fight against particular corrupt officials—that is, it often amounts to replacing a particular disloyal, corrupt person with one's own politically loyal corrupt official.

The Search for a Theoretical Framework for a Regional Political Regime

Defining "regional political regime" is important in the first instance in order to understand the operational capabilities of this term and the conceptual specifics of its application. Definitions of this term usually proceed along one of two paths: the legal-juridical path, or the sociological path. In the legal-juridical case regional regimes are interpreted through the lens of the formal-constitutional institutional features of a particular political unit. Sociological definitions, on the other hand, focus on the informal institutional parameters required for the formation of regional political regimes that are separated from the central regime because of actual (real) policy differences or institutional disintegration of the state system (e.g., as a consequence of the degradation of public administration).[19] In the sociological case the functions of the absent state are carried out by quasi-state regional systems of leadership, and the system of regional power itself is built on local informal institutions, backroom agreements, regional party machines, and the shadow economy as a resource basis for the regional regime. In fact, in situations of "denationalization" of certain regions and spheres of social and economic activity, we find the emergence of stable regional systems: regional patrimonial political regimes.

---

[18]   K. Rogov, "Rezhim miagkikh pravovykh ogranichenii," *InLiberty.ru*, 22 July 2013, http://www.inliberty.ru/blog/1175-rezhim-myagkih-pravovyh-ogranicheniy. Emphasis in original.

[19]   For more detail, see R. Turovskii, "Regional'nye politicheskie rezhimy v Rossii: K metodologii analiza," *Polis* 2 (2009): 77–95.

In most studies of the regional (local or regional) political process, the political regimes are political objects of analysis; that is, they are political units (polities). These polities as forms of autonomous social domination are characterized by a certain autonomy from the central state governance apparatus and its political actors, behaving instead as autonomous agents of regional influence[20] with resources and strategies of social domination, as well as a set of informal political institutions and practices that contribute to the business and political isolation of the regional polity from the central system of public administration. They operate, as Vladimir Gel'man points out, through "the aggregation of actors (subjects) of the political process, institutional forms of organization of political power, resources and strategies for the struggle to achieve and/or retain power."[21]

Thus the regional political regime can be considered the complex of methods, means, and practices through which the ruling elites make or implement political, economic, ideological, and power management in the region. If the political regime is understood as a form of governance, then the regional regime can be understood as a form of management of a particular region localized in a certain sense; that is, a certain autonomy is achieved through a combination of formal and informal practices and institutions. In fact, in developing an understanding of the regional political regime in general, we come to the definition of a regional or local political government, one of whose features is the holding of elections in competitive but unfree conditions.[22]

---

[20]   By this I mean regional actors whose resources originate outside the region (e.g., state funding rather than municipal funding, international grants), regional actors who are included in the structure of national or transnational monopolies or corporations.

[21]   V. Gel'man, "Regional'naia vlast' v sovremennoi Rossii: Instituty, rezhimy, praktiki," *Polis* 1 (1998). See also V. Gel'man, S. Ryzhenkov, and M. Bree (eds.), *Rossiia regionov: Transformatsiia politicheskikh rezhimov* (Moscow: Ves' mir, 2000), 19–20.

[22]   As the post-Soviet practice shows, business political competitiveness can coexist with a public "lack of freedom"—a fierce competition for power in a city or region between different sets of "bad guys" (ethnic groups, local groups, criminal business groups, etc.).

One of the specific features of such regional political regimes is the presence of incumbents who are not afraid to lose power as a result of competitive unfree elections as they are capable of mass mobilization of the electorate and of accessing the entire set of resources of local elites in order to achieve the desired electoral result. In the Ukrainian situation, as well as in post-Soviet space more broadly, "million-person cities" (cities with more than or close to one million inhabitants), urban agglomerations, and "regional capitals" (including centers of historical regions with different ethnographic specifics) have traditionally functioned as spaces for the formation of civil culture and the post-Soviet inversion of democratization (chiefly the translation of alternative national projects and the creation of party machines and non-patrimonial regional elites).[23] In contrast to the Russian post-Soviet situation, in which the regional divergence of political regimes is the key element in the formation of regional regimes[24] (i.e., individualization of the institutional and political specifics of the regions, divergence of the trajectories of the institutional transformation of the center and regions, sometimes taking into account the sociocultural specifics of ethnonational autonomies), the Ukrainian situation is not characterized by such regional diversity and develops much more through imitation of the national model of patrimonial management at the local or regional level.[25]

My attempt to explain the emergence of various regional political regimes in Ukraine draws on an analysis of individual cases of

---

[23] For more detail, see N. Zubarevich, "Goroda kak tsentry modernizatsii ekonomiki i chelovecheskogo kapitala," *Obschestvennye nauki i sovremennost'* 5 (2010): 5–19.

[24] For more detail, see V. Nechaev, "Regional'nye politicheskie sistemy v post-sovetskoi Rossii," *Pro et Contra* 5, no. 1 (Winter 2000): 80–95.

[25] To understand the difference in the current regional specifics of Ukraine and Russia, it will be useful to refer to the work of the Russian researcher Natalia Zubarevich, which shows that the modern regional dimension of the Russian Federation is significantly different from the Ukrainian situation; N. Zubarevich, *Regiony Rossii: Neravenstvo, krisis, modernizatsiia* (Moscow, 2010), 22–28; and N. Zubarevich, "Four Russias: Rethinking the Post-Soviet Map," *Open Democracy* website, 22 March 2012, https://www.opendemocracy.net/od-russia/natalia-zubarevich/four-russias-rethinking-post-soviet-map.

Ukrainian regions in which million-person cities (densely populated urban agglomerations) are located at the center, namely: Kharkiv, Dnipro, Odesa, Kyiv, and L'viv. Among these cities a central role is played by Kyiv, the capital of Ukraine, a region with a special constitutional status, where the position of the mayor of the city and the head of the city state administration are combined in one elected mayoral candidate (the role of head of the city state administration strengthens the mayor of Kiev, making him a significant figure with powers that mayors of other cities lack, but at the same time the procedure for appointing the elected mayor head of the Kyiv city state administration also makes him more dependent on the central power than other mayors). Until 2014, the regional oligarchic elites understood control of Kyiv to be a mandatory precondition for seizing power in the country because control of Kyiv meant control of the central bureaucracy. In the period before the Maidan of 2014, the only center of attraction was Kyiv, which had been seized in both business and political terms by representatives of the Donetsk group in 2010–2013, after the 2010 election of Viktor Yanukovych as president. Yanukovych's unprecedented dismissal of Kyiv mayor Leonid Chernovets'kyi from his duties as chairman of the Kyiv city state administration[26] and the appointment of the first vice-mayor, Oleksandr Popov, who was absolutely loyal to the central government and the Party of Regions, is indicative. In 2012, three years before the next planned mayoral elections in Kyiv, under pressure from the central government, Chernovets'kyi resigned as mayor, and the power in the capital passed to Popov, who was absolutely controlled by the central government.

The Regional Dimension of the Ukrainian Political Process before and after the Revolution of Dignity

Regional oligarchic structures of business and power constitute a phenomenon that is inseparable from modern Ukrainian reality—in

---

[26]   On 16 November 2010 Leonid Chernovets'kyi was removed from the post of the head of Kyiv city state administration by decree of President Yanukovych, but he retained the post of the mayor of Kyiv.

fact, they are the backbone of Ukrainian politics. During the years of state independence, political oligarchism went through several stages of development and sometimes, depending on the political situation, turned into a quite respectable phenomenon in public opinion.[27] Oligarchism has penetrated the state system so deeply that sometimes it seems that the fight against the oligarchic influence on state administration must inevitably lead to a decrease in the manageability of the state apparatus itself. In a situation of institutional weakness of the Ukrainian state, the assistance and support of the oligarchs seems to be a natural phenomenon to many Ukrainians, who in return provide electoral and public support to the oligarchs and their clients.

An illustrative example is the participation of the oligarchs in state "image" projects. A case in point is the oligarchs' participation in the state's preparation for the 2012 football European Championship, and specifically in the implementation of infrastructure projects in the host cities, Donetsk and Kharkiv. These projects entailed the construction or renovation of stadiums, airports, and hotels, which was carried out with the significant financial and organizational participation of the regional oligarchic business: Oleksandr Yaroslavs'kyi implemented these projects in Kharkov and Rinat Akhmetov in Donetsk, while in L'viv and Kyiv they were implemented by the state because there were no local oligarchs in command of enough resources to do so.

At the regional and local level, with the help of controlled business, controlled local bureaucracies, and charity funds, the oligarchs have turned majoritarian constituencies into electoral strongholds where incumbents (their representatives, or the oligarchs themselves if the representatives' costs are too high or carry additional risks in a situation of high uncertainty) possess a

---

[27]   Ninety percent of Ukrainians believe that the oligarchs continue to be an influential political and economic force in the country. However, only 11 percent of Ukrainians believe that "the state must conduct a strict demonopolization in all areas where the oligarchs are monopolists." See "Kazhdyi chetvertyi ukrainets khochet 'raskurkulit'" oligarkhov," *ZN,UA*, 2 January 2015, https://zn.ua/ECON OMICS/kazhdyy-chetvertyy-ukrainec-hochet-raskurkulit-oligarhov-162888_.h tml.

monopoly on electoral resources.[28] As a result, regional oligarchs who do not have relevant party projects prefer to be elected during parliamentary elections from the majority electoral constituencies under their control, with guaranteed access to the parliament.[29]

Historically, Ukrainian oligarchism was created in the early 1990s in the Donetsk-Dnipro economic region, which was the most industrialized region in the country. As far as the oligarchy's own development is concerned, its influence began to penetrate actively into other regions of Ukraine (in the second half of the 1990s) that did not have their own strong political groups, in particular Kyiv. Kyiv was perceived as the country's "headquarters," and with the "capture" of Kyiv came the possibility of having access to disposal of the entire state infrastructure. The next city of interest was Kharkiv, the key to Ukraine's East. If in Soviet times Kyiv never had its own influential political elite, the situation was different with Kharkiv. The Kharkiv communist and economic elite was the dominant political group in the Ukrainian SSR. Later, however, lacking powerful export-oriented businesses, which would give access to significant foreign exchange earnings, Kharkiv oligarchs could not become an independent and self-sufficient group. Consequently, they have always acted as junior partners to other oligarchs, patrons of either the Donetsk group (e.g., Evgen Shcherban, Rynat Akhmetov, Viktor Yanukovych), or the Dnipropetrovsk group (Pavlo Lazarenko, Ihor Kolomoyskyi, Viktor Pinchuk). This relationship, however, has also allowed the local elites to balance between the two oligarchic centers and to retain both a relatively large degree of autonomy and a

---

[28] Representatives' costs are the costs of containing the private interests and/or personal motives of "representatives" (business managers, public policy makers, trade unionists, government officials, security forces, criminal leaders, judges). The interests of representatives can never be fully embedded into the interests of the party that hires them (owners, shareholders, citizens as voters), which is why the institutionalization of the costs that contribute to the complex but acceptable balance of representatives' interests and the interests of the party that hires them is required.

[29] For example, Aleksandr Fel'dman in the Kharkiv region, Sergei Taruta in the Donetsk region, Viktor Baloga in Transcarpathia region, Konstantin Zhevago in Poltava region, and others. For more detail, see http://w1.c1.rada.gov.ua/pls/site2/p_deputat_list.

certain business-political representation in the region, for they were strong enough to prevent the rise of a regional consolidated business-political group within their own sphere of political activity.

Thus the Kharkiv regional elites were co-opted by Donetsk or Dnieper groups into party machines, on the one hand, but on the other hand the local elites controlled access to most of the districts in Kharkiv region until 2012. Therefore, only the representatives of local business and political groups won elections in Kharkiv-majority districts. After the Donetsk group consolidated its power monopoly, the parliamentary elections of 2012 destroyed this consensus, and "parachute deputies"[30] appeared in Kharkiv-majority districts. This became one of the direct signs of the loss of autonomy on the part of the Kharkiv groups. A second sign was the complete absence of Kharkiv groups in the central bodies of executive power in the period 2010–2013.

One of the consequences of the regional weakness of the Kharkiv oligarchy is its pro-Russianness, its tendency to seek patrons and partners in Russia capable of protecting the oligarchs both against the Ukrainian state and against more powerful oligarchic groups. Prior to the strengthening of Putin's regime, the role of such patron partners was played by the Russian oligarchs Roman Abramovich and Oleg Deripaska. With Putin's centralization of the Russian oligarchy, attempts were made to establish patron-client relations with state structures through the mechanism of cross-border cooperation (though after the Russian military aggression in the Donbas, cross-border cooperation was frozen). Thanks to the influence of Russian patrons on the Kharkiv oligarchy as well as the established institutions of cross-border cooperation, it was Kharkiv

---

[30]   In political jargon this term refers to deputies elected in majority districts in regions to which they had no earlier connection. Their victory is ensured first and foremost by the central administrative resource.

region, along with Crimea, that was assigned[31] the role of being the region most loyal to Russia during the 2014 invasion.[32]

Odesa and L'viv have always had their own business and political groups, which prevented these cities' appropriation by external oligarchic elites (such as the Donetsk or Dnipro groups). However, from the second half of the 1990s, control over these cities was established by the central government through administrative control over the respective regions and through budget allocations and the power infrastructure (thus control over the central government amounts to control over these regions). In addition, L'viv and Odesa are the main "gateways" to the West and South, respectively (since 2014 Kharkiv lost the role of the eastern gate as a result of Russia's loss of its strategic role of transportation and bilateral communication), and this requires strategic control over these regions in order to prevent excessive strengthening of the local oligarchic elites.

The Russian occupation of Crimea[33] and parts of Donetsk and Luhansk regions destroyed one of the most dominant Ukrainian

---

[31] The commander of the National Guard of Ukraine, Yuryi Allerov, has claimed that the original goal of Russian aggression in the east of Ukraine was neither Donetsk, nor Lugansk, but Kharkov. For more detail see Liliia Ragutskaia, "Pered voinoi glavnoi tsel'iu Rossii byli ne Donetsk i Lugansk, a drugoi gorod—glava Natsgvardii," *Apostrof,* 4 July 2017, https://apostrophe.ua/article/politics/2017-07-04/pered-voynoy-glavnoy-tselyu-rossii-byili-ne-donetsk-i-lugansk-a-drugoy-gorod---glava-natsgvardii/13221.

[32] The Russian publishing house "Novaya Gazeta" obtained a Russian Presidential Administration document comprising a plan for Russia's capture of a number of Ukrainian territories, compiled in the days when Yanukovich was still the president of Ukraine. Among other things, it states that: "In these conditions [that is, the impossibility of Viktor Yanukovich's retaining power], it seems correct to play on the centrifugal aspirations of various regions of the country with the aim of initiating the annexation of its eastern regions to Russia in one form or another. Dominant regions for the application of efforts should be the Crimea and the Kharkiv region, in which there are already quite strong support groups for the idea of maximum integration with the Russian Federation"; Andrei Lipskii, "Predstavliaetsia pravil'nym initsiirovat' prisoedinenie vostochnykh oblastei Ukrainy k Rossii," *Novaia gazeta,* 24 February 2015, https://www.novayagazeta.ru/articles/2015/02/24/63168-171-predstavlyaetsya-pravilnym-initsiirovat-prisoedinenie-vostochnyh-oblastey-ukrainy-k-rossii-187.

[33] It is worth noting that Crimea (or the Autonomous Republic of Crimea) and the city of Sevastopol (two separate subjects of the regional process), located on the Crimean Peninsula, never were independent regionally. The Crimean elite was

regions, the Donbas (the Donetsk basin mega-region, which has a high population density and a high degree of industrialization). The seizure of the administrative and regional centers of the Donbas, Donetsk and Luhansk, resulted in the central government's losing control over a significant part of the Donbas region (15,341.2 km^2, or 2.5 percent of the territory of Ukraine; 3.7 million people lived in the occupied territory before the occupation, out of 6.5 million inhabitants of the Donbas). The part of the Donbas that remained under the control of the central government is governed by military-civil administrations[34] and does not have sufficient economic, political, or electoral resources to exert the kind of influence the Donbas had before the Revolution of Dignity.

The first regional elections after the Revolution of Dignity, in October 2015, were of key importance, since the expert community's and the public's hopes for rebooting the political system, both in general and in the regions, rested with a new composition of the local councils. These elections led to a new status quo among the regional political groups. Among the regions where the megacities that I analyzed are located, a coexistence of new and old political and business elites appeared as a result of the elections. Thus the following political forces proved to be the most represented in the city councils: in Kyiv, Petro Poroshenko Bloc Solidarnist' and Samopomich; in L'viv, Samopomich and again Petro Poroshenko Bloc Solidarnist'; in Odesa, Doveriai Delam (Trust the Deeds) and Petro Poroshenko Bloc Solidarnist'; in Kharkiv, Vidrodzhennia and

---

included in national and, usually, dominant electoral political projects, and representatives of the central government were appointed to the key positions in the regional political system (the head of the Council of Ministers of Crimea and the head of the City State Administration of Sevastopol). However, the exclusion of Crimea (representing the exclusion of 1.5 million mainly pro-Russian voters) from the Ukrainian electoral democratic process has significantly changed the geo-cultural configuration of the "pro-Western" and "pro-Russian" regions in the direction of implementing a pro-Western foreign policy strategy for the development of the state.

[34]   On 3 February 2015 the Verkhovna Rada of Ukraine adopted the Law "On Civil and Military Administrations." These administrations operate instead of local councils in the area of the Anti-Terrorist Operation (ATO) in the Donbas. For more detail see http://zakon2.rada.gov.ua/laws/show/141-19.

Samopomich; in Dnipro, UKROP (Ukrainske ob'iednannia patriotiv / Ukrainian Union of Patriots) and Opposition bloc.[35] At the same time, in all megacities the mayors who were elected headed the party lists, which ultimately implied the presence in the city council of a strong party faction, upon which the mayor could rely in his own policy implementation. Thus, in Kyiv, Mayor Vitali Klitschko, who headed the list of Petro Poroshenko Bloc Solidarnist' (winning 64 percent in the second round of voting) was elected; in L'viv, Andrii Sadovyi of Samopomich (61 percent in the second round); in Odesa, Hennadii Trukhanov of Doveriai Delam (51 percent in the first round); in Kharkiv, Hennadii Kernes of Vidrodzhennia (66 percent in the first round); and in Dnipro, Borys Filatov of UKROP (52 percent in the second round).

It should be noted that in all five cases, regional electoral and political particularities can be observed. Thus the Kyiv case, which can be characterized as "political union," reflects Klitschko's joining the presidential party Solidarnist' in 2014; the Kyiv mayor himself functions as a junior partner to President Poroshenko. The L'viv case, which we might label a case of "political expansion," illustrates the increasing reach of Samopomich, the political party of Andrii Sadovyi, which achieved significant results not only in L'viv (24 of 64 places) but also in Kyiv (22 of 120 places), and Kharkiv (13 of 84 places). The Odesa case, which can be described as a "political autarky," represents the bid of Hennadii Trukhanov to form the regional party Doveriai Delam and to achieve the maximum unification of the elite around the dominant regional political party in order to protect himself from the influence of extra-regional political forces, including political appointments from the center. Odesa region has always represented an important area for the extraction of both formal and shadow rents for the central government: it offers significant electoral resources (1.8 million voters), significant revenues from taxes and fees paid to the state budget, and shadow revenues from corruption schemes at Odesa customs offices and ports.

---

[35] For the results of 2015 regional elections in Ukraine, see the official website of the Central Electoral Commission: http://www.cvk.gov.ua/pls/vm2015/PVM00 5?PT001F01=100&pt00_t00if01=100.

The appointment of Mikheil Saakashvili as governor of Odesa region in 2015 essentially was done with the goal of democratizing and reforming the region, including by eliminating the regional political regime that had begun to form around the mayor of Odesa, Hennadii Trukhanov.[36] For maximum success in carrying out these tasks, Saakashvili received unprecedented support from Petro Poroshenko (no other regional governor ever received such support, either before or after). People loyal to Saakashvili were appointed to key positions in the region, including David Sakvarelidze, who was appointed to the posts of regional prosecutor and deputy prosecutor general; Giorgi Lortkipanidze, who became chief of the National Police in Odesa region; and later Iuliia Marushevskaia, the protégée of Saakashvili, was appointed head of Odesa customs. Since Saakashvili failed to adequately deal with his mission, the de-oligarchization and democratization of Odesa region, the central regime has been forced to take into account the Trukhanov regime and cooperate with Trukhanov in order to maintain influence in the region.

The Kharkiv case, which can be characterized as "political outsourcing," entailed the use of Hennadii Kernes of Vidrodzhennia to change political patrons, which meant "a change of senior partners from the Donetsk grouping to the Dnipro grouping."[37] The

---

36   Poroshenko appointed Saakashvili governor of Odesa region on 30 May 2015; see http://www.bbc.com/ukrainian/ukraine_in_russian/2015/05/150530_ru_s_s aakashvili_appointment_odesa. At 5:37 a.m. on 30 May 2015, Poroshenko tweeted: "Ukraine will not have the power of the oligarchs. There will be discipline! These are the tasks that I put to the new head of Odesa Regional Administration Mikheil Saakashvili!" (https://twitter.com/poroshenko).

37   At the expert level, there is a consensus around the belief that the Dnipro oligarch Ihor Kolomoyskyi is the main business sponsor and patron of the party Vidrodzhennia. (In an interview, Igor Kolomoiskyi calls himself a sympathizer of Vidrodzhennya party and he completely refuses to confirm any kind of his involvement in this party; https://ukr.lb.ua/news/2018/04/11/395013_gennadiy_kernes_zaraz_poroshenko.html). The necessity to change patrons or promoters for Hennadii Kernes became one of the tools of political survival in the period 2014–2015 as Kernes's involvement in the Party of Regions required him to take actions aimed at his own rehabilitation and separation from the political group Donetsk People, which united in a new political project, Opposition bloc, in 2014. In order to demonstrate a high degree of loyalty to the central government, Kernes through his control of the city's political and legal process did not allow the registration of the Opposition bloc for the elections to

Dnipro case can be described as "political dualism." Here we find a deep renewal of the deputy corps through the victory of patriotic party UKROP (Ukrainskeob'iednannia patriotiv), but it was not enough to achieve a stable majority, and as a consequence, the mayor of Dnipro, Borys Filatov, has been forced to attempt cooperation with the Opposition bloc (consisting mainly of former members of the Party of Regions) to build a more effective regional governance system.

The regimes that are thus coalescing are building their relationship with the central government using different strategies. A confrontational strategy is the choice of the L'viv regional regime and the Dnipro regional regime. In the case of L'viv, the confrontation is between the mayor of L'viv, Andrii Sadovyi (and his party, Samopomich), and the central government. The confrontation made history on the back of such events as the "garbage war"[38] and the blockade of the "trade in blood,"[39] or trade with the rebel-held areas. The Dnipro regional regime has used a confrontational strategy in its relations with the central government (both with the government of Arseniy Yatsenyuk and with the government of Volodymyr Groysman) as a result of losing control of the Privat group (Ihor Kolomoyskyi and company) and the state's oil and gas and banking infrastructure. The Kharkiv, Kyiv, and Odesa regional regimes have opted for a cooperative strategy. Political processes in

---

the City Council. It is worth noting that Kernes, despite constant conflicts with civil activists from the pro-democracy camp and also criminal prosecution by law enforcement bodies, maintains effective control over Kharkiv. So, for example, the Vidrodzhennia party has an absolute majority in the Kharkiv City Council (57 of 84 places), which is a record among all city councils in Ukrainian megacities. Kernes also has indirect control over the Kharkiv communal economy and the local justice system, which makes him a key political actor in Kharkiv region.

[38] Mayor of Lviv Andrii Sadovii accuses the central authorities of waging a "garbage blockade" against Lviv. For more details, see https://focus.ua/opinions/368683/; https://lb.ua/news/2017/06/09/368652_sadoviy_obvinil_tsentralnuyu _vlast.html.

[39] See "Samopomich" party website for more detail: https://samopomich.ua/ru/rik-z-pochatku-blokady-torgivli-na-krovi-strashylky-ne-spravdylysya/;   and https://samopomich.ua/ru/torgivlya-na-krovi-z-okupatsijnoyu-vladoyu-ye-ne pryjnyatnoyu-ta-nyshhivnoyu-dlya-ukrayiny-samopomich/.

these megacities throughout 2014–2018 have not demonstrated any significant confrontation with the central government and with the President of Ukraine Petro Poroshenko personally. On the contrary, the mayors of Kharkiv and Odesa—Hennadii Kernes[40] and Hennadii Trukhanov[41]—have already announced their support for Petro Poroshenko in the upcoming presidential elections in May 2019. It is noteworthy that Trukhanov and Kernes have both named his successful decentralization policy/reform as the key argument for their support for Petro Poroshenko.

The key aspect that determines a regional regime's choice of strategy is the amount of resources—economic, political, electoral, and power—a regional regime can draw on. The volume of these resources, and the ability to extract them from regional business and political groups or to control them, is an important element in the choice of a strategy for relations with the central government. One important type of such resources is the presence or absence of paramilitary formations under the control of the regional political elite, which can provide leverage on the central government. An example is the Oplot (Bastion) paramilitary vigilante group, which was supported by Kharkiv mayor Hennadii Kernes; another is the association of veterans of the battalion "Donbas," over which Samopomich in L'viv and Kyiv has some control. A third example is the "municipal police" in Dnipro (the communal security service of mayor Boris Filatov). An important role is also played by the presence of regional governors who have direct access to the leaders of the executive vertical—to the president of Ukraine, the head of the presidential administration, or the prime minister. Direct access to the leaders of the executive vertical is an important and rather rare institutional and political resource in regional politics. This resource allows

---

[40]   Kernes said that he would support Poroshenko in future presidential elections; Sonia Koshkina, "Gennadii Kernes: 'Seichas Poroshenko proiavliaet sebia kak lider natsii,'" *LB.ua*, 11 April 2018, https://lb.ua/news/2018/04/11/395013_genna diy_kernes_seychas_poroshenko.html.

[41]   Trukhanov said that he would vote for Poroshenko in the upcoming presidential elections, as he had done during the last elections. For more details, see Sonia Koshkina, "Gennady Trukhanov: 'Ia gotov progolosovat' za Poroshenko,'" *LB.ua*, 7 March 2018, https://lb.ua/news/2018/03/07/392038_gennadiy_truha nov_ya_gotov_povtorno.html.

governors to attract additional state financial resources (which are often distributed manually, through separate decisions of the Cabinet of Ministers or by order of the president of Ukraine). It also increases the loyalty of the law enforcement personnel in the regions, and enhances the governor's status in the regional political process. For example, Ihor Rainin, governor of Kharkiv region in 2015–2016, Saakashvili, governor of Odesa region in 2015–2016, and Kolomoyskyi, governor of Dnipro region in 2014–2015, all had direct access either to the president of Ukraine or to the head of his administration. All three were not only the key architects of regional policy, actively confronting the influential political opposition in their regions, they were also active in national politics.[42]

The most dramatic example of the interworkings of regional power relations with the center, important both for the central government and for the country in general, is Odesa. After the victory in the extraordinary elections held on 25 May 2014, Hennadii Trukhanov, the representative of the local elites and a member of the Party of Regions, became the mayor of Odesa. Several weeks earlier Ihor Palytsia, a close associate of the leader of Privat group Ihor Kolomoyskyi, who headed Dnipropetrovsk region at that time, was appointed governor of Odesa region. This period, before Kolomoyskyi's resignation as governor of Dnipropetrovsk region on 24 March 2015 and Palytsia's own resignation as governor of Odesa region on 30 May 2015, was a time of unconditional influence of the Privat group on the Ukrainian regional political process. Privat group maintained direct or indirect control over the strategic Dnieper and Odesa regions; the volunteer battalions Dnieper-1 and Dnieper-2; and one of the most influential media outlets in the country, 1 + 1, as well as other media resources. The subsequent strengthening of the center's power (represented by Petro Poroshenko) occurred through two measures: (1) the weakening of the influence of Privat

---

[42]   The practice of establishing direct access to the "first persons of the state" is something of a tradition in Ukrainian politics. For example, the governor of Kharkiv region (2005–2010) Arseniy Avakov appointed Yaroslav Yushchenko, the twenty-three-year-old nephew of the then president of Ukraine, Viktor Yushchenko, to the post of vice-governor of Kharkiv region so as to have direct communication with and access to the president through his deputy.

group in the regional political process; and (2) prevention of acts of political revenge in the regions of south-eastern Ukraine. Poroshenko coped more than successfully with the first task: by the end of 2016 Privat group had almost completely lost its influence in the regional political process in Ukraine (the final straw was the nationalization of Privatbank, the largest Ukrainian bank and a key asset of Dnipro's Privat group). However, the second task turned out to be more complicated. In the Ukrainian megacities, the city agencies are headed by regional leaders who are not affiliated with Poroshenko's party. The method of applying pressure to local elites (who enjoy indisputable electoral advantages) through a governor loyal to the president, in this case Saakashvili, who, as we have seen, had been appointed governor of Odesa region in May 2015, was tested in Odesa. The key task required of Saakashvili was to "clear the hornet nest" of local reactionary elites and turn Odesa region into a laboratory of reform.[43] However, implicitly, the powers of Ukrainian regional governors are significantly limited by the central bodies of executive power. The governor is not an autonomous political figure but is inscribed in the hierarchy of executive power. Emboldened by his sense of Western support,[44] Mikheil Saakashvili joined the struggle with the government of Arseniy Yatsenyuk, the leader of the People's Front. By mid-2015 Yatsenyuk had lost most of his electoral capital through unpopular government decisions (a reduction in budget outlays, an increase in gas tariffs for the population, a reduction in the number of state employees)[45] and had

---

[43]   On the tasks assigned to Saakashvili by Poroshenko, see further: http://dum skaya.net/news/petr-poroshenko-predstavil-novogo-glavu-odesskoj-047074/.

[44]   Jeffrey Piett, U.S. ambassador in Ukraine, said: "The United States Government fully supports Governor Saakashvili and his team and we will do everything to make them successful"; cited in "Saakashvili provel vstrechu s mezhdunarodnymi donorami," *Unian.net*, 1 July 2015, https://www.unian.net/politics/1095 888-saakashvili-provel-vstrechu-s-mejdunarodnymi-donorami-dlya-privlecheniya-investitsiy-v-odesskuyu-oblast.html.

[45]   For more details about the unpopular political and economic measures of the Yatsenyuk government, see "Pravitel'stvo poidet na nepopuliarnye mery dlia policheniia kredita MVF–Iatseniuk," *Korrespondent.net*, 28 February 2014, https://korrespondent.net/ukraine/politics/3312721-pravytelstvo-poidet-na-ne-populiarnye-mery-dlia-poluchenyia-kredyta-mvf-yatsenuik.

turned into a lightning rod for the central government. Acting as the key lever of pressure on Ihor Kolomoyskyi to replace Yatsenyuk,[46] Saakashvili nevertheless did not himself receive the portfolio of the head of government. In developing his political platform, the Movement of New Forces, Saakashvili increasingly criticized the activities of the government of Volodymyr Groysman and the policies of Petro Poroshenko. On 7 November 2016 he resigned as governor of Odesa region and moved to adopt a position of political opposition to the central government. The consequence of Saakashvili's political activity and his personal opposition to Petro Poroshenko since November 2016 has been loss of his Ukrainian citizenship on controversial formal grounds.

One Ukrainian regional and political specificity is that the systems of regional business and political leadership have always been based on three institutional components: (1) the availability of a disciplined electoral base (electoral political resources, such as the ability to get people out into the streets or to handle regional problems related to national security); (2) the existence of an administrative base (which allows mobilization of administrative resources, i.e., control over regional law enforcement and fiscal institutions, and the ability to provide parallel formal and shadow economies and "to be useful" both for the state budget and for the neo-patrimonial elite in the central institutions of power); and (3) the presence of powerful economic contributors to the budget in the region, including knowledge-intensive industries or export-oriented businesses (the economic specifics within or around Ukrainian megacities allow local elites to engage in dialogue with the central government about the need to redistribute tax revenues in favor of the regions rather than the center).

The events of 2014–2015, however, changed the configuration of the institutional components of regional business and political leadership somewhat. The powerful economic contributors to the

---

[46] M. Saakashvili, "Ty ispol'zoval menia," *YouTube*, 3 September 2017, https://www.youtube.com/watch?v=vHQq1xegxPg; and A. Gerashchenko, *Facebook* post, 7 November 2016, https://www.facebook.com/anton.gerashchenko.7/posts/1187450514675127.

regional budgets now lost their importance, and their proximity to the zone of the Anti-Terrorist Operation (ATO) in the Donbas came to the fore instead. In this situation, Dnipro and Kharkiv turned into "front-line" megacities, and L'viv and Odesa became the western and southern gates of Ukraine (the common border of Odesa region and the unrecognized Transnistrian republic also makes Odesa, in a certain sense, a front-line megacity).

Such transformations yielded some bonuses for the local elites: the central government turns a blind eye to their corrupt past in exchange for political loyalty in the present and the future (including personal loyalty to Petro Poroshenko). This deal relies on the misalignment between the city and regional authorities in the regions. The cases of Odesa and Kharkiv are good examples of this misalignment. The mayors of these cities received a kind of political amnesty from the central government in exchange for loyalty to local governors and for distancing themselves from "anti-presidential political projects" (the mayor of Odesa created a regional party machine, Doveriai Delam, that does not take part in the political process at the national level, and the mayor of Kharkiv, who topped the list of the Vidrodzhennia party in the elections to the Kharkiv City Council, distanced himself from the Opposition bloc, which by autumn 2015 had moved into systemic opposition to Poroshenko and the government of Arseniy Yatsenyuk). The fact that the Opposition bloc was not admitted to the elections to the Kharkiv City Council has also helped strengthen the position of Hennadii Kernes. The stability of this configuration is evident in the sluggish progress of the criminal cases initiated against Trukhanov[47] and Kernes,[48] which, should political will be exercised by the central authorities, might remove these regional leaders from regional policy making. The opposite situation is equally plausible: in the event of further decentralization of the system of political governance and weakening of the central government's influence on the regions in Ukraine, administrative and electoral misalliances may disintegrate and a weak central government may be left to deal with regional systems of strong business and political leadership—in other words, neo-patrimonial regional regimes.

Conclusions

The institutional architecture of the Ukrainian political system is built on the principle of the dominance of the informal sphere over the formal one and for this reason it is urgently in need of political and institutional modernization. After the destruction of the authoritarian-patrimonial system of public administration of Viktor Yanukovych's regime, Ukraine has established a regime that in its external form has both democratic and autocratic institutional characteristics, strengthened by the weakness of the state; that is, it is

---

[47] From February 2016, Hennadii Trukhanov has been the object of an investigation by the National Anti-Corruption Bureau of Ukraine regarding a major case of embezzlement of the local budget by officials of Odesa City Hall. For more on this, see: "V NABU soobshchili detali masshtabnykh obyskov v Odesskom gorsovete," *TSN.ua,* 24 March 2017, https://ru.tsn.ua/groshi/v-nabu-soobschili-detali-masshtabnyh-obyskov-v-odesskom-gorsovete-829008.html. Trukhanov is also the object of an investigation by the SBU (Security Service of Ukraine) into subversive activities of the UOC-MP (Ukrainian Orthodox Church of Moscow Patriarchate). For more information, see: "U Trukhanova opiat' problemy," *Ivasi.news,* 6 June 2017, http://ivasi.news/religion/u-mera-snova-problemyi-sbu-rassleduet-finansirovanie-odesskogo-patriarhata/.

[48] The trial of Hennadii Kernes has been underway since March 2015 (on 3 February 2015, the General Prosecutor's Office of Ukraine announced that Kernes was suspected of the kidnapping and beating of Euromaidan activists), however he continues to act as mayor of Kharkiv.

close to the unstable and ineffective situation of anocracy, as defined by Gandhi and Vreeland.[49]

The deficit of state capacity in the patrimonial system of state administration has led to a fragmentation of the pyramid of centralized patron-client networks in the political regime. One of the consequences of the degradation of the authoritarian-patrimonial system is a decrease in the level of controllability of the public administration system (a reduction in control over both the formal segment and the sphere of informal institutions of politics and power), which is mistakenly perceived by society as a movement toward democratizing and liberalizing the Ukrainian state.

Another consequence of this transformation of the public administration system is the formation of a number of local regimes that lay claim to drawing autonomously not only economic but also political rent from the region. In other words, the single, monolithic, centralized pyramid of patrimonial authoritarianism of the Yanukovych regime has been substituted by several local pyramids of neo-patrimonial regional regimes.

As all the central political leaders of Ukraine, the presidents, have traditionally seen a drop in their rating during their tenure, the central chieftaincy, the leader regime, permanently suffers from a lack of electoral legitimacy (since an authoritarian leadership faces a large element of uncertainty while participating in nationwide electoral competitions). Local leaders do not suffer from a lack of electoral resources as they have much greater and more consolidated electoral support than central political leaders.

To replace the central regime of the Donetsk clan, a network of regional regimes with centers in Kharkiv, Dnipro, Odesa, L'viv, and Kyiv has appeared. Those million-person cities are emerging as new centers of institutional attraction for the patrimonial regional elite. Mayors of Ukrainian megacities, the leaders of regional regimes, by heading regional party lists and gaining a qualifying majority of votes in elections reduce the electoral formation of

---

49   Jennifer Gandhi and James Vreeland, "Political Institutions and Civil War: Unpacking Anocracy," *Journal of Conflict Solutions* 52, no. 3 (June 2008).

dominant regional party machines. It is the mayors of Ukrainian megacities who are the key elements in the formation of regional regimes, in contrast to the indiscriminate governors, appointed "from the center," who often have a low electoral rating, and who do not have obvious competitive advantages (in fact, the political function of the governor under such conditions is to contain the mayor of a Ukrainian metropolis seeking a business-political autonomy).

In the medium term, the formation of regional regimes may lead to a de facto political federalization of Ukraine. If before 2014 the political process developed along the lines of electoral presidential cycles, after which power changed hands, in the current situation a change in presidential regime does not appear to be a cornerstone of political development. The role of stabilizer in the political process will be played not so much by the central government as by regional regimes, which will not need the president as arbiter. The successor institution as a stabilizing factor will lose its functional purpose.

Regional regimes are formed primarily as electoral-authoritarian control systems. In a situation of limited competition in the electoral process, the key opposition to regional regimes is posed not so much by outsider politicians (both internal and external) as by representatives of civil society. The political opposition in the regional regime is either blocked by incumbents or excluded from the regional political economy. Ultimately, in this situation, losing its independence, or facing a threat to its very political survival, all political opposition comes to a halt.

Russian Regionalism in Action: The Case of the North-Western Federal District (1991–2017)

Sergey Sukhankin

Abstract: The issue of regionalism and the "center-periphery" relationship in Russia has once again re-entered academic discourse in the context of the economic hardships and external isolation that the Russian Federation has faced since the outbreak of the Ukrainian crisis in late 2013. This article traces the development of these concepts, using Russia's North-West (after the reform of 2000, the North-Western Federal District) as a case study. It provides an exploratory description of the 1991–2017 period, based on a longitudinal analysis of trends and tendencies experienced by this macro-region. The article argues that while there have been some changes during this period, these have been largely superficial; overall, the North-West macro-region has not overcome its traditional deficiencies, such as sluggish economic growth and massive outflow of the population (and of young and qualified people in particular). Moreover, some problems have taken even more dangerous forms, leading to a growing gap between more developed and less vibrant parts of the North-West. The author employs a broad variety of primary and secondary sources, primarily relying on studies produced in Russian. The theoretical framework of the article includes a brief discussion of regionalism, and of how it is understood and perceived in Russia. In addition, the paper argues that the notion of "regionalism" (in its Western understanding) has been largely misconstrued by Russian ruling elites, which has led to its improper application in the practices of the local authorities.

Introduction

Relations between the center and the periphery (*tsentr i okrainy*) have been one of the most complicated and debated topics throughout Russia's history. Russia's size, the multicultural, multiethnic, and multireligious composition of its population, its uneven demographic and economic development—these factors have contributed to the complex and often contradictory nature of center-periphery relations at different stages of Russia's history. At the same time, Russia's drive toward centralism and long-standing fear of decentralization as a potential source of instability and chaos (a fear which is undoubtedly deeply rooted in historical experience) have on many occasions contributed to the internal shocks sustained by the state in various historical periods.

The collapse of the USSR, followed by pompous rhetorical effusions hailing a new era in center-periphery relations, cloaked in liberal garb yet lacking in proper calculation of the consequences,[1] launched truly tragic developments and a new period of instability in the 1990s. The beginning of the new millennium seemed to have ended this "new Time of Troubles," as it brought some economic growth and political stabilization. This temporary calm did not mean that the deeply rooted problem of center-periphery relations had disappeared, however. There are many reasons for the enduring nature of this problem. In this article, I shall argue that an important factor in the post-Soviet period has been a fundamentally misconceived structure of these relations, which stems from the Russian elite's (mis)reading or misinterpretation of regionalism as a political phenomenon, and its corresponding inability or unwillingness to consider the experience of other actors or factors. It will be argued that suppression of the regions' ability to expand external relations and the denial of their right to interact with more economically developed geographic regions (a denial often arising out of fear of separatism) brings economic stagnation and serves to further increase the disparity between more buoyant and less economically vibrant regions.

It should be noted that the period of economic growth in the 2000s meant that the Kremlin was able to paper over problems in relations between center and periphery by allocating additional federal resources to cover local needs. It remains to be seen how

---

[1]   Such as Yeltsin's (in)famous phrase, "Swallow as much sovereignty as you can!"

Moscow will approach financial assistance to the regions in the new circumstances, now that this period of relative prosperity has ended and the economic prognoses are rather pessimistic. The task will surely be particularly difficult in economically depressed and unevenly developed regions that are unable to capitalize on natural resources as a way to cover local expenditure. One such region is the North-Western Federal District.

This article explores the development of regionalism in Russia's North-West from 1991 to 2017. The relatively broad chronological scope was selected in order to enable coverage of key developments and transformations in the region as they unfolded over time. To this end, the article proceeds with the following objectives:

- To outline the mainstream Russian perception of "regionalism" and the distinctiveness of this view as compared to the standard European concept of regionalism;
- To provide a chronological analysis of the socio-economic development of Russia's north-western region using as examples Pskov oblast', the Republic of Karelia, and St. Petersburg, as seen through the prism of the shifting political paradigm in Moscow in the period 1991–2017;
- To outline the complexities of and barriers to the development of regionalism in Russia through an examination of the shifting fortunes of Kaliningrad oblast'; and
- To analyze the impact of post-Crimean developments on Russia's north-west in light of the area's geographic proximity to the EU and NATO member countries.

The Russian Perception of Regionalism: Soviet Prejudices and New Challenges

Regionalism is not a new phenomenon. Yet its essence was significantly transformed in the aftermath of the Cold War, when the metrics of inter-regional cooperation were no longer reduced to economic prosperity or security-related concerns, but were taken to a different level, with expansion of transborder ties based on political liberalization and intensification of existing inter-regional ties playing an essential role.[2] Regionalism can be described as a "multi-dimensional form of integration which includes economic, political, social and cultural aspects and thus goes far beyond the goal of creating region-based free-trade regimes or security alliances."[3] The current regionalist tendency involves the unit of the region becoming a powerful player in political and economic development, which in the Russian context would represent a profound change to the previous pattern of core-periphery relations.[4] The tendency of regions to act more comprehensively in the political and economic arena has led some authors to argue that the new regionalism is becoming an essential factor for the unification of Europe.[5]

The Baltic Sea region affords one of the best examples of the practical implementation of the key postulates of the "new regionalism."[6] To a large degree this became possible because of the dissolution of the USSR, which led to stronger cross-border cooperation, and decreasing military- and security-related concerns, all of which created space for economic development and the proliferation of cross-border ties.[7]

Throughout the 1990s and the early 2000s, it was hoped that the Russian regions bordering the Baltic Sea would be integrated into the rapidly developing Baltic Sea rim, through joint (and mutually lucrative) economic projects, cooperation, and dialogue. With the passage of time, however, it became clear that Russian and European readings of regionalism differed in important ways. This disparity can be attributed to three main factors. First, the deeply rooted differences in political culture did not disappear with the

---

[2]   Hettne Björn, Inotai András, and Sunkel Osvaldo (eds.), *Globalism and the New Regionalism* (Basingstoke: Macmillan, 1999).

[3]   Hettne Björn, "The New Regionalism: A Prologue," in *ibid.*, xvi.

[4]   Hettne Björn and Fredrik Söderbaum, "Theorising the Rise of Regionness," *New Political Economy* 5, no. 3 (2000): 457–74.

[5]   Kepa Sodupe, "The European Union and Inter-regional Co-operation," in *Paradiplomacy in Action: The Foreign Relations of Subnational Governments*, eds. Francisco Aldecoa and Michael Keating (London: Frank Cass, 1999), 58.

[6]   Urpo Kivikari and Esko Antola, *Baltic Sea Region: A Dynamic Third of Europe* (Turku: City of Turku, 2004).

[7]   Leena-Kaarina Williams, *The Baltic Sea Region: Forms and Functions of Regional Co-operation* (Berlin: Humboldt University, 2001), 8.

breakdown of the Soviet ideology. A considerable share of Russia's ruling elites (the majority of whom made their careers during the Soviet period) saw the West's overtures and policy recommendations as aimed fundamentally at diminishing Russian influence and power, both in the so-called "near abroad" and within Russia itself. A second factor was the historical baggage that the nascent independent Russian state had inherited from its predecessor: the late Soviet system had cultivated a highly centralized system that heavily shaped the mode of relations between center and periphery.[8] The Soviet prioritization of industrialization and the needs of the military-industrial complex had a negative effect not only on the economy per se but also on the development of the regions, which was disfigured through being under-resourced, resulting in increasing tensions, instability, and eventually, in some cases, separatism. Third, the abrupt collapse of the USSR meant that the process of adjusting to the new reality of a federation with a different structure was largely haphazard, and extremely painful (especially in the case of Kaliningrad oblast'). The situation in the regions was aggravated by the lack of a concrete strategy in Moscow, where various groups and factions clashed for power, ignoring mounting problems in the regions.[9]

The experience of the 1990s greatly contributed to the Russian misperception of regionalism, which came to be seen as a "revolutionary and purely Western phenomenon" that "challenged traditional Russian norms and principles."[10] This negative view was based on the dramatic increase in regional autonomy during this period, such that "by the end of the 1990s the federal center had lost the main leverage of influence upon the situation in the regions."[11] This loss of control was viewed as a sign of the upcoming further

---

[8]   For more information, see Boris Khorev, *Regional'naia politika v SSSR* (Moskva: Mysl', 1989).

[9]   For more information, see: "Chechenskii kapkan. 1 seriia. Zagovor" (REN TV, 2004), available at: https://www.youtube.com/watch?v=HZRhwJrOlEw&t=21s.

[10]   Kamaludin Gadzhiev and Valerii Kovalenko (eds.), *Federalizm: Entsiklopediia* (Moskva: Izdatel'stvo MGU, 2000), 419.

[11]   Irina Busygina, "How Does Russian Federalism Work? Looking at Internal Borders in the Russian Federation," *Journal of Borderlands Studies* 32, no. 1 (2017): 110.

fragmentation of the country, which in turn appeared to threaten complete collapse. Meanwhile, the role of the West in these processes was erroneously construed in Russia. For instance, the Clinton administration's efforts to help build democracy and a functioning market economy in the states of the former Soviet Union were increasingly seen as the West meddling in Russia's internal affairs, even on those occasions when Western assistance was directed to other countries of the former USSR.[12] During this period, however, the brewing discontent with the West among Russian ruling elites and intellectuals was to some degree toned down by liberal forces still present within Russian political architecture, as well as Russia's inability to openly challenge the West given the lack of resources and piling internal difficulties. Moreover, still economically weak, Russia was interested in obtaining economic assistance from the EU for its western regions (for example, for Kaliningrad oblast', whose economic needs were to some extent covered by European financial support. The most telling example occurred in 1998, when amidst economic crisis the oblast' was given economic assistance from European countries to mitigate consequences of the shock). After 2003, however, when political relations between Russia and the West started to show visible fissures, the so-called geopolitical perspective, which views regionalization in general and cooperation with other regions (especially European) in particular as a potential challenge, gained some popularity,[13] leading to a change in Moscow's stance on the issue of Russian regional cooperation with external actors.

On the other hand, some Russian intellectuals warned that the increasing dominance of the interests of the center over the

---

[12]   Alfred B. Evans, "The Failure of Democratization in Russia: A Comparative Perspective," *Journal of Eurasian Studies* 2 (2011): 40–51.

[13]   For more information, see Zuriet Zhade, "Geopoliticheskaia identichnost' v usloviiakh formirovaniia rossiiskoi identichnosti," in *Rossiia i sovremennyi mir: Problemy politicheskogo razvitiia. Materialy II Mezhdunarodnoi mezhvuzovskoi nauchnoi konferentsii Moskva, 13–14 aprelia 2006 g. v 2 chastiakh* (Moskva: Institut biznesa i politiki, 2006), chast' 1, 134–46; and Zuriet Zhade, "Regional'naia identichnost' s tochki zreniia geopolitiki," *Vestnik Adygeiskogo gosudarstvennogo universiteta* (2006), https://cyberleninka.ru/article/n/regionalnaya-identichnost-s-tochki-zreniya-geopolitiki.

needs of the regions could lead to "Russia becoming a highly centralized state actively using authoritarian methods."[14] Authors such as Andrey Makarychev, Aleksandr Sergunin, Natalia Smorodinskaia, and Sergei Kortunov argued that Moscow should draw on the Western, mainly European, experience to develop a new type of center-periphery relation. In particular, liberal-minded Russian scholars and experts referred to Russia's North-west as an ideal venue for testing models of cooperation between Russian and European regions.[15]

At this juncture, the year 2000 had a truly pivotal meaning for the development of regionalism in Russia. Not only did it mark an important transformation of the Russian political system more broadly (with a visible drive toward political centralization accompanied by gradual elimination of political opposition and elevation of the *siloviki* faction), it also paved the way for a dramatic change in relations between the center and the periphery, with a new emphasis on centralization and curtailing the rights of regions. With the initiation of regional reforms that introduced the federal districts headed by Plenipotentiary Representatives (2000), and tax reform (launched in 2000 and finalized in 2004) that resulted in the transfer of the revenues from the regions to the federal center,[16] some regions were left to the mercy of Moscow when it came to financial injections, which would become the main support for existence and survival. Moreover, the centralization process in Russia had yet another side: the regions' right and ability to maintain foreign ties, both politically and economically, were becoming much more limited.

Worsening political relations with the West as well as internal developments in Russia between 1999 and 2004 resulted in a

---

[14] Ruslan Smishchenko, "Regionalizm i modeli regionalizatsii v sravnitel'noi perspektive," *Izvestiia Altaiskogo gosudarstvennogo universiteta* (2011), 281, https://cyberleninka.ru/article/n/regionalizm-i-modeli-regionalizatsii-v-sravnitelnoy-perspektive.

[15] Sergei Kortunov, "Kaliningrad kak vorota w Bol'shuiu Evropu," *Russia in Global Affairs*, 27 December 2004, http://www.globalaffairs.ru/number/n_4210.

[16] For more information, see Gulnaz Sharafutdinova and Rostislav Turovsky, "The Politics of Federal Transfers in Putin's Russia: Regional Competition, Lobbying, and Federal Priorities," *Post-Soviet Affairs* 33, no. 2 (2017): 161–75.

complete rejection of the European reading of regional integration, a sentiment that later transformed into harsh criticism of the European way, now counterposed to the "Russian model."[17] After 2014 this tendency became even more pronounced, leading many domestic and foreign observers to the corollary conclusion that the movement toward greater centralization at the expense of the regions would only continue to increase in future.[18] This had (and continues to have) a direct effect on the north-western regions in particular, because of their physical proximity to the EU.

Russia's North-West: The General Picture (1991–2013)

As a result of the abovementioned reforms of regional administrative structures, the north-western part of the Russian Federation became the North-Western Federal District on 13 May 2000.[19] Consisting of Arkhangelsk oblast', Vologda oblast', Kaliningrad oblast', the Republic of Karelia, Komi Republic, Leningrad oblast', Murmansk oblast', the Nenets Autonomous Okrug, Novgorod oblast', Pskov oblast', and St. Petersburg, its total population amounts to merely 13.6 million (roughly 9.4 percent of Russia's total population),[20] residing on a vast swath of land covering 1,687,000 square kilometers. Any assessment of the district's strong points must include four key factors. The first is the district's unique geography, which makes it the only Russian administrative entity to border EU and NATO member states and, especially important, the Baltic Sea. Second is the virtual absence of factors that could undermine local security (unlike the situation in some other Russian regions, which

---

[17] "Sergei Naryshkin vystupil na mezhdunarodnoi konferentsii 'Prezident, parlament, integratsiia,'" *Novosti Predsedatelia Gosudarstvennoi Dumy*, 24 November 2014, http://www.duma.gov.ru/news/%20274/858084/?sphrase_id=18657 50#photo5.

[18] Yekaterina Mikhailenko, "Slozhnosti postroeniia rossiiskogo regionalizma na postsovetskom prostranstve," *Vestnik Tomskogo gosudarstvennogo universiteta* 400 (2015): 81–87.

[19] Ukaz Prezidenta RF ot 13 maia 2000 g. N 849, "O polnomochnom predstavitele Prezidenta Rossiiskoi Federatsii v federal'nom okruge" (s izmeneniiami i dopolneniiami), http://base.garant.ru/12119586/#block_2000.

[20] Almost half the population resides in St. Petersburg and Leningrad oblast'.

have been assailed by ethnic conflicts and instability). Third, histor-ically, a good local security situation underwrites the possibility of cooperation. Fourth is the abundance of natural resources (e.g., tim-ber, various metals, hydrocarbons) that could be used as factors of transborder economic cooperation and a source of improved living standards.

Russia's North-West: The Place and Role of the Region through the Prism of History

Historically, the Baltic Sea region has played a decisive role for Rus-sian statehood. For instance, it stood at the foundations of Kievan Rus'. At the same time, through participating in the powerful Han-seatic League, which dominated regional trade flows, Pskov and Novgorod republics were included in regional economic affairs and trade in the Baltic Sea basin and beyond.[21] This balance, however, was changed with the advent of the Great Duchy of Moscow (begin-ning with the reign of Ivan III Vasilyevich) and the outbreak of the Livonian War (1558–83), two events that were a manifestation of the political centralization of the Russian state through the policy of "the gathering of the Russian lands."

Subsequent developments also pointed to a qualitative trans-formation of the role of the Baltic Sea area for Russia. In addition to the empire's deeply vested economic and security interests in the region, it became a prime source of Russian modernization and "Eu-ropeanization," resulting in a decisive separation from the Latin–Polish cultural tradition (through the Polish–Lithuanian Common-wealth, in which Kyiv played a decisive role) in favor of a pivot to-ward northern Europe. Thus, in the final analysis, it was the active military–diplomatic involvement of the Russian state in this region that made the Russian Empire, with its capital in St. Petersburg, a full-fledged participant in the European balance of power. Over time, as the Russian Empire began projecting its might over the re-gion (1725–1871), the Baltic Sea area ceased to play the same role it

---

[21]   Valentin Valerov, *Novgorod i Pskov: Ocherki politicheskoi istorii Severo-Zapad-noi Rusi XI–XIV vekov* (St. Petersburg: Alteia, 2004).

once had and was eclipsed by other regions. Yet, after unification and the rapid rise of the German Empire, the region turned into a playground between Berlin and St. Petersburg. Subsequently, in the aftermath of two global military conflicts, World War I and World War II, the powerful Soviet Union viewed the region through the lens of security-related concerns and the power play with NATO.[22]

The post–Cold War developments on the Baltic Sea were greatly influenced by the collapse of the USSR, the emergence of the EU, which encouraged a new round of regional cooperation, and initiation of the demilitarization process (enabled by the termination of the Warsaw Pact), which promised to turn the area into a less militarized zone of peace and prosperity.[23] This picture of a bright future, however, contrasted with the Russian perception: despite having lost great power status, Moscow did not abandon the aspiration to regain that status in the future. Russia's neighbors were acutely conscious of this; speaking in Hamburg in 1994, for example, Estonia's president Lennart Meri warned of the prospect that the Baltic Sea region might become one of the main targets of Russian power politics.[24]

Socio-economic Crisis and the Russian North-West: Challenges, Prospects, and Solutions

The economic crises that struck the Russian Federation and dealt a severe blow to the legacy of the Soviet Union and self-perception of the Russian population, first in 1991 and subsequently in 1998, negatively affected the north-western region. This was the result of a number of factors, chief among which was the region's unequal economic and demographic development, a problem inherited from the

---

[22]   See further Sergey Sukhankin, "From 'Bridge of Cooperation' to A2/AD 'Bubble': The Military Transformation of Kaliningrad Oblast," *Journal of Slavic Military Studies* 31, no. 1 (2018): 15–36.

[23]   Ari Puheloinen, *Russia's Geopolitical Interests in the Baltic Area* (Helsinki: National Defence College, 1999), 45.

[24]   "Rech', iz-za kotoroi Putin vyshel, khlopnuv dver'iu. Chto sluchilos' v Gamburge v 1994 godu," *Nastoiashchee Vremia*, 6 July 2017, https://www.currenttime.tv/a/28598781.html.

Soviet era. With the collapse of the USSR, the North-West became even more unattractive, leading to a massive depopulation of Pskov, Novgorod, and Karelia, while St. Petersburg and Leningrad oblast' together accounted for more than 50 percent of the total population of the North-West.[25] This differential highlighted the growing gap between the center and the periphery, making the difference between traditionally economically depressed areas and more developed parts even more striking than during the Soviet period.[26]

Out of a broad variety of choices for addressing this problem, Moscow picked the most short-sighted one, with the following elements:

- the allocation of subsidies (of course, after removing the regions' power to tax) as a means of stimulating local economic growth;
- greater centralization, with a view to enabling control over local processes; and
- the merger of economically weak areas with more buoyant areas (including intensification of cooperation), which was intended to stimulate less developed areas to catch up with more developed ones.

This model did not meet with universal approval.[27] An alternative proposal envisaged allocation of more autonomy to Russia's border territories (especially Kaliningrad oblast' and Karelia), using those as "pilot" regions (primarily Kaliningrad) for cooperation with EU member states and candidates. This arrangement implied the granting of greater autonomy to the regions, which stood in contrast to the course and logic of Russia's internal development after 1996, which was marked by a growing conservatism.

---

[25]   Boris Prokhorov (ed.), "Sotsial'no-ekonomicheskie osobennosti federal'nykh okrugov Rossii i zdorov'e naseleniia," in *Nauchnye Trudy INP RAN* (Moskva: Maks-Press, 2008).

[26]   Natalia Zubarevich, "Sotsial'noe razvitie regionov i poselenii Rossii: Izmeneniia 90-kh godov," *Vestnik Moskovskogo universiteta*, ser. 5, *Geografiia* 6 (2002): 56.

[27]   Andrei Manakov, "Federalizm i yedinstvo Rossii," *Pskovskii Regionologicheskii Zhurnal* 2 (2006): 36–41.

Europe's Position: "Euroregions" and the Northern Dimension Initiative

Russia's European partners, however, saw the solution from a different perspective, insofar as the centralization promulgated prior to 1991 turned out to have multiple flaws. From the European point of view, it was desirable for Moscow to grant Russia's border regions more freedom and autonomy as a way to increase competitiveness and attract more foreign direct investment (FDI).[28] For this purpose, Europe offered a number of programs that were intended to facilitate the transition of Russia's North-West from the previous model to a European market participant through the exchange of experience and expertise.

One such instrument was the Technical Assistance to the Commonwealth of Independent States (TACIS) program, which offered a cooperative framework that included a broad range of areas and dimensions.[29] TACIS was also intended to provide economic assistance to developing countries, with the expectation that it would directly bring more than $54 million in FDI into Russia's North-West.[30] The efficiency of the program was profoundly undermined, however, by frequent misuse and the illegal redistribution of financial means (discussed below).

Another initiative offered by Russia's partners was to form "Euroregions," which had been successfully practiced by Western European countries for decades. The idea was to integrate Russia's border regions in the Baltic Sea rim through joint projects in such domains as economics, education and culture, transportation, green energy, and ecology. Proliferating cooperation was expected to result in increased local problem solving without the involvement of the center. The Euroregions (with the participation of Russian

---

[28]   N. Y. Oding and G. M. Fedorov, "Aktivizatsiia rossiiskogo uchastiia v transgranichnom sotrudnichestve na Baltike," *Vestnik Rossiiskogo gosudarstvennogo universiteta im. I. Kanta* 3 (2009): 64.

[29]   TACIS, *European Commission*, Press Release Database, http://europa.eu/rapid/press-release_MEMO-92-54_en.htm.

[30]   Alexander Frenz, "The European Commission's Tacis Programme 1991–2006," *European Union External Action*, https://eeas.europa.eu/sites/eeas/files/tacis_success_story_final_en.pdf.

north-western entities) in existence in 1997–2010 are listed in Table 1.

Table 1. Russian Euroregions 1997–2010.

Euroregion	Year of creation	Territorial coverage (in Russia)
Neman	1997	Gur'evsk, Krasnoznamensk, and Ozersk districts (Kaliningrad oblast')
Baltic	1998	Kaliningrad oblast'
Karelia	1998	Republic of Karelia
Saule	1999	Slavsk district (Kaliningrad oblast')
Lyna-Lave	2004	Kaliningrad oblast'
Šešupė	2004	Kaliningrad oblast'
Pskov-Livonia	2004	Pskov oblast'
Yaroslavna	2007	Kursk oblast'
Donbas	2010	Voronezh oblast'

In the final analysis, the Euroregions initiative (unlike the Baltic states and Poland) did not result in a breakthrough, suffering from lack of interest on the Russian side. The general Russian assessment was summed up in the statement by political scientists Aleksei Vovenda and Vladislav Plotnikov that "this form of integration has not brought any visible results."[31] Some authoritative Russian media outlets even suggested that the roots of the 2008 economic crisis lay in the failure of regionalism.[32]

On the other hand, the Northern Dimension (ND) initiative, which emerged in 1997, prioritized the development of a transborder partnership between northern Europe and parts of the Russian

---

[31] Aleksei Vovenda and Vladislav Plotnikov, "Evroregiony kak faktor uspeshnoi mezhdunarodnoi integratsii v sovremennykh usloviiakh," *Vestnik Rossiiskogo gosudarstvennogo universiteta im. I. Kanta* 4, vypusk 10 (2011): 66.

[32] N. Mezhevich, "Vstrecha Sarkozi i Merkel'—popytka otdelit'sia ot slabykh stran Evrozony," *RIA Novosti*, 29 June 2012 (previously available at http://strateg y2020.rian.ru/news/20110817/366127391.html; URL inactive as at 12 July 2018).

Federation, with particular emphasis on Kaliningrad oblast'. By 2010, however, Russian experts had not formed any definitive opinion on the project, primarily concentrating on its "deficiencies."[33] In general, the Russian perception of interregional cooperation was expressed in the following maxim, put forward by scholars evaluating this initiative: "The development of transborder and interregional cooperation is one of several objectives, but is not the main goal of strategic development of the North-West. The goal is the development of human potential based on economic growth of an innovative type."[34] This posture vividly demonstrated the strategy, based on "complex development of the macro-region,"[35] did not in fact leave any room for initiatives promulgated by Russia's European partners. This policy resembled the Soviet vision of center-periphery relations. This vision seemed to have been abandoned after 1991; alas, as later developments made clear, this was not the case. In the end, Russian participation in the Northern Dimension initiative was reduced to meaningless formalities.

Russian "Prosperity" and the North-West

The period between 2000 and 2012 is frequently referred to as one of Russian economic exuberance. In fact, this is often misconstrued— the real picture is more complex.[36] Nonetheless, it is certainly the case that the period was characterized by micro- and macro-economic growth, fueled by growing exports of oil, petroleum products, and natural gas at rising world market prices. Growing economic

---

33   Ekaterina Bolotnikova, "Obnovlennoe 'Severnoe izmerenie': Kontseptual'nye aspekty," in *Nauchnye trudy Severo-Zapadnoi Akademii Gosudarstvennoi Sluzhby, Sovremennaia vneshniaia politika Rossii v global'nom i yevropeiskom izmerenii*, vol. 1, no. 1 (Sankt-Peterburg: Baltiiskii Region, 2010), 115–26.

34   A. A. Zhabrev, N. M. Mezhevich, and A. N. Leont'eva, "Razvitie prigranichnogo sotrudnichestva—tsel' i sovokupnost' zadach strategicheskogo razvitiia Severo-Zapada Rossiiskoi Federatsii," *Pskovskii Regionologicheskii Zhurnal* 12 (2011): 4.

35   N. Mezhevich, "Infrastrukturnyi faktor w sovremennoi ekonomicheskoi geografii makroregiona 'Severo-Zapad,'" *Pskovskii regionologicheskii zhurnal* 16 (2013): 3–11.

36   It should be noted that the powerful image of "prosperity" was in many ways built on raising energy prices, whereas signs of potential (and existing) economic difficulties were skilfully concealed by Russian propaganda.

capabilities were widely used by Russian official propaganda in various information campaigns designed for both internal and external consumption.[37] It is worthwhile reviewing briefly how the northwestern part of the Russian Federation was developing at the time and to what extent Russian economic growth changed both the living conditions of local residents and growth rates in the North-West.

By 2010–2011, the North-Western Federal District's share in Russia's cumulative GRP (gross regional product) was approximately 10 percent, of which St. Petersburg's contribution alone had increased from 32 to 43 percent. The city was home to 483 major organizations and business corporations (out of 527 in the North-West) and to key branches of high-tech industry oriented toward both civilian use and the needs of the military-industrial complex.[38] This positive trend sharply contrasted with the overall image of Russia's domestic economics, which was that of a huge and rapidly growing imbalance between center and periphery.[39] Owing to the lack of an integrated strategy, poorly developed parts of the North-West had to rely on financial injections from the federal center, which was hardly a prudent solution.

The challenges faced by the north-western region in 2000–2012 included the following:

1. *An excessive number of unprofitable businesses.* The leading oblasti in this respect were Karelia (where 47.5 percent of businesses were unprofitable) and, rather disappointingly, Kaliningrad oblast' (47.3 percent).[40]

---

37   See, for example, "Russia Second by Economic Performance among G20: Survey," *RT*, 23 November 2012, https://www.rt.com/business/russia-economic-performance-rating-396/.

38   A. I. Prygunov, "Perspektivy razvitiia regional'noi khoziaistvennoi sistemy na Severo-Zapade Rossii," *Vestnik MGTU* 10, no. 4 (2007): 680–92.

39   V. A. Shliamin, Rossiia v *"Severnom izmerenii": Monografiia* (Petrozavodsk: Petrozavodsk State University, 2002), 192.

40   O. Tolstoguzov, Ye. Nemkovich, T. Shmuilo, and M. Kurilo, "Sotsial'no-ekonomicheskoe sostoianie prigranichnykh regionov Severo-Zapadnogo Federal'nogo Okruga," *Regional'naia ekonomika: Teoriia i praktika*, Institut ekonomiki Karel'skogo nauchnogo tsentra 22, no. 349 (2014): 34.

2. *Uncontrollable draining of human resources* from economically weak to more attractive regions.

3. *Appalling demographic conditions.* The poor demographic picture stemmed from both low birth rates and skyrocketing death rates,[41] resulting in part from deviant behavior and pervasive alcoholism among local populations.[42]

3. *Weak or inadequate level of foreign economic cooperation.* In this regard, Kaliningrad oblast"s much touted leadership was mostly illusory: its foreign economic contacts were premised on a huge imbalance between imports (8.1 percent of the cumulative imports of the Russian Federation) and exports (Western goods were simply transferred to the Russian mainland).[43] Karelia did develop several projects, yet these were rather insignificant and did not bring any visible relief to the republic, making the gap with neighboring Finland all the more striking.[44]

That said, it should also be pointed out that Russian policies aimed at improving socio-economic conditions in Russia's North-West could not possibly have been effective since they did not give proper consideration to the nature of the problems at hand, which were deeply rooted in the Soviet past. Moscow ignored the fact that increasing financial support to the region while closing it to the outside world amounted to creating a twenty-first century Potemkin village. Instead of providing a solution, these policies became the source of new challenges for the region.

Unfortunately, the ideas and projects elaborated by both domestic and external experts and members of civil society were given short shrift, if indeed they were considered at all. One of these proposals was the "road map" presented in 2009 by the prominent

---

41   For instance, the number of deaths in Pskov oblast' in 2000–2012 was twice the number of births in the same period.

42   *Regiony Rossii: Osnovnye kharakteristiki sub"ektov Rossiiskoi Federatsii. Statisticheskii sbornik* (Moskva: Federal'naia sluzhba gosudarstvennoi statistiki, 2012), 662.

43   For more information, see Sergey Sukhankin, "Kaliningrad: Russia's Stagnant Enclave," *European Council on Foreign Relations*, 31 March 2016, http://www.ecfr.eu/article/commentary_kaliningrad_russias_stagnant_enclave_6052.

44   T. Druzhinin and P. Kukhareva, "Sotrudnichestvo prigranichnykh regionov: Karel'skaia praktika," *Regional'naia Ekonomika: Teoriia i Praktika* 8 (2012): 2–9.

Kaliningrad-based economist Gennadii Fedorov, who emphasized reliance on innovation, integration in the Baltic Sea rim, and cross-border cooperation as three main preconditions for sustainable growth and development in Russia's North-West.[45] Other notable experts also acknowledged that the simple allocation of subsidies to less developed regions could trigger nothing but growth on paper while at the same time "destroying any motivation for development."[46] These voices, however, were ignored or dismissed.

In the final analysis, the period of economic growth experienced by the Russian Federation in 2000–2012 had ambiguous consequences for the North-West. On the one hand, the overall image of prosperity and growth was largely associated with St. Petersburg, which obscured problems faced by other parts of this macro-region. At the same time, high oil prices and multiple contentious issues between Russia and the West (issues were increasingly obvious and repeatedly underscored) even well before the outbreak of the Ukrainian crisis resulted in a lessening of cooperation between Russia's North-West and the macro-region's European partners. Subsequent developments did not change the essence of the overall picture, merely highlighting previously observed trends.

Russia's North-West Post-Crimea

Events in Ukraine—first the outbreak of the Euromaidan in 2013, and subsequently the tragic developments in the country's South-East—have become an acid test for relations between Russia and the West. Growing anti-European and anti-American rhetoric and counter-sanctions in response to sanctions imposed on Russia brought certain changes to the Russian regions, especially those sharing a border with an EU country. This section discusses the impact of post-2014 changes on Karelia and Pskov oblasti as Russia's "Euroregions" (and the least developed parts of the North-Western

---

[45] N. Y. Oding and G. M. Fedorov, "Aktivizatsiia rossiiskogo uchastiia v transgranichnom sotrudnichestve na Baltike," *Vestnik Rossiiskogo gosudarstvennogo universiteta im. I. Kanta* 3 (2009): 63–69.

[46] Sergei Yevdokimov, "Konkurentosposobnost' Pskovskoi oblasti i sosednikh regionov Severo-Zapada Rossii," *Pskovskii Regionologicheskii Zhurnal* 9 (2010).

Federal District), and on St. Petersburg as the most developed entity and Russia's most "European" city.

Karelia: Patriotism and Isolationism in Lieu of Development

In September 2017, the Republic of Karelia held its first elections since 2002, and Artur Parfenchikov was elected the new head of the republic. The result, though predictable, still brought with it an element of surprise: the popular turnout was only about 29 percent of the Karelian electorate.[47] This poor showing pointed to spreading indifference and aloofness among local residents, as well as underscoring the flawed policies of the previous incumbent, Putin appointee Aleksandr Hudilainen (2012–2017), whose activities had led to a severe economic crisis and massive public protests.[48]

A disintegrating economy is not the only distinctive trait of post-2014 Karelia: the republic's development has been shaped negatively by the outbreak of witch-hunts and repressions launched against those unable or unwilling to prove their loyalty. One of the first measures was closure of the Department of Baltic-Finnish Philology and Culture at Petrozavodsk University, the only such academic department in Russia, an action that should be seen as an attempt to uproot any vestiges of ties between the region and neighboring Finland. In 2015 Galina Shirshina, acting mayor of Petrozavodsk, whose political position was distinct from that of the ruling United Russia party, was sacked. This started a trail of political repressions aimed at eliminating opposition candidates. For instance, the leader of the local Russian United Democratic Party Yabloko, Vasilii Popov, was forced to flee to Finland in search of political

---

[47]   Vadim Shtepa, "Russian Karelia: Further Repressions Instead of European Integration?" *Jamestown Foundation Blog*, 28 September 2017, https://jamestown.org/russian-karelia-further-repressions-instead-of-european-integration/.

[48]   Vadim Martynov and Andrei Korolev, "Kareliia: Vesennie posadki," *Radio Svoboda*, 9 April 2015, https://www.svoboda.org/a/26945288.html.

asylum.[49] His departure virtually eliminated the party from the race and paved the way for the victory of Putin's appointee.[50]

In 2016, repressions in Karelia took a different turn: spiraling ideological confrontations resulted in a new round of information warfare,[51] which led to the prohibition of any reading of Soviet history differing from the officially presented one. For Karelia, where a huge number of Soviet concentration camps had been established in the Stalinist period, this became an especially troubling issue. In 2016 Yurii Dmitriev, a prominent amateur historian and activist engaged in restoring the memory of the Stalinist terror in the region, was detained under seemingly false and politically motivated charges.[52] His detention signaled a new round of strife with the "fifth column."

The Kremlin's current concern with Karelia needs to be viewed in the context of events that took place in 1990, when the Supreme Council of the Karelian ASSR passed a declaration of sovereignty of the republic.[53] The "shadow of separatism" reappeared in 2014, when the republican movement of Karelia emerged. The local authorities reacted immediately: after the organizational statute had been adopted, the local Ministry of Internal Affairs' Center for Counteracting Extremism demanded that the notion of, and all

---

[49] "Vasilii Popov iz partii 'Yabloko' poluchil ubezhyshche v Finliandii," *Radio Svoboda*, 17 February 2017, https://www.svoboda.org/a/28316133.html.

[50] Valerii Potashov, "Kareliia gotovitsia k postanovke," *Posle Imperii*, 8 June 2017, http://afterempire.info/2017/06/08/postanovka/.

[51] Sergey Sukhankin, "The 'Trump Cards' of the Russian Propaganda and Disinformation Operations," *Notes Internacionals* (Barcelona: Barcelona Centre for International Affairs [CIDOB], June 2017), https://www.cidob.org/en/publications/publication_series/notes_internacionals/n1_176/the_trump_cards_of_the _russian_propaganda_and_disinformation_operations.

[52] Aleksandr Gnetnev and Yelizaveta Maetnaia, "Liudi v nego veriat," *Radio Svoboda*, 1 June 2017, https://www.svoboda.org/a/2852060.html.

[53] For more information, see "Deklaratsiia o gosudarstvennom suverenitete Karel'skoi ASSR," in *Sbornik dokumentov KPSS: Zakonodatel'nykh aktov, deklaratsyi, obrashchenii i prezidentskikh ukazov, posviashchennykh probleme natsional'no-gosudarstvennogo supereniteta* (Moscow: Institut teorii i istorii sotsializma TsK KPSS, 1991), 267–70, available at: http://soveticus5.narod.ru/ 85/sborn91.htm#p267.

language pertaining to, regionalism be removed from the document.[54] This telling episode vividly demonstrated the Russian (mis)perception of regionalism as a fundamentally political phenomenon.

Aside from this, in June 2014 the activities of the local online newspaper *Chernika*, recognized as a key source of independent information in Karelia, were "temporarily halted" by local authorities,[55] which was quite a broad hint. At the same time, Moscow explicitly threatened Karelian authorities with "withdrawal of funds and subsidies" in the event that the program of development was not fulfilled.

Threats and repressions have been supplemented by a vigorous campaign aimed at boosting "patriotic feelings" among Karelian residents—an unsurprising development in light of Russian internal developments. For this purpose, the local Ministry of Education has elaborated "recommendations" (dispatched from Moscow) for local schoolteachers and primary and secondary educational institutions that oblige them to carry out a series of events dedicated to the "unification of Russia and Crimea." It was reported that a full week of in- and extra-curricular activities covering such topics as "Russia and Crimea—We are together," "Unification of Russia and Crimea," "Defense of Sevastopol during the Great Patriotic War," "Inclusion of Crimea and Sevastopol in the Russian Federation," and "Unification of the Crimean Republic" was to be carried out in local schools.[56]

In the final analysis, it seems reasonable to argue that the geographic proximity of Karelia to the EU has turned to be, as political scientist Oleg Reut has put it, "a source of imaginary threats, not a factor of development,"[57] a view that has undoubtedly received new impetus after the outbreak of the Ukrainian crisis. The likelihood is

---

54   Valerii Potashov, "Chinovniki boiatsia regionalizma," *Vesti Kareliia*, 10 February 2014, http://vesti.karelia.ru/news/chinovniki_boyatsya_regionalizma/.

55   "'Chernika' ukhodit na kanikuly," *Chernika*, 31 May 2017, https://mustoi.ru/chernika-uxodit-na-kanikuly.

56   "Karel'skikh shkol'nikov budut tseluiu nedeliu muchit' Krymom," *Posle Imperii*, 4 March 2017, http://afterempire.info/2017/03/04/karjala-crimea/.

57   Oleg Reut, "Prigranichnost' dlia Kremlia—istochnik vydumannykh ugroz, a ne resurs razvitiia," *Chernika*, 25 February 2016, https://mustoi.ru/prigranichnost-dlya-kremlya-istochnik-vydumannyx-ugroz-a-ne-resurs-razvitiya/.

that this is the reality Karelia will be facing in the short and intermediate term.

Pskov Oblast': Back to the USSR?

Pskov oblast' has traditionally been viewed as one of the least developed parts of Russia's North-West. A scarcity of natural resources
has made reliance on heavy industry and serving the military-industrial complex the key components of the local economy. Economic
hardship followed the collapse of the USSR, and lack of innovation
has severely damaged those components, jeopardizing the economic development of the oblast'. At the same time, plummeting
living standards turned the demographic crisis (already acute during the Soviet period, yet largely ignored[58]) into sheer disaster, resulting in a massive outflow of qualified workers and young people
to more economically buoyant parts of the North-West, mainly St.
Petersburg and the Leningrad oblast'.

At this juncture, it should be noted that the Ukrainian crisis
did not dramatically change the trajectory of development of Pskov
oblast'. The key problems and challenges faced by the oblast' have,
however, been magnified by worsening economic conditions caused
by the economic sanctions. Researchers specializing in local affairs
have presented a dreary picture in which stagnating industry, a disintegrating agrarian sector, weak services, inadequate health care, a
low and falling FDI, and decreasing governmental support are all
mixed in together, thus contributing to the overall image of a dying
region.[59]

In addition, worsening relations between Russia and the West
have affected the perceptions of local residents, especially in light of

---

[58]   Andrei Manakov, "Depopuliatsionnye protsessy v Pskovskoi oblasti na fone poliarizatsii naseleniia severo-zapadnoi Rossii," in *Voprosy geografii: Problemy regional'nogo razvitiia Rossii*, eds. V. M. Kotliakov, V. N. Streletskii, O.B. Glezer,
and S. G. Safronov (Moskva: Izdatel'skii dom Kodeks, 2016), 317–37; and Andrei
Manakov, *Dinamika naseleniia pskovskogo regiona na fone poliarizatsii naseleniia severo-zapada Rossii* (Pskov, 2014), 55.

[59]   Tat'iana Puzynia, "Otsenka investitsionnoi privlekatel'nosti Pskovskoi oblasti,"
in *Regional'naia ekonomika: Teoriia i praktika* (Velikie Luki, 2014).

the region's role in Russia's security-related calculations (the famous 76th Guards Air Assault Division is located in Pskov). According to CNN journalist Clarissa Ward, who travelled to the oblast' in 2017, the majority of respondents were more concerned with plummeting living standards than with political developments.[60] On the other hand, many local residents are very supportive of the course pursued by Vladimir Putin and "feel safe" because of the level of militarization, which, according to some respondents, "will protect us from NATO" as the arch-enemy of Russia. Nostalgia for Soviet times is also quite widespread, and this profoundly intensifies the overall atmosphere of obscurantism and stagnation.

St. Petersburg: The "Russian European" in an Age of Russo-European Crisis

On the surface, St. Petersburg would appear to be one of most successful examples of the post-Soviet transformation. The city managed to overcome the hardships of the early 1990s, having earlier developed the most diversified economy in the entire North-Western Federal District.[61] In addition to its powerful industrial backbone, the city can boast of significant innovative potential, and its cultural attractions draw millions of tourists each year.[62]

In May 2014 the government of St. Petersburg adopted a new strategic plan that stipulates key areas of development for the city up to the year 2030.[63] Aside from the rather optimistically ambitious tasks the city sets for itself in the document, including strengthening its industries, improving competitiveness, increasing

---

[60]   "CNN: V Pskove boiatsia ne NATO, a bednosti," *RT*, 18 January 2017, https://russ ian.rt.com/inotv/2017-01-18/CNN-v-Pskove-boyatsy-ne.

[61]   A. Batchaev and B. Zhykharevich, "Sankt-Peterburg v postsovetskii period: Ekonomicheskie strategii i razvitie," *Ekonomicheskie i sotsial'nye peremeny: fakty, tendentsii, prognozy* 34, no. 4 (2014): 69.

[62]   Anna Murav'eva, "Peterburg v 2016 godu pobil rekord po chislu turistov," *Peterburgskii dnevnik*, 16 January 2017, https://www.spbdnevnik.ru/news/2017-01-16/peterburg-v-2016-godu-pobil-rekord-po-chislu-turistov/.

[63]   Pravitel'stvo Sankt-Peterburga, Postanovlenie ot 13.05.2014 N 355 "O Strategii ekonomicheskogo i sotsial'nogo razvitiia Sankt-Peterburga na period do 2030 goda," http://spbstrategy2030.ru/?page_id=102.

investment, and developing a greater innovative potential, a closer look brings to light ongoing contradictions and uncertainties. Needless to say, the document itself was not uniformly supported by its creators, causing heated debate.[64] The strategic plan was criticized from various quarters as "utopian"[65] and at the same time "indecisive."[66]

What clearly emerges from a careful reading of the document is that the plan's adoption was greatly influenced by external developments and the spiraling political confrontation between Russia and the West. This cannot possibly imply anything but an intention to increase isolation from the West (and increase control from Moscow), in sharp contradiction to history and the essence of St. Petersburg as Russia's cultural capital.

Another disturbing element of the strategic plan is its explicit emphasis on the development of heavy industry as the city's economic core, an emphasis that brushes aside the importance of "nonmaterial" contributions to the city's economy, such as culture, tourism, or the fine arts. One of the most logical questions that could be posed is why the two aspects cannot be developed simultaneously. The question is especially apropos in light of the ongoing crisis in heavy industry. One might be tempted to blame the "anti-Russian sanctions" imposed by the West in 2014 for the backward-looking emphasis on heavy industry, yet this would be incorrect. In fact, the tendency started in 2008 and was progressively increasing up to 2013,[67] which underscores the fact that the economic sanctions merely worsened previously existing problems. On another front, Russian sources have on a number of occasions referred to the inefficiency of the local authorities, who have failed to establish a

---

[64] Daria Fazletdinova, "RANy Strategii-2030," *Baltinfo*, 17 December 2013, http://www.baltinfo.ru/2013/12/17/RANy-Strategii-2030-397389.

[65] Yelena Danilevich, "Chto unizhaet gorod? Lev Lur'e—o nesmelom rukovodstve i uezzhaiushchikh talantakh," *Argumenty i fakty* 51, 18 December 2013, http://www.spb.aif.ru/culture/person/1068284.

[66] Mikhail Shevchuk, "Programma spokoistviia," *Delovoi Peterburg*, 21 August 2014, https://www.dp.ru/a/2014/08/21/Programma_spokojstvija/.

[67] Feliks Rybakov, "Sovremennyi oblik promyshlennosti Sankt-Peterburga (predvaritel'naia otsenka rynochnoi transformatsii)," *Promyshlennaia politika v Rossiiskoi Federatsii* 10-12 (2013): 37–42.

dialogue and reach an understanding with the business elites. This lack of understanding of modern business directions has remained one of the main scourges of post-1991 Russia.[68]

Unfortunately, a quite sizable pool of Russian experts seems to be searching for a solution in the wrong places, namely, in the idea of a "new GOELRO plan" (which valorizes so-called "locomotive branches of production")[69] and in the postulates enunciated by Yevgeny Primakov, former minister of foreign affairs, stressing natural resources as "Russia's best ally." These views seem to be gaining huge popularity among the local elites.[70] Projects of this kind remind one forcibly of the Soviet experience—characterized by a high level of centralization, the uncontrolled draining of natural resources from other regions, and import substitution—an economic program that proved flawed and, in the final analysis, unsustainable.

Meanwhile, given Russia's current pivot to the East, which is actively promulgated by influential domestic conservative experts,[71] the issue of Chinese investments in St. Petersburg has become one of the most widely discussed topics in the Russian academic community. It has been argued that in light of the decreasing rates of Western FDI after 2014, financial capital from China could become a viable substitute.[72] Even though this scenario might yield some results in the future, it seems imprudent to vest excessive hopes in the "Chinese vector." First, the general trend pertaining to the amount of Chinese investments in the Russian economy remains rather pessimistic. Second, St. Petersburg itself cannot boast any major

---

[68]   T. Feofilova and A. Litvinenko, "Razvitie malogo predprinimatel'stva v obespechenii ekonomicheskoi bezopasnosti regiona," *Voprosy bezopasnosti* 6 (2014): 98–149.

[69]   The GOELRO plan (State Commission for Electrification of Russia) was the first-ever Soviet plan for national economic recovery and development promoted by Lenin.

[70]   Iu. Kosov, M. Meiksin, N. Mezhevich, and V. Yag'ia, "Promyshlennaia politika v usloviiakh vneshnikh vyzovov: vzgliad iz Sankt-Peterburga," *Upravlencheskoe Konsul'tirovanie (Sankt-Peterburgskii gosudarstvennyi universitet)* 9 (2016): 12.

[71]   See, for example, Sergei Karaganov, "Povorot k Azii: istoriia politicheskoi idei," *Rossiia v global'noi politike, GlobalAffairs.ru*, 13 January 2016, http://www.global affairs.ru/pubcol/Povorot-k-Azii-istoriya-politicheskoi-idei-17919.

[72]   E. Semenova, "Legkorel's s kitaiskoi perspektivoi," *Peterburgskii dnevnik*, 25 November 2015.

Chinese investments or projects. This means that the city cannot fully "reorient to the East"; cooperation with countries of the Baltic Sea rim remains the most logical and prudent solution. Unfortunately, profitability and common sense tend overwhelmingly to be trumped by ideology—once again, calling to mind parallels with the Soviet experience.

Professor Aleksandr Khodachek, President of the Higher School of Economics, has outlined three main scenarios of development for St. Petersburg:[73]

1. *Realistic scenario*. Because of its huge geopolitical and geostrategic importance, the city continues to follow a more or less similar trajectory of development as observed over the past ten to twelve years.

2. *Optimistic scenario*. The city wins the competition with the Baltic states in terms of logistics, thereby attracting new investments, resulting in steady economic growth.

3. *Pessimistic scenario*. The city continues losing its attractiveness to investors, due to its inability to compete effectively with other countries of the Baltic Sea region. This might result in a reorientation of the city away from international trade and toward domestic needs, which would be reflected in decreasing foreign cooperation and an increasing emphasis on ties with the rest of the North-Western Federal District.

Here, one could argue that the case of St. Petersburg is different to the two preceding examples of Pskov and Karelia. Because of its economic might and strategic importance, it is highly unlikely that the city would encounter the same problems faced by the peripheral regions. What is apparent, however, is that abridging existing external ties with the EU in the absence of any visible alternative will have a negative effect on the economic development of the city and its image. In theory, Moscow should not be interested in pursuing isolationist policies in regard to St. Petersburg since doing so would increase the support from the national budget that would have to be allocated for local needs. Despite the obvious drawbacks,

---

[73]   A. Khodachek, "Stsenarnye usloviia razvitiia Sankt-Peterburga," *Problemy sovremennoi ekonomiki* 45, no. 1 (2013): 137–40.

however, the political course chosen and upheld by the Kremlin may once again prevail over economic sense.

From "Pilot Region" to A2/AD "Bubble": The Case of Kaliningrad

Because of its history and geography, Kaliningrad oblast', which is part of the Russian Federation but physically detached from the mainland, presents an ideal venue for interregional cooperation with foreign partners. Its territorial proximity to buoyantly developing Poland and Lithuania, its myriad historical and cultural ties with economically powerful Germany, and its near-ideal geostrategic location have prompted many authors to refer to Kaliningrad as Russia's answer to Hong Kong. Unfortunately, the parallel has failed to materialize economically or socially. A quarter of a century after the collapse of the Soviet Union, it would not be an exaggeration to suggest that Kaliningrad has returned to its roots as a "militarized bastion" against the West, with ever diminishing external contacts.[74]

Between Great Hopes and Bleak Reality: Kaliningrad at the Crossroad of History (1991–2005)

The collapse of the USSR had a dramatic and unequivocal effect on Kaliningrad. Besides physical isolation and the disruption of previously established economic ties, the first post-Soviet decade witnessed plummeting living standards and unprecedented political chaos. This turned a previously semi-privileged Soviet oblast' into the "black hole of Europe" and "Russia's HIV/AIDS capital."[75] Needless to say, this transformation dealt a severe blow to local residents,

---

[74]   Sergey Sukhankin, "Kaliningrad's Changing Role on the Geopolitical Chess Board of Europe (1991–2015): Does History Repeat Itself?" in *Problemy bezpieczeństwa Europy i Azji*, ed. Arkadiusz Czwołek (Torun: N. Copernicus University, 2016), 223–45.

[75]   Sergey Sukhankin, "Kaliningrad—the Troubled Man of Europe," *NewEasternEurope.eu*, 29 July 2016, http://neweasterneurope.eu/2016/07/29/kaliningrad-the-troubled-man-of-europe/.

many of whom started to blame their misfortunes on the "liberal experiment"—as was quite typical for the rest of Russia as well.

At the same time, the demise of communism presented a rare opportunity: through programs promoted or sponsored by the EU, Kaliningrad was offered a unique chance to overcome the isolation/isolationism previously artificially imposed by Moscow and to transform from a hyper-militarized, largely inefficient economy based on subsidies in the direction of a genuine market economy based on competition and cross-border cooperation. Unfortunately, this potential path was also truncated, for two main reasons. First, the local residents and businesses were not well prepared to compete. It seems that the Soviet patterns, which guaranteed economic subsidies for areas facing a "challenging past," were rooted much deeper in the outlook of the Kaliningrad residents than in neighboring Poland and Lithuania. Second, even if the local residents and businesses had demonstrated greater flexibility, the result still would probably have been the same. Apprehensive of separatism, the Kremlin was concerned about eventually "losing the oblast'" to the West. With the passage of time, those voices became much more audible, leading to an assault on local rights and liberties.

Meanwhile, EU-backed initiatives in fact seemed inefficient, for reasons which, however, had nothing to do with the EU or the way those projects were organized. The reasons were much more trivial and mundane. First, the Kremlin, acting through loyal local elites, hampered cooperation between Kaliningrad and its geographic neighbors.[76] Second, European funds earmarked for the oblast' were fraudulently redistributed among the local elites, a process which was accompanied by numerous international corruption scandals (some of them dragging on to this day).[77] Third, the local

---

[76] For example, it took several years and huge effort to initiate business contacts between the oblast and German investors. At the same time, foreigners were not granted visa-free status, which made it exceedingly difficult for them to conduct any entrepreneurial activities in Kaliningrad.

[77] "Novye ochistnye v Guseve rekonstruiruiut iz-za vysokikh ekonorm v Rossii," *Gusev-onlin.ru*, 1 April 2015, https://gusev-online.ru/news/politika/4845-novye-ochistnye-v-guseve-rekonstruiruyut-iz-za-vysokih-ekonorm-v-rossii.html; and "Tsukanov: Poka net ochistnykh, vse stoki sbrasyvaiutsia v Baltiiskoe more," *Novyi Kaliningrad*, 28 January 2015, https://www.newkaliningrad.ru/news/br

authorities launched a campaign vilifying the EU for an "inadequate level of support" and lack of knowledge of local specifics,[78] at the same time conveniently forgetting the true extent of the support provided by the EU.

Another line of criticism was concerned with the upcoming enlargement of the EU, which "threatened" to "encircle" Kaliningrad, thus "cutting it off from the rest of Russia." Curiously, however, Moscow appears to have been well aware (and well in advance) of the upcoming EU's enlargement, but opted to stay on the side lines and refrain from any concrete negotiations on the matter.

The weak voices of the local liberals, who protested that Kaliningrad's prosperity and stability were and are inseparable from the oblast''s European connections, were muted by 2005. Thanks to huge oil revenues, Moscow managed to increase subsidies to the oblast'; the local population, for its part, did not hesitate to "trade stability for tranquillity."[79]

Kaliningrad and the Fateful Turn (2005–2013)

In 2005, Kaliningrad oblast' celebrated with great pomp and ceremony the 750th anniversary of the founding of the city of Kaliningrad (as Königsberg). This occasion was exploited by Moscow in an attempt to create an anti-NATO (anti-American) platform based on a "continental alliance" between Russia, Germany, and France. Incidentally, this was also one of Moscow's first attempts at testing European cohesion by purposefully taking an anti-Polish, anti-Lithuanian line, without, however, finding any support among leaders of European states. A year later, Kaliningrad was declared a Special Economic Zone (SEZ) in a show of support for the new governor.

---

iefs/community/5187842-tsukanov-poka-net-ochistnykh-vse-stoki-sbrasyvayu tsya-v-baltiyskoe-more.html.

78   "Kaliningradskaia oblast': Gubernator Vladimir Yegorov zaiavil, chto programma tekhnicheskogo sodeistviia TASIS sebia ischerpala," *Regnum*, 27 March 2003, https://regnum.ru/news/101123.html.

79   Sergey Sukhankin, "Kaliningrad: Baltic Hong Kong No Longer," *Foreign Policy Research Institute (Philadelphia)* website, 26 April 2017, https://www.fpri.org/article/2017/04/kaliningrad-baltic-hong-kong-no-longer/.

The SEZ status was supposed to contribute to the region's economic growth but turned out to be merely a hedge against foreign investors' interest and a tool for Moscow to expand its control over the local economy.[80]

At this juncture, it is useful to look at the broader picture, against the backdrop of the evolution of the Kremlin's foreign policy in 2007–2008. Starting with Putin's notorious Munich speech and Russia's withdrawal from the Treaty on Conventional Armed Forces in Europe (CFE), and moving on to the Bucharest NATO summit and the outbreak of the military conflict with Georgia, a number of events in a relatively short time frame proved fateful for Kaliningrad.

Previously perceived as an irrelevant and dilapidated backwater, the oblast' now found itself at the center of the Kremlin's power play against the West in the Baltic Sea region. This took the form of remilitarization of the oblast', which effectively canceled any hopes for greater demilitarization of the Baltic Sea, and the oblast' became an integral part of the *"Russkii mir,"* the Russian World project that emerged in 2007, a factor that would play a crucial role in the future. In the final analysis, one could justly argue that by 2013, the oblast' that once was referred to as the "Kaliningrad puzzle" had been transformed into the "Kaliningrad headache."[81] The worst, however, was yet to come.

Kaliningrad in the Post-Crimea World: Russia's "Bastion" against the West

Without question, the events that took place in south-east Ukraine from 2014 have had a huge impact on the trajectory of development of Kaliningrad oblast', altering its status from a hypothetical to a

---

[80] Nataliya Smorodinskaya, "Kaliningrad on Its Crooked Way to Economic Modernization," *The 6th EU Framework programme, UNDEUNIS project*, January 2007.

[81] Sergey Sukhankin, "Kaliningrad: From Boomtown to Battle-Station," *European Council on Foreign Relations*, 27 March 2017, http://www.ecfr.eu/article/comm entary_kaliningrad_from_boomtown_to_battle_station_7256.

very real source of unease for the entire Baltic region.[82] The related challenges can be provisionally separated into security-related and "soft" issues.

The security-related issues pertain to the rapid (re)militarization of the oblast' and its transformation into Russia's most advanced Anti-Access/Area-Denial "bubble,"[83] conceived as a military outpost against the West. This policy to some extent reiterated the Soviet actions that had made the oblast' into one of the most militarized zones in Europe (and probably in the world), a status it lost in the 1990s owing to the decrease in military spending and Moscow's new-found obligation to follow international agreements. The process of gradual remilitarization was initiated in 1999, when the oblast' co-hosted strategic military exercises under the code name "Zapad." Subsequently, exercises under the same code name were conducted in 2009, 2013, and 2017,[84] all based on clearly anti-NATO scenarios.

Yet it was the crisis in Ukraine (especially after 2015, when Russia officially abandoned the CFE Treaty) that ushered in a new wave of militarization of the entire Western Military District, and Kaliningrad in particular. This process has been marked by the deployment in Kaliningrad oblast' of the world's most cutting-edge military hardware, such as the Iskander-M tactical missile complexes (which may have been withdrawn from the oblast' on completion of military exercises); the S-400 Triumf anti-aircraft weapon system; the Bastion-P and the 3K60 Bal coastal defense missile systems, equipped with nuclear capability; and the P-800 Oniks supersonic anti-ship cruise missile. As a result, Russia has achieved full conventional superiority over NATO forces in the Baltic (taking into

---

[82] For more information, see Stephan Frühling and Guillaume Lasconjarias, "NATO, A2/AD and the Kaliningrad Challenge," *Survival* 58, no. 2 (2016): 95–116.

[83] Sergey Sukhankin, "The Kaliningrad Oblast Today: A 'Military Bastion 2.0,' Not a 'Bridge of Cooperation,'" *Diplomaatia* 165, May 2017, https://www.diplomaatia.ee/en/article/the-kaliningrad-oblast-today-a-military-bastion-20-not-a-bridge-of-cooperation/.

[84] Sergey Sukhankin, "Zapad-2017: What Did These Military Exercises Reveal?" *Diplomaatia* 170, October 2017, https://www.diplomaatia.ee/en/article/zapad-2017-what-did-these-military-exercises-reveal/.

account the military might of the entire Western Military District) while at the same time creating an "arc of counter-containment"[85] that now stretches from the Black Sea (Crimea) to the Baltic Sea, jeopardizing security on NATO's eastern flank, especially since certain NATO member states had been reducing their armed forces prior to 2014. These developments have had a chilling effect on previously neutral Sweden and Finland (where talk about eventually joining NATO is much more audible today than several years before), as well as on states traditionally apprehensive of Russian actions, including Estonia, Latvia, Lithuania, Poland, and now Ukraine. According to the US-based RAND Corporation, in the event of a military encounter between NATO and Russia, it might take Russia a mere thirty-six hours to occupy the Baltic states,[86] with Kaliningrad playing a decisive role as a springboard for military attack. Regrettably, this change of outlook and worsening political environment in the region is hardly separable from Russia's actions and the new-old role ascribed to Kaliningrad oblast'.

The soft issues pertain to Kaliningrad's transformation into a beacon of the Russian World initiative and an outlet for anti-Western propaganda. Partly, this owes to the Russian experience in Ukraine and Russia's subsequent involvement in the Syrian civil war, which convinced Russian military strategists that "information" and "information space" will play key roles in future wars.[87]

Apart from the military aspects, Kaliningrad's changing role has owed a great deal to the development and sophistication of the Russian World project, which was supplemented by an "ecclesiastical" ingredient after Kirill (who had been metropolitan of Smolensk and Kaliningrad since 1984) became Russian patriarch in 2009. The role played by the Russian Orthodox Church (Moscow Patriarchate)

---

[85]   Sergey Sukhankin, "Russian Electronic Warfare in Ukraine: Between Real and Imaginable," *Eurasia Daily Monitor (Jamestown Foundation)* 14, no. 71 (24 May 2017), https://jamestown.org/program/russian-electronic-warfare-ukraine-real-imaginable/.

[86]   David A. Shlapak, "Michael Johnson, Reinforcing Deterrence on NATO's Eastern Flank," *RAND*, https://www.rand.org/pubs/research_reports/RR1253.html.

[87]   See for example V. Gerasimov, "Po opytu Sirii," *Voenno-promyshlennyi kur'er*, 7 March 2016, https://vpk-news.ru/articles/29579.

and the personality of Kirill have been decisive factors in Kaliningrad becoming a pivotal element of the new version of the Russian World concept.[88] This trend was greatly amplified as a result of the debacle in political relations between Russia and the West.

After 2014, Kaliningrad was openly pronounced a "border" separating "Russian and non-Russian lands" and Russia's response to a morally stagnant Europe, which had departed from its historical roots and Christian values.[89] The campaign (one might be tempted to call it a crusade) against the oblast"s German cultural legacy (which survived the age of the Soviet barbarism) was headed by Patriarch Kirill, who called the remnants of German architecture "old stones" that should not be praised at the expense of Russian culture and national traditions.[90]

This "war on the past" received new impetus after implementation of the law on "foreign agents" (2014). This resulted in closure of the German-Russian House, a cultural and educational center that was the oldest and most reputable foreign NGO in Kaliningrad. These developments heralded a vigorous campaign against so-called "creeping Germanization." In the context of worsening relations with the West and the need for greater internal mobilization, this theme acquired new meaning. Two episodes should be mentioned in this connection. The first is the scandal over an anonymous letter that accused Professor of Sociology at the Baltic Federal University (BFU) Anna Alimpieva of "criticizing the government," "promulgating homosexual relations," and "defending Kaliningrad separatism."[91] Subsequent events showed that the matter originated with the so-called "international information-analytical Russian

---

88   Sergey Sukhankin, "The "Russkij mir" as Mission: Kaliningrad between the 'Altar' and the 'Throne' 2009–2015," *Magazine Ortodoxia (University of Eastern Finland)* (2016).

89   Russkaia Pravoslavnaia Tserkov', Vystuplenie Sviateishego Patriarkha Kirilla na I Kaliningradskom forume Vsemirnogo russkogo narodnogo sobora, 14 March 2015, http://www.patriarchia.ru/db/text/4013160.htm.

90   *Ibid.*

91   Tatiana Ziberova, "Na obychnykh listakh v kletku: podrobnosti skandala vokrug BFU im. I. Kanta," *Novyi Kaliningrad*, 29 September 2017, https://www.newkalin ingrad.ru/news/community/15110393-na-obychnykh-listakh-v-kletku-podrobn osti-skandala-vokrug-bfu-im-i-kanta.html.

language news portal" *NewsBalt*. Even a cursory glance at the range of topics covered by the agency, such as "Russophobia in the Baltic Sea Region," "Consequences of Ukrainian 'Eurointegration,'" and "Germanization of Kaliningrad," exposes its sharply ideological posture. The scandal caused a huge uproar in the oblast' that could be ignored neither by local authorities nor by the intellectual community. As a result, sixty-four leading professors from the BFU drafted a letter expressing serious concern over the attacks on their colleague.[92]

The vigorous campaign against the "Germanization" of Kaliningrad has also been joined by ultraconservative outlets such as *Exclav.ru, Russkii Krai,* and *Regnum.* In 2016, after Michael McFaul posted a reasonable question on *Twitter*—"Königsberg was a German city for centuries. Does that mean Germany has a right to annex Kaliningrad now?"—the level of tensions skyrocketed. This question triggered a heated debate in Kaliningrad. In his contribution to the debate, the editor-in-chief of *NewsBalt* stated that "the fifth column is getting stronger. It has become a matter of *bon ton* to use German names for objects located in Kaliningrad Oblast'."[93] This piece was followed by a torrent of similar pieces accusing the West (in addition to Germany and the United States, Poland and Lithuania joined the roster of potential irredentists) of harboring clandestine plans to "annex" the oblast' from Russia.

Indeed, the myth about the Germanization of Kaliningrad did not come out of nowhere at the beginning of the Ukrainian crisis and the resulting crisis in relations between Russia and the West; its origin can be traced to the early 1990s. Yet the current situation is far more dangerous. At a time when Russia's state ideology is based on a conflict with the West that serves as a source of legitimacy and a factor in the mobilization of public support through fifth-column rhetoric and claims of a witch-hunt, this myth could be exploited to

---

[92]   "Uchenye BFU im. I. Kanta opublikovali otkrytoe pis'mo v zashchitu kollegi ot anonimnogo donosa," *Novyi Kaliningrad,* 5 October 2017, https://www.newkaliningrad.ru/news/briefs/community/15182453-uchenye-bfu-opublikovali-ot-krytoe-pismo-v-zashchitu-kollegi-ot-anonimnogo-donosa.html.

[93]   "Vashington dal start: teper' u Rossii budut otnimat' Kaliningrad," *NewsBalt,* 21 March 2016, http://newsbalt.ru/reviews/2016/03/washington-kaliningrad/.

eradicate the opposition and further diminish any connection between Kaliningrad and its neighbors.

Russia's position on Kaliningrad can best be summed up in a
rather straightforward statement by the head of the Department of
Regional Security Problems at the Russian Institute for Strategic
Studies, Igor Nikolaichuk, who said in April 2016 that the oblast'
would never become a demilitarized "region of peace."[94]

Conclusions

The twenty-six years that have passed since the dissolution of the
Soviet Union have not led to profound changes to the essence of
center-periphery relations in Russia. On the contrary, one might argue that the period of growth and prosperity—in many respects artificial, albeit exquisitely presented by Russian media and state-
sponsored propaganda—only deepened the gap between the economically vibrant and the less developed parts of the Russian Federation. On the basis of the arguments and data presented in this
article, it would be safe to suggest that Russia's North-Western Federal District could and should be seen as a telling example of this
thesis. Two post-Soviet decades have demonstrated that the gulf between St. Petersburg, on the one hand, and Pskov and the Republic
of Karelia on the other has widened to a greater extent than under
the Soviet regime and even during the tumultuous 1990s, a decade
widely associated in the Russian mass consciousness with widespread poverty and instability. On the other hand, Kaliningrad oblast', with its favorable geographic location and the huge hopes
vested in its development by both external and domestic (though
mostly liberal-minded) experts and observers, presents yet another
disheartening example.

These instances suggest that such concepts as regionalism, regionalization, and interregional cooperation have remained foreign

---

94   Sergey Sukhankin, "Kaliningrad as a 'New Ideological Battlefield' between Russia and the West," *Eurasia Daily Monitor (Jamestown Foundation)* 13, no. 80 (25
April 2016), https://jamestown.org/program/kaliningrad-as-a-new-ideological-
battlefield-between-russia-and-the-west/.

to the Russian political dictionary. Being misconstrued and largely misunderstood (in part due to the purposeful creation and dissemination of a negative image), the concepts behind these terms came to be associated not with dialogue, cooperation, and sustainable growth, but with separatism, chaos, and ethnically driven nationalism. Unfortunately, the experience of growing cooperation with the West in the early 1990s, an experience that was disappointingly short-lived and as a result inconclusive, did nothing to change this trajectory. On the contrary, the consolidation of political power in Russia (which was accompanied by monopolization of the state's power over information via state-sponsored mass media and other information outlets) incessantly draws on the alleged "nonconformity" of Western practices with Russian history and developmental trajectory. For this purpose, the experience of the 1990s was and still is being widely exploited, with the general support of multiple strata of the Russian population.

Among the main victims of the post-2000 transformations were the Russian regions, whose rights and liberties were and continue to be increasingly suppressed. This trend attained qualitatively new form in the context of growing tensions between Russia and its Western partners, a situation that would turn to distrust (1996), stagnate into a "cold peace" (2007), and eventually devolve into a complete debacle with the onset of the Ukrainian crisis. In this regard, Russian regions geographically proximate to the EU and the main centers of deployment of NATO forces in Europe have found themselves in the most precarious position. The virtual discontinuation of dialogue and cooperation between Russia and the West has had a negative impact on the trajectory of developments of the north-western part of the Russian Federation, causing even greater abridgment of interregional cooperation and further dissolution of ties.

At the same time, it would not be entirely accurate to blame events in Ukraine. The overall tendency (beginning in the early 2000s) suggested that what occurred after 2014 was not an unfortunate sequence of events but a logical continuation of the antecedent course. In effect, Russia's border regions never adequately engaged in EU-offered projects, for a number of reasons. One of them was the Kremlin's obsession with separatism—in the case of Kaliningrad oblast', "irredentism"—which eclipsed common sense and reasoning. On the other hand, the period between the collapse of the USSR and the Ukrainian crisis vividly demonstrated that in the Kremlin's view, the North-West has not changed much from Soviet days. Moscow still regards the area first and foremost as a source of vast natural resources and a lever against Russia's geopolitical foes.

Unfortunately, the unique opportunity granted to Russia's North-West in the 1990s to overcome the vicious circle of history was not taken advantage of. In this regard, this region's example in many ways reflects the entire post-1991 course of relations between Russia and the West: starting with high hopes, it moved into a phase of illusory progress, and ended in bitter disappointment.

Ukrainian Attitudes toward the United States during the Russian Military Intervention

Oleksandr Potiekhin and Maryna Bessonova

Abstract: This article sets out to draw some general conclusions about attitudes toward the United States in contemporary Ukraine, focusing on the period 2014–2017. During this period, critical attitudes toward the US were fueled by Washington's weak fulfillment of its promises under the Budapest Memorandum (1994) and its failure to meet expectations of American military aid during Russia's military intervention in Ukraine. At the same time, Ukrainians took a positive view on the general US policy with regard to the Russian war against Ukraine and on American political support for Ukraine more broadly. Traditionally, strong anti-American views have been expressed by the supporters of left-wing forces, but the latter's influence is clearly declining in post-Euromaidan Ukraine. Negative sentiments toward America continue to be closely correlated with strong pro-Russian and anti-Western views. But on the whole, while neutral attitudes toward America, pro-Americanism, and anti-Americanism are all present in Ukraine, Ukrainians hold mostly positive opinions about America.

The article also compares Ukrainian attitudes to the US with those to Europe, Russia, and NATO. The authors demonstrate that for the majority of Ukrainians, the main foreign policy priority is in fact not the US, but Europe. Attitudes toward Russia, whether positive or negative, were at one time the principal delineator of self-identification in Ukraine, but today we see a shift whereby the Russian Federation is quickly gaining in importance precisely as the constitutive Other for Ukraine. The US is primarily associated in public opinion either with the West as a whole, or with NATO, which is generally viewed as more important than the US itself. The issue of Ukraine's orientation toward NATO has often been divisive and controversial in

the past, but from 2014 a positive view on the prospect of NATO mem-
bership has come to prevail in Ukrainian society and an orientation
towards NATO is now widely viewed as the best way to ensure na-
tional security and sovereignty.

Overall, in 2014–2017, Ukrainians were primarily concerned
about the war, corruption, and reforms, and had mixed perceptions of
foreign involvement in developments in their country (such as the pro-
vision of aid to help win the war). Since 2014, after the Russian occu-
pation of Crimea and the invasion of the Donbas, Ukrainians have
viewed close relations with both the EU and the US as important, but
cooperation with the former is generally viewed as higher priority
than with the latter.

Introduction

This article sets out to draw some general conclusions about attitudes toward the United States in contemporary Ukraine, focusing
mainly on the period 2014–2017. The research is based on data from
public opinion polls, statistical databases, materials used in the pre-
election political campaigns, and state documents (for example,
those pertaining to Ukraine's national security strategy and military
doctrine). We examine the results of surveys conducted by reputable polling institutions, both international (Gallup Organization,
Pew Research Center) and Ukrainian (Kyiv International Institute of
Sociology, the Ilko Kucheriv Democratic Initiatives Foundation, the
Gorshenin Institute, the O. Razumkov Ukrainian Center for Economic and Political Research, and Rating Sociological Group, a non-
governmental polling organization). All research was based on traditional methods of sociological polling, and all polls conducted
since the spring of 2014 excluded the Autonomous Republic of Crimea, territory that is currently occupied by Russia, and the areas of
the Donetsk and Luhansk oblasts that are controlled by the Russian
Federation and Russia-supported separatists (so-called ORDiLO,
from "Ukrainian-occupied districts of Donetsk and Luhansk oblasts"). In most Ukrainian surveys, the following *macro-regions* are
marked out: the West, comprising Volyn, Zakarpattia, Ivano-Frankivsk, L'viv, Ternopil, Chernivtsi, and Rivne oblasts; the Center,

comprising Kyiv, Vinnytsia, Zhytomyr, Kropyvnytskyi (the former Kirovograd), Poltava, Sumy, Khmelnytskiy, Cherkasy, and Chernihiv oblasts; the South, consisting of Mykolaiv, Odesa, and Kherson oblasts; and the East, comprising Dnipro (the former Dnipropetrovsk), Zaporizhzhia, Kharkiv, and the Donbas (Donetsk and Luhansk oblasts).

We sought to evaluate what place the US occupies among Ukrainians' foreign policy perceptions. For this purpose we compared Ukrainians' attitudes toward the US with their attitudes toward Europe, Russia, and NATO. Is there any connection between sentiments toward the US and preferences for certain ways to solve major security problems? What kinds of attitudes toward the US are dominant among Ukrainians? Does the US feature in Ukrainian political discourse (for example, in domestic pre-election campaigns)? The state of bilateral US–Russian relations is not the focus of this article; we make some observations on this issue only where it is directly relevant for understanding the context of Ukrainian public opinion concerning the US. It should also be noted that it has not been possible for us to adhere to standard sociological language throughout the article, because some of our sources are drawn from the mass media. We chose to include sources of this kind because of the decisive impact that mass media exert on the images of countries and events that form in the public consciousness.

Traditionally, the Ukrainian populace had tended to be ambivalent in its preference for one or another foreign policy orientation. Europe and Russia were the two main vectors of alignment, in line with the standard West–East general dichotomy that has generally structured Ukrainian foreign policy orientation. For a long period between 1991 and 2013, these two foreign policy directions coexisted in the public consciousness without any feeling of conflict between them. It was difficult to impossible to understand the correlation between these vectors in the minds of Ukrainians and the place of the US inside or outside this dichotomy, which predominated overwhelmingly at the beginning of 2014, before the Revolution of Dignity and the annexation of Crimea by Russia.

Attitudes toward Russia, whether positive or negative, were at one time the principal delineator of self-identification in Ukraine, but today we are witnessing a shift whereby the Russian Federation is quickly gaining in importance primarily as the constitutive Other for Ukraine. This is not, however, accompanied by a rise in the importance of the US as an alternative to the Russian Federation.

Certain geopolitical myths, in particular a view of the world as an arena of struggle among giants —the US, Russia, and China— are still widespread in all strata of Ukrainian society. In people's minds, Europe is absent from this geopolitical power game—it represents the biggest soft power but is not viewed as a player in the hard-power struggle for "world domination." For the political elites (the ruling class) in Ukraine, the search for a foreign master is the natural state of mind; consequently, representatives of this group showed an intense interest in developments in US domestic politics in 2016–2017.[1] Many representatives of the pro-reform creative class,[2] by contrast, are rather skeptical about the real possibility of receiving decisive support from abroad, but both the political elite and the creative class understand the need for American assistance to enable Ukraine to stand strong against Russian aggression.

The war brought about by Russian aggression in the Donbas is a focal point in the minds of most people in today's Ukraine. The representatives of the so-called "party of peace," an artificial designation crafted by Kremlin propagandists,[3] still have influence in the East and South of Ukraine; they are mostly former leaders of Victor

---

[1]   See, for example, "Staly vidomi imena ukrayins'kykh politykiv, yaki vidvidayut' inavhuratsiyu Trampa" *ZN,UA*, 20 January 2017, https://dt.ua/POLITICS/stali-v idomi-imena-ukrayinskih-politikiv-yaki-vidvidayut-inavguraciyu-trampa-2306 69_.html.

[2]   According to different sociological estimates, this group comprises 15-20 percent of the electorate.

[3]   The notion of a division in Ukraine's ruling elites between a "party of war" and a "party of peace" was confected by Russian propagandists. There are, however, some grounds for accepting the reality of a party of peace; members of this group have repeatedly argued that the only way to end the war is to meet Russia's demands. Effectively they call for paying whatever price Russia wants Ukraine to pay—a solution which would entail Ukraine's complete and unreserved capitulation to becoming a quasi-state satellite of Russia. See further "'Partiya viyny': Lavrov prokomentuvav politychnu sytuatsiyu v Ukrayini," *TSN.UA*, 26 April 2017, https://tsn.ua/politika/partiya-viyni-lavrov-prokomen-tuvav-politichnu-situaciyu-v-ukrayini-920245.html.

Yanukovych's Party of Regions, now represented in the parliamentary "Opposition Bloc" by Yurii Boyko, Oleksandr Vilkul, Serhii L'ovochkin, Mykhailo Dobkin, Vadim Novinsky, and others.[4] They cannot openly side with the enemy in war, hence their attempt to promote an image of themselves as the "party of peace"; in practice, however, their position on how to "solve the Ukrainian crisis" is very closely aligned with that of the Kremlin.[5]

The war essentially destroyed the idealistic image of Russia among the bulk of Viktor Yanukovych's and the "Opposition bloc"'s electorate, and those voters are now confused: neither the EU nor the US can replace the Russian Federation (for older people, "Russia" still means the Soviet Union, not its successor state) in their minds. On the whole, the Ukrainian population is now divided into two large groups: those who consider the war their personal affair (for example, those who are actively involved in volunteer activities in this connection),[6] on the one hand, and passive "observers," on the other. The US does not occupy a significant place in the projections of either group as an important factor in ending the war.

---

[4]   Two of the group's leading oligarch backers warrant special mention: Rinat Akhmetov, and Dmytro Firtash, who is seeking political asylum in Austria and is under investigation for crimes by the US authorities.

[5]   An illustrative example is Yurii Boyko's advertisement featuring two unnamed veterans of the Great Patriotic War (WWII) and the slogan "We'll return peace to Ukraine," which appeared on thousands of billboards across Ukraine in 2017. On 29 March 2018 Vadim Novinsky announced the creation of a new people's movement "Party for Peace." He follows the Kremlin's rhetoric in referring to "civil war" in Ukraine, and not a Russian invasion: "Our politicians have talked a lot about peace but do so little for the victory of peace in our land... Peace starts when every soldier—from one and the other side—breaks through his pain and declares his readiness to shake hands with his former enemy ... Party of Peace will put a full stop to the bacchanalia of obscurantism, witch hunting, lies, hatred and low-profile propaganda that the government has been feeding people for the past four years." For more detail, see "Novyns'kyy oholosyv pro stvorennya rukhu 'Partiya myru,'" *Gordonua.com*, 30 March 2018, http://gordonua.com/ukr/news/politics/novinskij-ogolosiv-pro-stvorennja-ruhu-partija-miru-239022.html.

[6]   These volunteer activities include supporting and helping the Ukrainian army and refugees from occupied Crimea and the Donetsk and Luhansk oblasti, working to further the process of lustration and reforms, and other forms of civic activity.

In this article, we set out to evaluate a set of different attitudes in Ukraine toward the US: its rank among Ukrainians' foreign policy priorities; the crude proportion of neutral, pro-American, and anti-American sentiments among Ukrainians; and the reaction of Ukrainians to the 2016 US presidential campaign and the new American president.

Ukrainian Priorities and America

To better understand Ukrainians' perceptions of the US, it is useful to place these in the context of current developments in Ukraine. In evaluating the place of the US in current Ukrainian attitudes, we stress that this country does not occupy top place in public opinion. Ukrainians are mainly focused on domestic affairs, especially economic development and reforms; military rivalry with Russia-supported forces in the East and the Russian occupation of Crimea; corruption; and living standards.

The latest surveys from a range of different research institutions show that the top concern of the Ukrainian population is the war and the Russian occupation in the East of Ukraine. When asked (in May 2016) which social issues most concerned them,[7] and (in December 2015 and December 2016) what should be the main focus of the authorities' efforts,[8] the issue most commonly mentioned by Ukrainians was resolving the situation in the Donbas and achieving peace; this issue was chosen by 78.5 percent of respondents in December 2015;[9] by 72% in May 2016;[10] and 75% in December 2016.[11] The results of a December 2016 national survey showed that Ukrainians believed that the government should focus on three main objectives: achieving peace in the Donbas (75%); regulating prices,

---

[7]   Respondents were able to name a maximum of three issues.
[8]   Respondents were able to name a maximum of five issues.
[9]   "Reformy v Ukraini: Hromads'ka dumka naselennia," *Ilko Kucheriv Democratic Initiatives Foundation* website, 14 February 2017, http://dif.org.ua/article/reformi-v-ukraini-gromadska-dumka-naselennya1234_4334312.
[10]   Tatyana Piaskovska, "Issues the Ukrainians Are Concerned About," *Kyiv International Institute of Sociology* website, 27 July 2016, http://kiis.com.ua/?lang=eng&cat=reports&id=640&page=1.
[11]   "Reformy v Ukraini: Hromads'ka dumka naselennia."

especially with respect to lowering utility rates (56%), and stimulating the economy, creating favorable conditions for business (48%); and fighting corruption (46%).[12] In May 2016, issues concerning foreign policy and international relations occupied sixth place (relations with Russia) and ninth place (relations with the EU),[13] while in December 2016 issues of integration with the EU were only in twelfth place[14] in the actual priorities of Ukrainians.

The issues of nation building and patriotism are also very important for Ukrainians now. Despite all the difficulties, the majority of Ukrainians (67%, according to a survey conducted in 2015) are proud to be citizens of their state.[15] In August 2016 almost half the population (49%) was sure that "Ukraine could overcome the problems and difficulties it faced in the long run"; 17% hoped that "this would happen over the next few years"; and 24% believed that "Ukraine would not be able to do it at all."[16]

Among the main driving forces of Ukrainian reforms, as perceived by Ukrainian survey respondents, the West in general (without division between Europe/the EU and the US) occupies only fourth place (selected by 21% of respondents in a December 2016 survey), after the government (33.5%); the president (29.5%); and NGOs and volunteers (23%). In other words, Ukrainians are mostly oriented toward relying on themselves in dealing with domestic problems. On the other hand, this represented an almost two-fold increase in expectations that the West would provide the engine of Ukrainian reforms compared to July 2015, when 11.5% of respondents reported such expectations.[17] The reason for this jump was the populace's dissatisfaction with the slow progress in the reforms being

---

[12]   *Ibid.*
[13]   Piaskovska, "Issues the Ukrainians Are Concerned About."
[14]   "Reformy v Ukraini: Hromads'ka dumka naselennia."
[15]   "Do Dnia Nezalezhnisti Ukraiiny: Shcho Ukraintsi dumaiut' pro Ukrainu," *Ilko Kucheriv Democratic Initiatives Foundation* website, 21 August 2015, http://dif.org.ua/article/do-dnya-nezalezhnosti-shcho-ukraintsi-dumayut-pro-ukrainu.
[16]   "Ukraini—25: Dosiagnennia ta porazky. Gromads'ka dumka," *Ilko Kucheriv Democratic Initiatives Foundation* website, 22 August 2016, http://dif.org.ua/article/ukraini-25-dosyagnennya-ta-porazki-gromadska-dumka.
[17]   "Reformy v Ukraini: Hromads'ka dumka naselennia."

conducted by the Ukrainian parliament and government. The "creative class" of reformers in Ukraine is looking for stimulus from the West to the ruling class of Ukraine. National attitudes toward foreign involvement, however, are mixed. The same December 2016 survey showed a growing confidence among Ukrainians in the ability of their country to survive without foreign aid. Here there is a notable dichotomy between the West (Europe and the US) and the East (Russia). For example, in 1991, 37% of the population was sure that Ukraine could survive only with Western economic aid, whereas in 2006 this belief had decreased to 14.3%. In 2016 there was a slight uptick in this indicator, to 19%, but this was still almost half as low as in 1991.[18] Opinions as to the necessity of help from Russia demonstrated the opposite trend: the share of supporters increased in the period 1991–2011 from 32% to 40.4%, but it fell almost fourfold by 2016, when only 11.2% of Ukrainians agreed with the statement that Ukraine could survive only with the help of Russia.[19] In any case, Ukrainians are well aware of the problems their country faces, and large numbers of them believe that Ukraine can survive without aid from the West (47% of respondents) or Russia (68%).[20]

The country that represents the top perceived threat to Ukraine is Russia. According to the results of a Gallup poll undertaken in the summer of 2015, 52% of Ukrainians saw the Russian Federation as the biggest threat to their country.[21] In the fall of 2014 more Ukrainians believed that it was more important to have close relations with the EU and the US, even if it might hurt relations with neighboring Russia, than to have close relations with Russia and risk damaging their country's dealings with the West. If we compare data on attitudes toward the EU and the US, we find that 43% of Ukrainians said it was important for their country to have close relations with the EU, even if doing so hurt relations with Russia, but only 37% chose close relations with the US over close relations with

---

18   "Ukraini—25: Dosiahnennia ta porazky."
19   *Ibid.*
20   *Ibid.*
21   Neli Esipova and Julie Ray, "Eastern Europeans, CIS Residents See Russia, U.S. as Threats," *Gallup.com,* 4 April 2016, http://www.gallup.com/poll/190415/eastern-europeans-cis-residents-russia-threats.aspx.

Russia.[22] Given that the proportion of respondents supporting the possibility of Ukraine having close relations with both Russia and the EU/US is the same, 27%, the clear preference for relations with the EU over relations with the US is striking.[23] If we compare the approval ratings of the EU, Germany (as the leader of the EU), and the US, as indicated by the Gallup poll, we see that Ukrainians are slightly more favorably inclined toward the EU (41% in 2013, 46% in 2014) and Germany (48% in 2013, 41% in 2014) than toward the US (38% in both 2013 and 2014).[24]

For the majority of Ukrainians, it is Europe, not the US, that is the key foreign policy priority. In part this reflects the EU's closer geographical proximity. According to a December 2016 poll, 58% of respondents supported joining the EU as the main vector of Ukraine's integration (the figure was 47% in 2013), while the proportion favoring joining Russia in the Eurasian Customs Union as the main vector of integration decreased from 36% to 11%.[25] Pro-European sentiment in Ukraine increased after February 2014, indicating that the rise was mostly due to Russian aggression.[26] According to the survey, if a referendum on whether Ukraine should join the EU had been held in February 2017, 49% of residents of Ukraine would have voted for Ukraine's accession to the EU; 28% would have voted against; and the remaining 23% would have been undecided or would not have participated in the voting. If we assume that those who were undecided as to how to vote would not have turned out to participate in a referendum on EU accession, then about 77% of

---

[22]   Elizabeth Keating and Cynthia English, "Ukrainians Prefer European Union, U.S. to Russia", *Gallup.com*, 16 December 2014, http://www.gallup.com/poll/180182/ukrainians-prefer-european-union-russia.aspx.

[23]   *Ibid.*

[24]   Julie Ray and Neli Esipova, "Ukrainian Approval of Russia's Leadership Dives Almost 90%," *Gallup.com*, 15 December 2014, http://www.gallup.com/poll/180110/ukrainian-approval-russia-leadership-dives-almost.aspx.

[25]   "2016-i: Politychni pidsumky—zagal'nonatsional'ne opytuvannia," *Ilko Kucheriv Democratic Initiatives Foundation* website, 28 December 2016, http://dif.org.ua/article/2016-y-politichni-pidsumki-zagalnonatsionalne-opituvannya.

[26]   "Support for Joining EU Rises One year after Revolution of Dignity—poll," *Interfax-Ukraine* website, 19 March 2015, http://en.interfax.com.ua/news/general/255939.html.

all those who had the right to vote and who resided in unoccupied territory would have voted, and the votes would have been distributed as follows: 64% for joining the EU and 36% against (these data are the closest indication we have of the possible results of a referendum had one been held in February 2017).[27]

In the foreign policy orientations of Ukrainians in the years of independence (since 1991) the US did not make it into the top three places, which are, in accordance with tradition, occupied by the EU, Russia, and the CIS countries. A number of surveys conducted in 2012–2015 confirmed that the US as a priority for Ukrainian foreign policy was selected by only a very small share of respondents: 1.2% (November 2012); 1.1% (April 2014); 6% (March 2015); and 3.4% (December 2015) of Ukrainians who participated in the surveys.[28] (In 2012 and 2014, the share of those selecting the US as a top priority for Ukraine's foreign policy orientation was close to zero, and fell within the range of statistical error.)

The US was not a significant focus when poll questions asked about possible options for guaranteeing Ukraine's security. The top priority in the period 2007–2016 was divided between (1) a possible neutral status for Ukraine (a minimum of 20.9% in December 2014, a maximum of 42.1% in April 2012); (2) a possible union with Russia and the other CIS countries (a minimum of 6.4% in December 2016, a maximum of 31.3% in December 2007); and (3) the possibility of joining NATO (a minimum of 13% in April 2012, a maximum of 46.4% in December 2014).[29] In 2014–2016, when a military alliance with the US was among the alternatives proposed, it was selected by fewer than 4% of respondents (a minimum of 1.5% in May 2014, a maximum of 3.9% in December 2016).[30]

---

[27]   Yulia Sakhno, "Geopolitical Orientations of the Residents of Ukraine: The European Union, Customs Union, NATO (February 2017)," *Kyiv International Institute of Sociology* website, 15 March 2017, http://kiis.com.ua/?lang=eng& cat=reports&id=689&page=1.

[28]   "Identychnist' hromadian Ukrainy v novykh umovakh: Stan, tendentsii, regional'ni osoblyvosti," *Natsional'na bezpeka i oborona* 161–62, nos. 3-4 (2016): 45, http://razumkov.org.ua/uploads/journal/ukr/NSD161-162_2016_ukr.pdf.

[29]   "2016-i: Politychni pidsumky."

[30]   *Ibid.*

When it comes to the abovementioned West–Russia dichotomy, the Ukrainian public does not generally view the US as a separate power. Rather, the US is mostly associated in public opinion either with the West as a whole or with NATO. From 2014 on, alignment with NATO has prevailed in public opinion as the best way to ensure the national security of Ukraine. Compared to 2012, the proportion of those who think an alignment with NATO is better than other security options increased more than threefold: from 16.2% in April 2012 to 47.8% in May 2016 (from the total number of respondents prepared to participate in a referendum). Among 62.2% of the respondents who declared a readiness to turn out to vote in December 2016, 71.5% were prepared to vote for Ukraine entering NATO.[31]

In recent years, regional support for NATO has changed dramatically. In 2012 the only domestic macro-region where a relative majority supported NATO membership was Ukraine's West, which registered 37% support for NATO membership, while 34% preferred a non-aligned status. In other regions the proportion of those who were oriented toward NATO as a guarantor of security ranged from 1% (in the Donbas) to 14% (Central region).[32]

Preferences for an alignment with NATO started to increase everywhere in Ukraine beginning in 2014. Strikingly, the most significant growth in orientation toward NATO in public opinion took place in Ukraine's East and the Donbas macro-region. According to a May 2016 poll conducted in the East, membership in NATO as a guarantee of security was selected by 29% of respondents (in April 2012 the figure was 1.7%), and in the Donbas it was selected by 24.4%—up from only 0.8% in April 2012.[33] The results of the most recent survey show that if a referendum on Ukraine's accession to NATO had been held in February 2017, and if all those who had decided on their choice had come out to vote, the turnout would have amounted to about 73% of those eligible to vote in the unoccupied territory, and the choices of the participants would have been

---

[31]   *Ibid.*

[32]   "Hromads'ka dumka pro NATO: Novyi pohliad," *Ilko Kucheriv Democratic Initiatives Foundation* website, 6 July 2016, http://dif.org.ua/article/gromadska-dumka-pro-nato-noviy-poglyad.

[33]   *Ibid.*

distributed as follows: 57% for Ukraine joining NATO, and 43% against.[34] Growing support for NATO membership has been accompanied and fueled by disappointment in the idea of non-alignment and in a military alliance with Russia and the other CIS countries.

In Ukraine, joining NATO is now seen in the same frame as it was in Poland and the Baltic states in the late 1980s–early 1990s: the main aim is not primarily to join the alliance as such, but to do so as a means of protecting the country's sovereignty and distancing it from Russia. In this respect, in Ukrainian public opinion NATO (which is directly affiliated with the US in the minds of many) is more visible and important than the US itself.

Pro-Americanism and Anti-Americanism in Ukraine

The Pew Research Center's surveys, which were compiled in its Global Indicators Database under "Opinion of the United States," confirmed that Ukrainians have very positive attitudes toward the US.[35] When asked the question, "Does the US government respect the personal freedoms of its people?" the majority of respondents gave a positive answer (65% in 2014 and 72% in 2015). The same poll showed that the proportion of Ukrainians who had a favorable view of the US remained relatively stable, at 68% in 2014 and 69% in 2015, while the proportion of those who held unfavorable opinions decreased slightly during the same period, from 25% in 2014 to 22% in 2015. Attitudes toward the American president (Barack Obama) with respect to his handling of world affairs were more critical: 54% of Ukrainians in 2014 and 51% in 2015 expressed confidence in Obama on this issue, while the percentage of Ukrainians responding "No confidence" did not change; it was 38% in both 2014 and 2015.[36] The reason for the lack of confidence was likely disappointment with the weak US response to the annexation of Crimea.

---

[34]   Sakhno, "Geopolitical Orientations of the Residents of Ukraine."

[35]   See the website: http://www.pewglobal.org/database/indicator/1/survey/all/. Surveys in Ukraine were only conducted in 2014 and 2015.

[36]   "Opinion of the United States," Ukraine, Global Indicators Database, *Pew Research Center, Global Attitudes & Trends* website, http://www.pewglobal.org/database/indicator/1/country/229/.

Later surveys also showed Ukrainians maintaining their positive attitude toward the US but displaying a more negative attitude toward US leadership. In a February 2016 rating of positive attitudes by the Gorshenin Institute, in response to the question, "How would you describe your attitude toward the following countries?" the US was in eighth place, with 62.8% of respondents supporting it, behind Belarus (83.6%), Poland, Georgia, Canada, Germany, France, and Turkey; just ahead of China (58.5%); and well ahead of Russia (28.4%). The American president received only 26.6% positive responses to the question, "Do you trust...?" and 54.6% negative—though it should be noted that, in comparison with the Russian president's ratings (President Putin received 87.7% negative and only 6.8% positive opinions), this was a good result.[37] Traditionally, US leaders' approval rating falls by the time they leave office, but in the case of Ukrainian attitudes the decline was mostly caused by Obama's decision not to provide defensive lethal arms to Ukraine.

The US is one of Ukrainians' preferred destinations for migration. Migration from Ukraine to the EU is better studied than migration to the US, but even incomplete data show that the US is among the top five preferred migration destinations. The Gorshenin Institute survey shows that when asked the question, "Were you to consider moving permanently, where would you go?" (respondents could choose two options), 68.4% of Ukrainians would opt to stay in Ukraine; 4% selected the US, which was in fourth place, after Germany (5.3%), Canada (5.2%), and Poland (4.5%).[38] Thus, while the majority of Ukrainians still prefer to stay in Ukraine, they find the US an attractive country.

Relations with the US are noticeably present in Ukrainian politics. But the political platforms of the top candidates in the 2010–2014 elections made few direct references to an international agenda or to the US in particular (especially in the parliamentary races). The EU and Russia (the CIS) garnered the most attention.

---

[37] "All-Ukrainian Sociological Survey: Geopolitical Choice," *Gorshenin Institute* website, 11 March 2016, http://gorshenin.eu/media/uploads/036/57/56e2913bd089f.pdf.

[38] *Ibid.*

In election programs the international organizations with US leadership—namely, NATO, the IMF, and the WTO—were mentioned more often than the US itself. Joining NATO was declared to be a political goal by *Nasha Ukraina* (Our Ukraine) in 2012 and by *Svoboda* (Freedom) and *Batkivshchyna* (Fatherland) in 2014. The ultra-nationalist political party *Pravyi Sektor* (Right Sector) mentioned cooperating with NATO (2014), while the opposite point of view was put forward in the program of the Communist Party, which promised its voters to "put up a reliable wall" against pro-NATO intentions (2014).[39]

An overview of the attitudes toward the US that are represented in the election platforms of Ukrainian presidential candidates shows that almost all candidates put foreign policy issues on their agenda but focused mainly on relations with Europe and Russia. We found very few statements of this kind touching on the US. There were promises to "provide a strategic partnership with the US and EU" (Yanukovych, 2010); to "conclude bilateral agreements with the US and Britain for military assistance in the event of military aggression against Ukraine" (Tiagnybok, 2010 and 2014); to "build partnerships with the US and China" (Yatsenyuk, 2010); to engage as "the strategic partners of neutral Ukraine … the EU, China, India, Brazil, Japan, the USA" (Bohoslovska, 2010); to establish "cooperation with the US and Britain as guarantors of the security and territorial integrity of Ukraine" and "deepen trade and economic cooperation with the US, China, South-East Asia and the Arab world" (Yarosh, 2014); to "provide a strategic partnership with the US, EU states" (Konovaliuk, 2014); and to "convince our allies—the US, EU, and NATO—to equip the Ukrainian army with the latest technology and weapons" (Liashko, 2014). In other words, the US was always mentioned together with other potential partners, and never on its own. The platforms of candidates on the left, for their part, included the traditional criticism of the US, replete with Soviet-era clichés

---

39   See the election programs, *Tsentral'na vyborcha komisiia Ukrainy* official website, at http://www.cvk.gov.ua.

(their opponents were "acting on the old recipes of America"; Symonenko, 2014).[40]

As the ongoing war in the East of Ukraine is an urgent priority, attitudes toward the US should be considered within the framework of Ukrainians' evaluation of the American reaction to this war. As during the Orange Revolution (2004) and the Revolution of Dignity (2013–2014), among the pro-Russia-oriented part of the citizenry of Ukraine, popular opinion strongly considers there to be a "Western [read: American] footprint" associated with these events. The war has also revealed anti-Americanism of the part of some of the population. In December 2015, 20.2% of survey respondents considered the conflict in the East of Ukraine "a struggle between Russia and the US for spheres of influence which took place on the territory of Ukraine," while 59.5% considered it to be "an aggressive war of Russia against Ukraine."[41]

Ukrainians mainly assess positively US policy with respect to Russia's undeclared war against Ukraine. According to a July 2015 survey, 46% of respondents approved and 35% disapproved of the American position, but there were significant regional differences. The US position was regarded favorably in the West and the Center, but in the South, the East, and the Donbas negative assessments dominated: 48%, 45%, and 54%, respectively. In comparison with attitudes toward EU policy in the context of the Russian–Ukrainian conflict, the US position was assessed positively in all macro-regions except the unoccupied part of Ukrainian Donbas, where 46% negatively perceived the actions of the EU and 36% did so positively.[42]

The end of the era of confrontation and the collapse of the Soviet Union did not lead to the complete disappearance of the Soviet traditional worldview, of which anti-Americanism is the

---

[40]   See the election programs, *Tsentral'na vyborcha komisiia Ukrainy* official website, at http://www.cvk.gov.ua.

[41]   "Identychnist' hromadian Ukrainy v novykh umovakh," 17.

[42]   "Zovnishnia polityka Ukrainy: Otsinky i ochikuvannia naselennia," *Ilko Kucheriv Democratic Initiatives Foundation* website, 24 September 2015, http://dif.org.ua/article/zovnishnya-politika-ukraini-otsinki-y-ochikuvannya-naselennya.

cornerstone.[43] The current negative attitudes toward NATO are rooted in Soviet-era stereotypes about the alliance. When asked the question, "Why are you against Ukraine joining NATO?" among those who did not support joining NATO the most popular answers were the following (respondents could choose three categories out of a larger number): "This may involve Ukraine in NATO military operations" (62.6% in April 2012, 50.3% in July 2015); "NATO is an aggressive imperialist bloc" (46% in April 2012, 36.6% in July 2015); "It will ruin relations with Russia" (23.2% in April 2012, 14.2% in July 2015), "Foreigners and foreign capital would rule the roost in Ukraine" (23.8% in April 2012, 28.6% in July 2015), and "Western culture and morality would extend into Ukraine" (6.6% in April 2012, 14.2% in July 2015).[44] Regional differences are confirmed by the data: among respondents negatively inclined toward NATO as "an aggressive imperialistic bloc," the majority were from the South (49%) and East (40.6%).

Anti-American views are mainly expressed by the supporters of left-wing forces. Often anti-American slogans are used in declarations of resistance to Ukraine's joining NATO, NATO's eastward expansion, and Ukraine's membership in the WTO and IMF. It is easy to find evaluations that are very close to the Soviet stereotypes in their lexical patterns, which include such formulaic expressions as "clientele of the IMF," "pressure of US leadership," "preventing the formation of a multipolar world," "the requirements of the International Monetary Fund aimed at the colonization of Ukraine by

---

[43]   Maryna Bessonova, "Antiamerikanizm na postradianskomu prostori: Rossiiskii ta ukrainskii vymiry," in *Spolucheni Shtaty Ameriki u suchasnomu sviti: Polityka, ekonomika, pravo, suspil'stvo*, proceedings of the Second International Scientific and Practical Conference, Lviv, 15 May 2015, 1: 13–19, http://internati onal.lnu.edu.ua/wp-content/uploads/2015/06/USA_in_modern_world_Lviv_15 .05.15-Volume-I.pdf.

[44]   "Referendum shchodo vstupu v NATO buv by vyhranyi, prote tse pytannia dilyt' Ukrainu," *Ilko Kucheriv Democratic Initiatives Foundation* website, 14 August 2015, http://dif.org.ua/article/referendum-shchodo-vstupu-do-nato-buv-bi-vi graniy-prote-tse-pitannya-dilit-ukrainu.

the USA," "the political dependence of Ukraine on the US," and "international speculative capital."[45]

Pro-American and anti-American views coexist, and most of them are energized by the political forces that share the same goal: to attract the sympathies of the voters. The image of the US is more positive than negative. But for Ukrainians, America is neither a shining city upon a hill, nor a strong backer in their struggle for survival as independent state, nor a serious alternative to Russia (as enemy) or the EU (as partner). The attitude of the majority of Ukrainians toward the US is rather neutral.

Ukrainian–American Relations and the 2016 US Presidential Campaign

Official documents are another helpful source for understanding the place of the US in Ukrainian governmental policy. In this section, we analyze references to the US, the EU, and NATO in a selection of laws, presidential decrees, and strategic national security documents. Our analysis shows that these documents reflect the overwhelming political importance of European and NATO institutions relative to that of the US for Kyiv.

Comparing different versions of these official documents across time allows us to trace continuity and change in the Ukrainian view on the main global players. In different editions of two Ukrainian laws, "On the Fundamentals of the National Security of Ukraine" (2003)[46] and "On the Principles of Domestic and Foreign Policy" (2010),[47] both of which (with some amendments) are still in force today, the main focus is on Europe and NATO. In earlier

---

45 For example, see the election programs of the political parties and of the candidates to the presidency, *Tsentral'na vyborcha komisiia Ukrainy* official website, at http://www.cvk.gov.ua.

46 "Zakon Ukrainy Pro osnovy natsional'noi bezpeky Ukrainy" (current edition), *Verkhovna Rada Ukrainy* official website, 7 August 2015, http://zakon2.ra da.gov.ua/laws/show/964-15.

47 "Zakon Ukrainy Pro zasady vnutrishnioii i zovnishnioii polityky" (current edition), *Verkhovna Rada Ukrainy* official website, 1 January 2015, http://zakon2.ra da.gov.ua/laws/show/2411-17.

versions of both laws the non-aligned status of Ukraine was emphasized, but the most recent versions reject non-alignment and declare
the goal of joining NATO.

In successive versions of the Military Doctrine we can see the
same focus on NATO and Europe. The Presidential Decree on the
Military Doctrine of Ukraine (in force 2004–September 2015) was focused on Ukraine's non-aligned status.[48] There was no mention of
the US, NATO, or the EU—either as potential allies or as opponents.
The new edition of the Military Doctrine of Ukraine (effective since
September 2015) was adopted against the backdrop of the war in
Donbas. In the new Doctrine the US is mentioned only twice (compared to 43 references to NATO and 16 references to the EU). Moreover, these references to the US appear in the somewhat strange
context of a point about "the increasing contradictions caused by
the division of spheres of influence between world centers of
power," and in particular "the escalation of confrontation between
the United States and the Russian Federation."[49] (In our view, these
general ideas are highly dubious formulas, seemingly imported from
the propaganda arsenal, and far from being an accurate reflection of
the true state of global international relations.) The US also features
here in connection with discussion of the possibilities for settling
the armed conflict in the East of Ukraine with reliance on US support. By contrast, NATO is mentioned many times in the context of
Ukraine's attempts to reform its own army, to deepen cooperation
with NATO, and, finally, to join the alliance.

Another set of official documents which can help to understand the place of America in Ukrainian defense is the successive
versions of the National Security Strategy of Ukraine, adopted in
2007, 2008, and 2015. These documents reflect the evolution of the
US role in Ukraine's vision for its national security. In 2007 the

---

[48] "Ukaz Prezydenta Ukrainy Pro voennu doctrinu Ukrainy" (2004 edition, with
      changes), *Verkhovna Rada Ukrainy* official website, 26 September 2015,
      http://zakon2.rada.gov.ua/laws/show/648/2004.
[49] "Ukaz Prezydenta Ukrainy Pro rishennia Rady natsional'noi bezpeky i oborony
      Ukrainy vid 2 veresnia 2015 roku 'Pro novu redaktsiiu Voennoi doktryny
      Ukrainy,'" *Verkhovna Rada Ukrainy* official website, 24 September 2015,
      http://zakon3.rada.gov.ua/laws/show/555/2015/.

National Security Strategy referred to the *extension of cooperation with the US.*[50] In 2008 it spoke of the *development of dialogue and cooperation* between Ukraine and the US within the framework of the US–Ukraine Charter on Strategic Partnership.[51] And finally, in the newest 2015 version, we find a reference to the *deepening of a strategic partnership* with the US as a guarantor of international security in the Euro-Atlantic area, which is seen as the main Ukrainian foreign policy priority.[52]

US–Ukrainian bilateral relations are regulated by 144 documents (treaties, agreements, memoranda, etc.).[53] The document most discussed in Ukrainian society in 2014–2015 was the December 1994 "Memorandum on Security Assurances in Connection with Ukraine's Accession to the Treaty on the Non-proliferation of Nuclear Weapons," signed by Ukraine, the US, Russia, and Great Britain, and known more commonly as the Budapest Memorandum. Through this agreement, three nuclear powers undertook to respect the independence and sovereignty and the existing borders of Ukraine; to refrain from using force or the threat of force against the territorial integrity or political independence of Ukraine; and to refrain from economic coercion designed to subordinate to their own interest the exercise by Ukraine of the rights inherent in its sovereignty and thus to secure advantages of any kind.[54]

After Russia's unlawful annexation of Crimea in 2014, in Ukrainian society and the Ukrainian establishment alike there was

---

[50]   "Ukaz Prezydenta Ukrainy Pro strategiiu natsional'noi bezpeky Ukrainy" (2007 edition, with changes), *Verkhovna Rada Ukrainy* official website, 29 May 2015, http://zakon2.rada.gov.ua/laws/show/105/2007.

[51]   *Ibid.*

[52]   "Ukaz Prezydenta Ukrainy Pro rishennia Rady national'noi bezpeky i oborony Ukrainy vid 9 travnia 2015 roku 'Pro Strategiiu natsional'noi bezpeky Ukrainy,'" *Verkhovna Rada Ukrainy* official website, 26 May 2015, http://zakon2.rada.gov.ua/laws/show/287/2015/.

[53]   "List of Bilateral Treaties and Arrangements," *Embassy of Ukraine in the United States of America* official website, 2017, http://usa.mfa.gov.ua/en/ukraine-us/legal-acts.

[54]   "Memorandum pro garantii bezpeky u zv'iazku z priiednanniam Ukrainy do Dogovoru pro nerozpovsiudzhennia iadernoi zbroi," *Verkhovna Rada Ukrainy* official website, 5 December 1994, http://zakon3.rada.gov.ua/laws/show/998_158.

widespread criticism of the US as a signatory to the Budapest Memorandum that had failed to meet its obligations. One of the first appeals to the US as a guarantor of Ukrainian sovereignty and territorial integrity was made by the Ukrainian parliament on 28 February 2014, just after events in Crimea began.[55] Here again, expectations that America would help were mostly connected to possible reactions by NATO, at least as a demonstration of support to Ukraine.[56] Since the beginning of the direct Russian aggression in 2014 the Budapest Memorandum remains the document most often mentioned by Ukrainian politicians, experts, and analysts in their opinions on the US. As noted above, the main criticism is connected with American non-fulfillment of the conditions of the Memorandum. This document, which is one of the basic for Ukrainian foreign policy after renunciation of nuclear weapons, is also referred to in an important bilateral agreement: the US–Ukraine Charter on Strategic Partnership, which was signed in December 2008.[57] The Charter emphasizes such points as protecting security and territorial integrity, cooperating for defensive and security purposes, and even Ukraine's candidacy for NATO membership.

Today, by contrast, Ukrainians' expectations of the US are mostly connected not with declarations of principles but with the need for American military aid in the context of Russia's military intervention in the Ukrainian Donbas. The issue of making American high-tech weaponry available to Ukraine was debated both in the US and in Ukraine. According to a 2015 Pew Research poll, Americans are divided on this issue: 46% support sending weapons and

---

[55]   "Postanova Verkhovnoi Rady Ukrainy pro zvernennia Verkhovnoi Rady Ukrainy do derzhav-garantiv vidpovidno do Memorandumu pro garantii bezpeky u zv'iazku z priiednanniam Ukrainy do Dogovoru pro nerozpovsiudzhennia iadernoii zbroi," *Verkhovna Rada Ukrainy* official website, 28 February 2014, http://zakon3.rada.gov.ua/laws/show/831-18.

[56]   "Stenogramma zasidannia Rady natsional'noi bezpeky i oborony Ukrainy vid 28 liutogo 2014 roku," *Rada natsional'noi bezpeky i oborony Ukrayiny* official website, 22 February 2016, http://www.rnbo.gov.ua/files/2016/stenogr.pdf.

[57]   "Khartiia Ukraina-SShA pro strategichne partnerstvo," *Verkhovna Rada Ukrainy* official website, 19 December 2008, http://zakon2.rada.gov.ua/laws/show/840_140.

43% oppose it.[58] America's European allies prefer providing Ukraine with economic aid and levying economic sanctions on Russia: there is a median level of support among NATO member states' citizens for sending arms to Ukraine; about 41% back such action.[59]

Overall, despite the desire and the high expectations of Ukrainians for military assistance, the bulk of the population is skeptical about the prospects for direct American military aid, but this issue is still salient in public attitudes toward the US. Expectations are always mainly gauged to the American president in office, the chief official with whom US foreign policy is associated. Naturally, special attention is paid to the US during presidential election years. The 2016 election was no exception.

In Ukraine, 55% of those polled at the time were following the course of the US presidential election.[60] The election aroused more interest in the West (67%) and less in the East (48%) of the country. Some 39% of Ukrainians overall sympathized with Hillary Clinton; one in ten sympathized with Donald Trump; and 42% were not sympathetic to any candidate. Among those who followed the elections, sympathies were distributed as follows: 62% sympathized with Clinton; and 15% with Trump. Trump's pro-Russia stance during the campaign and later was a popular topic on TV shows and in the Ukrainian press. Fewer than half (42%) of respondents did not expect any change in relations between Ukraine and the US after the victory of Donald Trump in 2016. However, a quarter thought that the relationship would change for the worse. Deterioration was mostly expected in the Center and South of Ukraine. Only 7% of Ukrainians believed that relations would improve.[61]

---

[58]   Katie Simmons, Bruce Stokes, and Jacob Poushter, "NATO Publics Blame Russia for Ukrainian Crisis, but Reluctant to Provide Military Aid," *Pew Research Center: Global Attitudes & Trends*, 10 June 2015, http://www.pewglobal.org /2015/06/10/nato-publics-blame-russia-for-ukrainian-crisis-but-reluctant-to-p rovide-military-aid/.

[59]   *Ibid.*

[60]   "Interes ta ochikuvannia ukraintsiv vid rezul'tativ vyboriv v SShA," *Reiting Sotsiologichna grupa* website, 21 November 2016, http://ratinggroup.ua/re-search/ukraine/interes_i_ozhidaniya_ukraincev_ot_rezultatov_vy-borov_v_ssha.html.

[61]   *Ibid.*

For Ukraine's ruling class and expert community, the victory of Donald Trump was surprising, even shocking. Trump's victory caused intense discussion in Ukraine on the topic of "Russian interference in the US elections." The "Opposition Bloc" and its media immediately distributed statements about the short-sightedness concerning international policy problems of President Poroshenko, his government, and particularly the Ministry of Foreign Affairs of Ukraine, which, the opposition claimed, had put all its eggs in one basket, staking everything on a Hillary Clinton win and "shunning" Donald Trump. For their part, representatives of the Ukrainian foreign policy establishment tried to fix their mistake by looking for contacts at the highest level of the Trump administration.

The general context of Trump's shock for the prospects of good American–Ukrainian relations was the opinion that "there is no place for Ukraine" in Trump's grand design, summed up in his slogan, "America first." Because of a rather widespread understanding among the Ukrainian public that Ukraine depends on American support (at least its political support) in preserving national independence in times of Russian aggression, the prospect of a deal between Washington and Moscow, which would entail the marginalization of Ukraine in exchange for Russian cooperation with Washington in Syria and against ISIS, was considered to pose a huge threat. As of 2017 and at the time of writing (early 2018), this threat appears to be a thing of the past because of current political developments in bilateral relations resulting from the visits of President Poroshenko to Washington and Secretary of State Rex Tillerson to Kyiv. The nomination of the American foreign policy establishment heavyweight Kurt Volker to the position of US Department of State special representative in Ukraine in July 2017 was probably the most important step in the direction of positive changes in American–Ukrainian cooperation. After the first six months of Donald J. Trump's incumbency in the White House, US policy toward Ukraine looked well defined: Trump would continue his predecessor's course. Just as Barack Obama's administration had, the Trump administration rejected direct US participation in the Normandy Format and left it up to European powers to resolve Ukraine's crisis.

Trump did not promise Ukraine everything that Ukrainians wanted. There was no public articulation of the message to the Kremlin in the spirit of the Budapest Memorandum that any attempt to intensify the war in Ukraine would lead to direct intervention by the US. Such a message, we surmise, would cost Washington nothing, but Obama did not make such a declaration, and neither, so far, has Trump.[62] The issue of supplying Ukraine with lethal defense weapons is on the agenda of the US–Ukrainian dialogue. Congress recommended it be implemented by the former presidential administration. In Kyiv's view, there was no serious motivation for Obama to refuse to give Ukraine defensive weapons other than Moscow's propaganda thesis, "If the US takes such a step, then Russia will go to full-scale invasion." However, unless Ukraine has suitable weapons of deterrence, full-scale aggression by the Kremlin against Ukraine is much more likely. Ukrainian military and political experts share this view.

Thanks to "Russia-gate" (the ongoing controversy around alleged Kremlin interference in the US presidential election and the unusual contacts of American officials with Russian colleagues) remaining on the agenda in Washington, the professionals in the US administration managed to convince Trump that Ukraine is an important country for US interests in Europe and himself personally. Thus, having shown his respect for Ukraine by meeting with his Ukrainian counterpart, we surmise that Trump may have played the Ukrainian card in order to refute charges that he is backed by Moscow. The US Congress managed, on a bipartisan basis and against the wishes of the Trump administration, to elevate Ukraine's status in Washington's foreign policy priorities.

It is very important for Ukraine to maintain the dynamics of the dialogue with the US and to obtain US help in implementing the main points of the Minsk agreements, including a ceasefire in the Donbas; cessation of the barbaric shelling of life support facilities; prevention of further losses among Ukrainian military and civilians

---

62 Oleksandr Potiekhin, "Druha 'kholodna viina': Poperedni pidsumky," *Zovnishni Spravy* 10 (2015): 14–17; and Oleksandr Potiekhin, "NATO bez Ukrainy," *Zovnishni Spravy* 11 (2016): 8–13, nas.academia.edu/oleksandrpotiekhin/papers.

along the dividing line; and prevention of further destruction of Donbas region infrastructure.[63] It would be difficult to impossible to force or persuade Putin to implement all points of the Minsk agreements through sanctions alone, even if they are tightened with the introduction of a new package.

The US policy toward Ukraine has been accompanied by abundant symbolic gestures of friendship and support. In August 2017, Secretary of Defense James Mattis visited Kyiv to celebrate, together with the Ukrainian leadership, the twenty-sixth anniversary of independence (this was the first visit by a US Secretary of Defense in ten years). In his speech in the Presidential Palace, Mattis stressed:

> As Secretary Tillerson said in July, the United States' goals are to restore Ukraine's sovereignty and territorial integrity, and to seek the safety and security of all Ukrainian citizens, regardless of nationality, ethnicity, or religion. We in the United States understand the strategic challenges associated with Russian aggression. Alongside our allies, we remain committed to upholding the widely accepted international norms that have increased global stability since the tragedy of World War II. Mr. President, we continue to support Ukraine and remain committed to building the capacity of your armed forces.[64]

If the US delivers on these promises, it will drastically improve the image of the US in the eyes of the Ukrainian public.

Conclusion

Ukrainian attitudes toward the US are generally structured by the standard dichotomy between East (Russia) and West (Europe, the US). For the majority of Ukrainians, Europe, not America, is the main foreign policy priority. In the opinion of the majority of

---

[63]   "Kompleks mer po vypolneniiu Minskikh soglashenii," *OSCE*, 12 February 2015, http://www.osce.org/ru/cio/140221.

[64]   "Secretary of Defense James Mattis Remarks with President Petro Poroshenko: Remarks as Delivered by Secretary of Defense James Mattis, Presidential Palace, Kyiv, Ukraine, Aug. 24, 2017," *US Department of Defense* official website, https://www.defense.gov/News/Speeches/Speech-View/Article/1291430/secretary-of-defense-james-mattis-remarks-with-president-petro-poroshenko/.

Ukrainians, the US does not make it into the top three spots, which traditionally are occupied by the EU, Russia, and other CIS countries. The US is primarily associated with the West as a whole, or with NATO. Attitudes toward NATO were very controversial for a long time, but from 2014 on a disposition toward NATO membership has prevailed in Ukrainian society as the best way to ensure national security. For the Ukrainian public, NATO (which is closely associated with the US in the minds of many Ukrainians) is more favored and more important than the US itself.

In 2014–2017, Ukrainians were more concerned about the war, reforms, and corruption, and had mixed perceptions of foreign involvement in developments in their country. Since 2014, after the Russian occupation of Crimea and the invasion of Donbas, Ukrainians have believed that close relations with the EU and the US are both important but that relations with the former are more important than relations with the latter.

While neutral attitudes toward America, pro-Americanism, and anti-Americanism coexist in Ukraine, Ukrainians hold mostly positive opinions about America. Critical views on the US have been fueled by that country's weak fulfillment of its obligations under the Budapest Memorandum and its failure to meet the expectations of American military aid during Russia's military intervention in Ukraine. In 2017 the issue of supplying Ukraine with lethal defensive weapons was still on the agenda of the American–Ukrainian dialogue, which has continued after President Trump's arrival in the White House.[65] Traditionally, strongly critical and anti-American views are expressed by the supporters of left-wing forces, whose

---

[65]   After months of heated debate in Washington and, reportedly, much reluctance on the part of US President Donald Trump, the White House approved the Javelin sale in December 2017. At the end of April 2018 Javelin anti-tank missile systems arrived in Ukraine; see further Christopher Miller, "U.S. Confirms Delivery Of Javelin Antitank Missiles to Ukraine," *Radio Free Europe/Radio Liberty*, 30 April 2018, https://www.rferl.org/amp/javelin-missile-delivery-ukraine-us-conf irmed/29200588.html. According to a US Department of Defense news release issued in July 2018, the US has provided over $1 billion worth of security sector assistance to Ukraine since 2014; *US Department of Defense* official website, 20 July 2018, https://www.defense.gov/News/News-Releases/News-Release-View/ Article/1580606/dod-announces-200m-to-ukraine/.

influence in Ukraine is declining. At the same time, Ukrainians assessed positively the US policy toward the Russian war against Ukraine and American political support for Ukraine. America is one of the preferred migration destinations. In sum, the image of the US is more positive than negative.

The image of the US in Ukraine is influenced by a combination of factors. These include current developments in international relations (and the perception of the US as an actual or potential ally), and the political situation in Ukraine. A factor whose importance is declining is that of Soviet heritage, which conditions the neutral or mostly negative sentiments toward the US among some demographic groups (generally older people) and regions (the East and South of Ukraine). Negative sentiments toward America are closely connected with strong pro-Russian and anti-Western views. As Russian aggression continues, it is becoming more difficult to sell the concept of a "Russkii mir" (Russian World) in Ukraine as a positive civilizational alternative to America and the West as a whole. At the same time, however, for Ukrainians, America is neither a shining city upon a hill, nor a stronghold in their struggle for survival as an independent state, nor a serious alternative to Russia (as enemy) or the EU (as partner). For the most part, when it comes to meeting the challenges currently faced by the country, rather than looking to mentors outside the country, ordinary Ukrainians prefer to rely on their own resources.

Images of the United States in Putin's Russia, from Obama to Trump

Victoria I. Zhuravleva

Abstract: *This article focuses on the evolution of the United States' image in Putin's Russia before and after the 2016 presidential election. It examines this evolution (through to February 2018, the time of writing) in correlation with both the Russian and American contexts, as well as within the context of the changing climate of Russia–US relations. The article applies a social constructivist approach with a view to deepening our understanding of the role played by the American Other in the Russian official and popular identity discourse. The author argues that the Russian Self–American Other opposition has retained its constitutive role in the interplay of meanings that defines Russian nationalism. This key opposition remains at the core of the public and political debates shaped by texts on the US, including speeches, cartoons, published articles, and opinion pieces.*

The author identifies a set of long-lived verbal and visual communicative strategies that have been integrated into the Russian discourse about America. First, American presidents are constructed in relation to the Russian leader (Putin)—either as Putin's antithesis (Obama), or as a kind of weak analogue of Putin (Trump). Second, American liberal-universalist values are contrasted with Russian traditional-conservative values. Third, crises and thorny issues in US politics and history are used in order to discredit and mock the American desire to school Russia in democracy and international law. Finally, the imagined reality of international relations is constructed through the universal language of popular culture with the aim of making patriotic discourse attractive to the younger generations.

The author argues that the periods of rapprochement between Russia and the US and, accordingly, the rejection of simplified schemes of mutual understanding have as a rule taken place in times of expansion of the Russian–American agenda out of a need to face a common enemy and address global challenges. Such rapprochement has also taken place during times of political reform and/or economic modernization in Russia.

Key words: Russia–US relations, anti-Americanism in Russia, Obama's presidency, the 2016 presidential election, Putin's Russia, Donald Trump's administration, Russian Self–American Other dichotomy

Introduction

During the Obama presidency (2009–2017), Russian–American relations changed dramatically, from the "reset" of the Medvedev era to the deepest crisis since the end of the Cold War. Bilateral cooperation was frozen in most spheres, and all the factors (both mutable and constant) that influence the process of mutual perception (the climate of Russian–US relations, the national sociocultural and political context, the historical legacy of past relations) worked against a clear-eyed view. This formed the basis for the "war of images" that was and still is one of the main characteristics of the crisis in bilateral relations during this period. In Russia, a demonic image of Obama was used to promote Putin's brand. Russian government and state-controlled outlets pinned their principal hopes on the presidency of Donald Trump, who became immensely popular after he announced his readiness to cooperate with Russia and began extolling the talents of Putin as a statesman and a political leader while devaluing Obama's abilities. For a while a positive attitude toward Trump in Russia was even a sort of marker of patriotism. But in the summer of 2017, after the US Congress imposed new sanctions on Russia for meddling in the 2016 presidential election and Donald Trump signed this legislation into being, the situation changed radically. The romantic image of Trump disappeared from Russian public and political discourse, especially in the context of the tit-for-tat expulsion of embassy personnel by the two sides that began in December 2016. This disappointment of previous hopes gave additional impetus to anti-American sentiments and foregrounded the image of the hostile American Other.

This article focuses on the oscillation in recent Russian attitudes toward the US from disappointment in Obama's America through hope in Trump's America to, once again, disappointment, and correlates it with the identity construction process in Putin's Russia. This process is traced through here to February 2018 (the time of writing). The evolution in perception examined in this article proves yet again that the American Other retains great significance for shaping identity in post-Soviet Russia. As the Russian sociologist Aleksei Levinson vividly put it:

> America is our only quintessential "Other." The rivalry with America does not unfold in the arena of the "real" world but in its reflection that exists in the Russian mass consciousness. And in this sphere, what matters is not defeating the Other but being completely certain that we "are not worse than them" ... In this worldview, examples of good relations with America are an acknowledgment that they are equal to us or similar to us, and we to them, as the only basis for mutual good feelings.[1]

The negative attitude toward the US in Russia today can largely be explained as a reaction to US global leadership and Russia's loss of its international standing in a post-bipolar world, on the one hand, and to domestic challenges, on the other. Vladimir Putin's high ratings stem from Russian citizens' belief in his ability to restore Russia's national greatness and international status. From this belief comes the attitude so popular in Russian public and political discourse: if they don't respect us, let them at least fear us. State-owned media and popular culture successfully promote this attitude since, though people experience the consequences of domestic policies in immediate and direct ways, their experiences of foreign policies are mediated through the agency of media contexts and images. In this case we are dealing with two types of anti-Americanism: issue-oriented (comprising emotional reactions to US foreign policy) and

---

[1]   Aleksei Levinson, "Amerika kak znachimyi Drugoi," *Pro et Contra* 11, no. 2 (2007): 69.

instrumental (aimed at maintaining anti-American sentiment in the general population for political purposes).[2]

My approach entails applying a social-constructivist paradigm to the study of international relations. According to this paradigm, a subject's self-knowledge is acquired through communication with its Other, and the relationship with the Other is based on an identity constructed via communication.[3] Accordingly, my analysis of the process of constructing identity in post-Soviet Russia focuses on the conceptual pair "Russian Self/American Other." Thus I am not limited to studying the process of mutual perception through the lens of narrative analysis, which would allow an assessment of how closely these images reflect actual reality. Instead, I wish to address a broader set of questions. Why do Russians imagine the US (its collective image) and its leaders (its personified image) in a particular way and not others? What kinds of discursive practices, both verbal and visual, have been used to create these images, and how malleable are they? How do these images function as means of both international communication and self-identification? My primary concern is with the motivations behind the image construction process that determines the hierarchy of images of America, giving some of them central roles and relegating others to the periphery.[4]

In taking up these questions, I draw on the methods used in popular geopolitics to analyze different kinds of media texts, from media presentations of politicians and public figures to political

---

[2]   On different types of anti-Americanism, see Alvin Rubinstein and Donald Smith, "Anti-Americanism in the Third World," *Annals of the American Academy of Political and Social Science*, 497, no 1 (1988): 35–45.

[3]   Alexander Wendt, "Anarchy Is What States Make of It: The Social Construction of Power Politics," *International Organization* 46, no. 2 (Spring 1992): 391–425; and Alexander Wendt, *Social Theory of International Politics* (Cambridge: Cambridge University Press, 1999).

[4]   For more detail on this methodology for studying Russian–U.S. relations, see Victoria I. Zhuraleva, "Izuchenie imagologii Rossiisko-amerikanskikh otnoshenii po obe storony Atlantiki," *Amerikanskii ezhegodnik, 2008/2009* (Moscow: Nauka, 2010): 142–66; and Ivan Kurilla and Victoria I. Zhuravleva (eds.), *Russian/Soviet Studies in the United States, Amerikanistika in Russia: Mutual Representations in Academic Projects* (Lanham, MD: Lexington Books, 2016).

cartoons, films, and radio and TV broadcasts. These texts, which serve as my leading primary sources, are crucial both for constructing the imagined reality of international relations and for defining Russia's place in it. The interdisciplinary approach of popular geopolitics brings together the fields of international relations, critical geopolitics, and cultural studies to explore international relations through images of the Other that are embodied in the new information-communicative environment in general and in popular culture in particular.[5]

Data from public opinion polls are another important input into my explanatory scheme. Such data help us understand how the images of the Russian Self and the American Other, which are conditioned by both international and domestic contexts, get translated into specific behavioral practices, and how these practices in turn act as feedback mechanisms for the constructed reality of Russian-American relations.

The article's conceptual framework relies on three kinds of context: (1) the Russian sociocultural context (which helps determine the dominant identity markers) and political context or agenda (which explains the mechanisms by which the image of the American Other is being used); (2) the American context (both domestic and international), which is actively exploited by the anti-American discourse being promulgated in Russia; and (3) the context of the changing climate of US–Russian relations.

Obama's America as the Demonic "Other": Anti-Americanism in Russian Public and Political Discourse at a Time of Crisis in US–Russian Relations

The open confrontation between Russia and the United States during Obama's second term began as a response to Ukraine's Euromaidan in November 2013, an event which was declared by Russia's political elite and by Putin himself to be an American project

---

5   Robert A. Saunders, *Popular Geopolitics and Nation Branding in the Post-Soviet Realm* (New York: Routledge, 2017), 71–88.

representing interference in the sphere of Russian national interests.[6] The annexation of Crimea in March 2014 and Russia's military support for the self-proclaimed Donetsk and Luhansk republics in eastern Ukraine led to the imposition of US-initiated sectoral and personal sanctions on Russia and, in turn, to Russia's countersanctions. The breaches of international law in Russia's own foreign policy were explained as necessary responses to external challenges to the country's national greatness posed by NATO's eastward expansion, by the US' destruction of the international security system, and by US attempts to expand American hegemony throughout the world. In reality, Russia's foreign policy in many ways arose out of the domestic political need to consolidate society around a national idea.[7] The image of the American demonic Other was and still is very useful for this purpose, not only because of the Cold War legacy but also because of events in the 1990s, when the asymmetric character of relations between the two countries was established. As Angela Stent has argued:

> The recognition of the reality that Russia is less important per se than indirectly is a continuing source of irritation to Russian officials. In this sense, the various American resets have represented attempts to engage Russia productively by persuading it to acknowledge and accept the asymmetries in the relationship and move forward on that basis. Putin's 2001 attempted

---

[6]   See, for example, "US Foreign Aid Agencies Paid for Kiev Street Violence," *Russia Today*, 17 March 2014, https://www.rt.com/shows/sophieco/ukraine-revolution-usa-support-246/; Andrew Higgins and Peter Baker, "Russia Claims U.S. Is Meddling Over Ukraine," *The New York Times*, 6 February 2014, https://www.nytimes.com/2014/02/07/world/europe/ukraine.html; and F. V. Mills, "Understanding the Euromaidan: The View from the Kremlin," in *Ukraine's Euromaidan. Analyses of a Civil Revolution*, eds., David R. Marples and Frederick V. Mills (Stuttgart: *ibidem* Verlag, 2015), 239–60.

[7]   On the correlation between Russia's foreign policy and national identity discourse, see, for example, Richard Sakwa, "Russia's Identity: Between the 'Domestic' and the 'International'," *Europe-Asia Studies* 63, no. 6 (August 2011): 957–75; Igor Zevelev, *Russian National Identity and Foreign Policy, A Report of the CSIS and Eurasia* Program (Washington, DC: Center for Strategic and International Studies, 2016); and Andrey P. Tsygankov, *Russia's Foreign Policy. Change and Continuity in National Identity* (New York: Rowman & Littlefield, 2016).

reset, by contrast, was a bid to establish a strategic partnership of equals, acting as if these asymmetries did not exist.[8]

Russia's actions in Ukraine and Syria have challenged the US-led post–Cold War order, including the asymmetric relationship between Russia and the US. Open confrontation with the West—especially over economic sanctions and the information warfare allegedly being waged against Russia—has given a powerful boost to Russian patriotism. In public speeches and in politics, President Vladimir Putin and high-ranking Russian officials have actively sought to destroy the "American teacher-Russian student" scheme created in the 1990s. Russia now aspires to play the role of a teacher itself by teaching the US about Russian national interests.

In 2014–2016, anti-Americanism became the dominant note in official and public discourse in Russia. In late 2014 to early 2015, Russian society experienced the highest level of anti-Americanism since the end of the Cold War, with 81 percent of Russians expressing a negative attitude toward the US.[9] According to a Levada Center opinion poll, half the Russian population was sure that America was impeding Russia's development, while 31 percent of poll respondents feared a military intervention and subsequent occupation by the US. At the same time, 33 percent were sure that, in the hypothetical case of a war against the US and its allies, Russia would be able to claim victory.[10] According to Pew Research Center polls, in June 2015 only 15 percent of Russians had a favorable opinion of America, down from 56 percent in 2011, and there was hardly any other nation in the world that attracted such a high level of resentment and of negative attitudes more broadly.[11] A March 2016 Levada

---

[8] Angela Stent, *The Limits of Partnership: U.S.-Russian Relations in the Twenty-First Century* (Princeton, NJ: Princeton University Press, 2014), xvi.

[9] Denis Volkov, "The Evolution of Anti-Americanism in Russia," *Carnegie Moscow Center* website, 22 June 2015, https://carnegie.ru/commentary/60457.

[10] "Ugroza dlia Rossii so storony SShA," *Levada Center* website, 12 May 2015, http://www.levada.ru/12-05-2015/ugroza-dlya-rossii-so-storony-ssha.

[11] Jacob Poushter, "Key Findings from Our Poll on the Russia-Ukraine Conflict," *Pew Research Center* website, 10 June 2015, http://www.pewresearch.org/fact-tank/2015/06/10/key-findings-from-our-poll-on-the-russia-ukraine-conflict/; and "Global Opposition to U.S. Surveillance and Drones, but Limited Harm to

poll found that 76 percent of Russians disapproved of the US approach to international problem solving and seven in ten Russians thought Russia should focus on limiting US power and influence (68%), compared to a third who favored cooperation with the United States (32%).[12]

Such sentiments were not new. After the collapse of the Soviet Union, there were four main outbursts of anti-American sentiment in Russia, in 1998, 2003, 2008, and 2014–2017. These episodes correlated with times when the two countries' positions, over conflicts in Kosovo, Iraq, Georgia, and Ukraine respectively, were in direct contradiction. But whereas during previous episodes, anti-American sentiment grew radically over the course of one or two months before falling again, in the most recent period a stable anti-American trend has been in place—a sign of the magnitude and depth of this crisis in Russian-American relations.[13]

On the one hand, anti-Americanism in Russian society has been and still is a function of propaganda. President Putin himself encouraged the political discourse to follow along these lines,[14] and the Russian federal television channels, the main source of news for more than 90 percent of Russians,[15] propagated an image of the US as a hostile country that views itself as the victor in the Cold War, wants to impose its dictates and double standards on the whole world and irresponsibly flirts with religious extremists and radicals to achieve its political goals. Anti-Americanism among the Russian populace has roots in the nationwide demand for "greatness" that

America's Image," *Pew Research Center* website, 14 July 2014, http://www.pew global.org/2014/07/14/chapter-1-the-american-brand/.

[12]   Dina Smeltz, Stepan Goncharov, and Lily Wojtowicz, "US and Russia: Insecurity and Mistrust Shape Mutual Perceptions," *Chicago Council on Global Affairs* website, 4 November 2016, https://www.thechicagocouncil.org/publication/us-and-russia-insecurity-and-mistrust-shape-mutual-perceptions.

[13]   Denis Volkov, "The Evolution of Anti-Americanism in Russia," *Carnegie Moscow Center* website, 22 June 2015, http://carnegie.ru/commentary/?fa=60457/.

[14]   See, for example, Vladimir Putin's Valdai speech on 24 October 2014, *Kremlin.ru*, http://en.kremlin.ru/events/president/news/46860.

[15]   Denis Volkov, Stepan Goncharov, "Rossiiskii medialandshaft: televidenie, pressa, internet," *Levada Center* website, June 2014, http://www.levada.ru/sites/default/files/levadareportmedia.pdf.

has emerged strongly in Putin's third presidential term as part of a new and unspoken social contract between the authorities and the people. This contract can be summed up as follows: "citizens give loyalty to the government, and in return receive great-power status and 'a thousand-year history'" (a phrase which, conveniently enough, was coined by Putin himself).[16] On the other hand, behind any anti-American or pro-American message stands a complex spectrum of love-hate feelings toward the US, all of which have deep historical roots in the public consciousness and have been present from pre-revolutionary imperial times through to the Soviet era and beyond.[17] In both cases (be it the function of propaganda or the specificity of perception) we are dealing with the conceptual pair of the Russian Self and the American Other.

The image of the US as the hostile Other was and is being used by Russian authorities to support a siege mentality and to construct the national identity discourse. The binary opposition of Russian conservative nationalism versus American universal liberalism plays a special role in this anti-American political and public discourse, casting into sharp relief those characteristics of the American model of development that are alien to the Russian idea, and appealing to ideological anti-Americanism, which reflects attitudes toward the US itself, including American values, culture, and way of life. The ranks of Russian conservatives started to swell during the crisis that began in 2014. They argue that in the 1990s, modern Russia had its own destructive "revolution," which was driven by the desire to break with the country's historical experience and to implement Western (American) prescriptions for political and economic development without taking into account existing conditions in Russia.[18]

---

[16]   Andrei Kolesnikov, *Russian Ideology after Crimea* (Washington, DC: Carnegie Endowment for International Peace, 2015), 1; and Andrei Kolesnikov, *The Burden of Predictability: Russia's 2018 Presidential Election* (Washington, DC: Carnegie Endowment for International Peace, 2017), 6.

[17]   See, for example, Vladimir Pechatnov, "Liubov'-gorech' k Amerike," *Mezhdunarodnye protsessy* 4, no. 1 (2006): 30–40.

[18]   On the conservative shift in Russia in 2012–2016, see Leonid Polyakov, *"Conservatism" in Russia: Political Tool or Historical Choice?* (Paris: Institute Français des Relations Internationales [IFRI], 2015); and Igor Zevelev, *Russian National*

Vladimir Putin himself has talked about the Russian "genetic code," the specificity of the Russian national character, and the special mission of Russian civilization.[19] Duma deputies, political and public figures, journalists, and other commentators echoed him. Foreign Minister Sergei Lavrov has made his personal contribution to this discussion about the unique Russian way of development. He has argued that fundamental differences exist between Russia and the West, developing Putin's argument about the Western threat to the Russian national identity.[20]

Sergei Obukhov, a Duma deputy and the Communist Party's Central Committee secretary, has described the close connection between anti-American and anti-liberal ideas with great clarity:

> The meaning of the word "liberal" in the mass consciousness has been completely changed, because the liberal project and its leaders have failed in Russia. To be more precise, what failed is what was carried out under the name and the banner of a liberal project, which was really a US global project... This project imposes US values on the entire world. Its understanding of human rights goes against our traditional cultural and mental values. In my opinion, these are the origins of the mass negative attitudes toward the word "liberal," which has become a curse word in our country.[21]

The "war of images" in Russian-American relations is a war of ideas and values. That is why many American organizations in Russia

---

Identity and Foreign Policy, A Report of the CSIS and Eurasia Program (Washington, DC: Center for Strategic and International Studies, 2016).

[19]   Vladimir Putin, "Meeting of the Valdai International Discussion Club," 19 September 2013, Johnson's Russia List, 20 September 2013, http://russialist.org/transcript-putin-at-meeting-of-the-valdai-international-discussion-club-partia l-transcript; Vladimir Putin, "Poslanie Prezidenta Federal'nomu Sobraniiu Rossiiskoi Federatsii," President of Russia official website, 12 December 2013, http://kremlin.ru/events/president/news/19825; and Vladimir Putin, "Poslanie Prezidenta Federal'nomu Sobraniiu Rossiiskoi Federatsii," President of Russia official website, 4 December 2014, http://kremlin.ru/events/president/news/47173.

[20]   Sergei Lavrov, "Russia's Foreign Policy in a Historical Perspective," Russia in Global Affairs website, 30 March 2016, http://eng.globalaffairs.ru/number/Russi as-Foreign-Policy-in-a-Historical-Perspective-18067.

[21]   "V znachenii 'poriadochnyi chelovek': 'Meduza' vyiasnila u politikov i obshchestvennykh deiatelei, kto takoi 'liberal,'" Meduza, 10 April 2015, https://meduza.io/feature/2015/04/10/v-znachenii-poryadochnyy-chelovek.

became the victims of the general campaign against "foreign agents,"[22] and why academic *Amerikanistika* has had to back off under pressure from low-quality anti-American journalism, especially on television. A stark example comes from the activities of the information group Rossiya Segodnya, established by a decree of Vladimir Putin in 2013 and headed by the fervid propagandist Dmitrii Kiselev. Hyperbolic, contemptuous criticism of the US and Barack Obama in Kiselev's television commentary created the background for extolling Russia and Putin, and conservative cultural, family, and political values were presented as "traditionally Russian."

In the information war between Russia and the US, we are dealing not with the reality of a renewed Cold War,[23] but with some expressive modes and tools from the Cold War discourse that have been retrieved and turned to new political purposes.[24] For example, just as was commonly done by Soviet propagandists, Russian media figures and politicians highlight the fact that America had and still has serious problems in its domestic and foreign politics and policies, and present US claims to the right to teach Russia the lessons of democracy and international law as ludicrous.

---

[22]   In October 2014 Russia cancelled the Future Leaders Exchange (FLEX) Program—the largest educational exchange program between Russia and the US; in September 2015 the Russian authorities closed the American Center at the Russian State Library of Foreign Literature in Moscow; in 2014–2015 American centers across Russia have been shut down. The Russian Federation Council's list of "undesirable organizations," which are deemed to constitute a "threat to the foundations of the constitutional system of the Russian Federation, its defense capabilities and its national security," includes many American organizations. Among them are the Open Society Foundation, the National Endowment for Democracy, the National Democratic Institute for International Affairs, the International Republican Institute, Freedom House, the Charles Stewart Mott Foundation. The MacArthur Foundation stopped its activity in July 2015, after the publication of Russia's "patriotic stop list."

[23]   Robert Legvold, *Return to Cold War* (Cambridge: Polity Press, 2016); and Andrew Monaghan, *"New Cold War"? Abusing History, Misunderstanding Russia* (London: Chatham House, 2015).

[24]   It should also be noted that Russian–American information warfare predates the Cold War. The first large-scale war of this kind between the two countries occurred over a century ago, during the crises of 1903–05, on which see Victoria I. Zhuravleva, *Ponimanie Rossii v SShA: Obrazy i mify 1881–1914* (Moscow: Russian State University for the Humanities, 2012), 407–786.

Since the beginning of the crisis in 2014, Russian state-controlled media have increasingly drawn public attention to the events in Ferguson and Baltimore and to the general upsurge in racial controversy in the US in general; to the spy scandals and Edward Snowden's revelations; to credible reports of torture in secret CIA prisons; to the failures of US foreign policy in hot spots ranging from Iraq to Syria; to the political and social problems in the US, which were exposed very clearly during the 2016 presidential election; and to the crisis in Russian studies in the US, which, detractors hold, confirms the poor quality of US expertise and that country's main responsibility for the crisis in bilateral relations. In this sense, the US continues to be consigned the role of a singular "dark twin" to Russia.[25]

Two top-rated films from this period hold a special place in Russia's propagandistic documentary filmmaking and exemplify the "I" concept of Putin's Russia in counterpoint to the West as a hostile Other in general and the US as the demonic Other in particular.[26] These are Andrei Kondrashov's *Crimea: The Way Home* (2015) and Vladimir Solov'ev's *The President* (2015), both of which use the American example in order to emphasize Russia's greatness and the purity of its president's intentions.

In the conversation with Kondrashov that features in *Crimea: The Way Home*, President Putin declared that Russians were moved to help Crimea's inhabitants because of "an outburst of nationalism in Ukraine." He acknowledged that he had overseen the Crimea operation personally, and stated that he would act in the same way in respect to the Crimea problem were history to repeat itself.[27] The

---

[25]   See, for example, Vitalii Podvitskii's cartoon in which Barack Obama is represented as saying, "If Russia cannot subdue the Ferguson rebels, the U.S. will respond with a new round of sanctions"; *Masterskaia karikatury Vitaliia Podvitskogo* website, 24 August 2016, http://cartoonmaster.livejournal.com/12344.html.

[26]   "Fil'm *Krym: Put' na rodinu* posmotreli 3 milliona moskvichei," *RIA Novosti*, 16 March 2015, https://ria.ru/culture/20150316/1052782460.html; "TNS. Fil'm *President* posmotreli okolo 39.1% moskvichei," *RIA Novosti*, 27 April 2015, https://ria.ru/society/20150427/1061134407.html.

[27]   The documentary also suggested that the American guided missile destroyer "Donald Cook" had played a role in the Crimean events; see "Kak Rossii udalos'

international community and the mass media reacted with indignation to Putin's declaration of his readiness to use nuclear weapons should a third party (he meant the US, of course) intervene in the conflict in Ukraine. The "hand of America" metaphor (in this case, referring to the notion of the US managing Ukraine's Euromaidan) was vividly evident both in this documentary and in the film *The President*.[28]

The *President* is a filmed interview with Putin made for the fifteenth anniversary of his first gaining the presidency. In it Putin talks about major turning points in high politics and about the direction in which he is leading Russia. Among his assertions is the allegation that Russian special security services had traced direct contacts between guerrillas in the North Caucasus and US special services representatives (another reference to the "hand of America" metaphor). The Western media noted that Putin used this assertion to justify Russia's actions in Ukraine and to emphasize his conviction that the US sought to weaken Russia.[29] In response to the Western media reaction, Vladimir Komoedov, head of the Duma's Defense Committee, stated that Russia "has always been a bone stuck in the throat" of both the US and Europe, "whatever road the country chose for itself: a Socialist-Communist one, a bourgeois-capitalist one, or the one during the tsarist period."[30] This was another appeal to the image of the US as the demonic Other. The principal task of both documentaries was to consolidate national sentiment around the idea of Great Russia. American presidents appeared as supporting actors, while Putin was cast in a favorable light as

---

[28] vziat' Krym bez boia," *BBC News*, 20 March 2015, https://www.bbc.com/russian/russia/2015/03/150320_crimea_film_battle.
It can also be found in Russian political cartoons from the same period; see, for example, Vitalii Podvitskii's cartoon, *RIA Novosti*, 29 October 2014, https://ria.ru/caricature/20141029/1030817004.html.

[29] Kathrin Hille, "Putin Accuses US of Supporting Separatist Militants inside Russia," *Financial Times*, 26 April 2015, https://www.ft.com/content/93c8b68c-ec2e-11e4-b428-00144feab7de.

[30] "V Gosudarstvennoi Dume ne soglasny s reaktsiei FT na slova Putina v fil'me Prezident," *RIA Novosti*, 27 April 2015, https://ria.ru/society/20150427/1061141425.html.

national leader and a world-class international politician and strategist.

In general, in the anti-American discourse, the image of Barack Obama as a weak president and a practitioner of double-standard politics was used widely in order to promote Putin's brand. Obama was especially harshly portrayed as the hostile Other in the cartoons of Vitalii Podvitskii, the official cartoonist of the state-controlled Russian Information Agency. Podvitskii is famous in the Russian segment of the internet for his patriotic, pro-Putin, and anti-American cartoons. He likes to emphasize his role in the information war against the West in general and the US in particular by drawing parallels between a cartoonist and a sniper, because "a visual shot can do much harm to the enemy in the current war of images."[31] In Podvitskii's cartoons, Obama is sometimes depicted in the Black Overlord's costume,[32] symbolizing his protection of the LGBT population in the US and thereby highlighting those characteristics of the American model of development that are alien to the Russian idea.[33] Obama has also been portrayed by this cartoonist in the likeness of Jabba the Hutt from the *Star Wars* films, with Putin cast as Jedi Luke Skywalker, proclaiming that "There is a Jedi for every dark side of the Force." Usually, American cartoonists recruited images of Darth Vader or Jabba the Hutt in order to label Russia the Evil Empire.[34] The Russian anti-American discourse, however, worked at reversing these leaders' roles in the imagined reality of international relations using the same popular culture artifacts, but switching roles so as to claim the side of Good for Putin. In order to underline

---

[31]   "Karikaturist Podvitskii 'snaiperskoi satiroi' zashchishchaet Rossiiu ot napadok Zapada," *PolitRussia.com*, 4 February 2016, http://politrussia.com/news/karikat urist-podvitskiy-laquo-spayperskoy-709/.

[32]   The Black Overlord is an internet meme of a tough-looking African American dressed in gay-style clothes who tirelessly fights evil in all its manifestations.

[33]   Vitalii Podvitskii, "Chernyi vlastelin," available at: http://caricatura.ru/daily/ podvitski/pic/735.jpg.

[34]   See, for example, Dick Locher's cartoon in *Chicago Daily Tribune*, 31 May 1988.

the hostility of the US Podvitskii used the Nazi swastika, a symbol familiar to every Russian.[35]

Podvitskii's Obama cartoons included a racist subtext that was part of a new trend in the anti-American discourse that developed against the background of American criticism of Russia's annexation of Crimea and the tit-for-tat sanctions war. This upsurge in racist imagery, foregrounded in racist jokes, targeted the first black president of the US. Anti-Obama (and hence anti-American) racist manifestations in popular culture included a chocolate bar named "Little Obama" ("Obamka"); cutting boards that featured two adult monkeys with their baby, on which Obama's face was superimposed; a series of posters calling the US president "Banan-Obama"; a light show projected onto the walls of the US embassy in Moscow showing Obama in a birthday hat and eating a banana; café restrooms with toilet paper featuring Obama's face and toilet mats in the red, white, and blue of the US flag; and a car wash called "Abama" that promised to "wash off all the black."[36] This everyday anti-American racism actually worked against the Kremlin's propagandistic attacks on the race controversy in the US and could be explained by the spread of xenophobic sentiments in Russian society itself as a consequence of the surge in nationalism and anti-immigration prejudices. Negative images of ethnic "aliens" (Central Asians and Caucasians, or the collective image of *Gastarbeiters*) activate the racial imaginary and are spread mainly through social media.[37] This trend, together with the overall confusion regarding

---

35   Vitalii Podvitskii, "Na vsiakuiu temnuiu storonu sily naidetsia svoi Dzhedai," Vitalii Podvitskii personal website, http://podvitski.ru/pictures/comix/1579/1579_big.jpg.

36   Jennifer Wilson, "Obama Banana 'Jokes' Show Soviet-Era Racism Remains Alive in Russia," *Guardian*, 12 May 2016, https://www.theguardian.com/world/2016/may/12/little-obama-jokes-soviet-era-racism-remains-alive-in-russia; and "Russia's 'Obama' Ice Cream Deepens Chilly Relations with US," *New York Post*, 6 May 2016, http://nypost.com/2016/05/06/russias-obama-ice-cream-deepens-chilly-relations-with-us/.

37   See, for example, Levada Center opinion polls: "Intolerantnost' i ksenofobiia," *Levada Center* website, 11 October 2016, https://www.levada.ru/2016/10/11/intolerantnost-i-ksenofobiya/; and "Ksenofobiia v 2017 gody," *Levada Center* website, 23 August 2017, https://www.levada.ru/2017/08/23/16486/.

race,[38] influenced the common Russian's perception of Barack Obama as the demonic Other.

The conformist and patriotic-minded segment of Russian youth also took, and continues to take, an active part in constructing a repertoire of meanings within the anti-American discourse. The group calling itself the Moscow Students' Initiative stood behind the banana light show on the walls of the US embassy.[39] Warranting special attention in this regard is the Studiia 13 project, created by the Young Guard (the youth wing of the United Russia party).[40] Studiia 13's slogan is "The Russian Misha as the protector of the world" ("Misha" being the diminutive of "bear" in Russian). This project combines the efforts of patriotic-minded Russian youth who are willing to take part in the information war against the West in general and against the US in particular. During Obama's presidency, project members drew posters and cartoons and made videos and animation clips in which Putin's Russia was contrasted with the US and Putin himself was contrasted with Barack Obama as the champion of a more just international order. For example, on 15 February 2016, in response to the anti-Russian messages that were coming from the White House, Studio 13 launched an exhibition of internet posters and cartoons titled *The True Faces of the US Presidents*.[41] The popular culture products created by Studiia 13 promote Russian "traditional values" and the Russian idea of patriotism by contrasting Russia with the American Other. One such exemplary product was a poster bearing the motto, "Each country has its own heroes." This poster visualized a conflict of ideas between the two countries over

---

38   For example, the Russian makers of the Obamka bar were inspired by the fictional African island of Chunga-Changa, which appeared in a popular Soviet children's animation and depicted black children as having the ability to magically communicate with the island's animals and sharing an affinity with them.

39   Adam K. Raymond, "Subtle Russian Light Show Depicts President Obama With a Banana in His Mouth," *New York Magazine*, 7 August 2014, http://nymag.com/daily/intelligencer/2014/08/obama-sucks-on-banana-in-russian-light-show.html.

40   See this project in social media: https://twitter.com/13studiya; and https://vk.com/13studiya.

41   "Studiia 13 pokazala istinnoe litso amerikanskikh prezidentov," *Molodaia Gvardiia* website, 15 February 2016, http://www.mger2020.ru/gallery/2016/02/15/86819.

what heroism is: the fictional character Captain America was contrasted with a "real-life" hero, a Russian grandfather who had fought in the Great Patriotic War and was admired by his grandson. The poster's message was that only real-life (Russian) heroism can provide true instruction in patriotism.[42]

Before Donald Trump's inauguration, Prime Minister Dmitry Medvedev, summarizing Obama's presidency, wrote on his Facebook page:

> The Obama Administration has destroyed relations between the United States and Russia, which are at their lowest point in decades. This is its key foreign policy mistake, which history will remember. We do not know yet how the new US Administration will approach relations with our country. But we are hoping that reason will prevail. And we are ready to do our share of the work in order to improve relations.[43]

The Russian leadership thus centered its principal hopes on the presidency of Donald Trump.

The 2016 Presidential Election: Clinton and Trump as Hostile "Other" and Friendly "Other"

In 2008, the neo-imperialist writer and columnist Aleksandr Prokhanov prophesied the death of America as a result of Obama's liberalism.[44] After the victory of Donald Trump, Prokhanov depicted Obama as "hellspawn," and "a peacemaker with cruise missiles in each fist," and celebrated Trump's election. Being inside the traditionalist conservative mainstream, the Russian columnist described the results of the 2016 US presidential election as an uprising of the original America, which had been "deceived by the sweet-singing liberal melodists, tied to the stake of tolerance, intimidated by gay pride parades, taken captive by bankers"; simultaneously, he

---

[42] "U kazhdoi strany svoi geroi," *13 Studiia* website, 24 January 2016, https://vk.com/13studiya?z=photo-65015436_456239494%2Falbum-65015436_00%2Frev.

[43] Dmitry Medvedev's official Facebook page, 19 January 2017, https://www.facebook.com/Dmitry.Medvedev/posts/10154053104646851.

[44] Aleksandr Prokhanov, "Osoboe mnenie," *Echo Moskvy*, 5 November 2008, http://echo.msk.ru/programs/personalno/551120-echo/.

condemned all the Russians (primarily liberals, of course) who were condemning Trump.[45]

Trump quickly turned into the favorite candidate of Russian officials and the state-run mass media, and his victory was greeted with euphoria in the State Duma, optimistic comments from the media, and enthusiasm on the part of ordinary people, who believed that Trump would improve relations with Russia and lift the sanctions.[46] During the entire presidential campaign the Russian public had been offered a romantic image of Donald Trump and a demonic image of Hillary Clinton (her "signals" to the Russian opposition, support for the "color" revolutions and the Arab Spring, and the intervention in Libya were all taken into consideration). The media also relished all the accusations Trump heaped on her, including the openly absurd and routinely sexist ones.[47]

In October 2016 Vladimir Zhirinovsky, ultra-nationalist ally of Putin and head of the pro-Kremlin Liberal Democratic Party of Russia (LDPR), who liked to compare himself to the US Republican Party candidate, told Reuters in an interview that Americans should vote for Donald Trump as president or risk being dragged into a nuclear war by Clinton. In typically sexist remarks, Zhirinovsky said that Clinton's gender should also bar her from the presidency: "Most Americans should choose Trump because men have been leading for millions of years. You can't take the risk of having one of the richest,

45   Aleksandr Prokhanov, "Trump, priezzhai!" *Russkaia Vesna*, 16 November 2016, http://rusvesna.su/news/1479279369.
46   See, for example, "Peskov zaiavil o fenomenal'nom skhodstve podkhodov Putina i Trampa k vneshnei politike," *Vedomosti*, 10 November 2016, http://www.vedomosti.ru/politics/news/2016/11/10/664438-fenomenalnom-putina-trampa; "Volodin zaiavil o skhozhesti mnogikh pozitsii Putina i Trampa," *Vedomosti*, 13 November 2016, http://www.vedomosti.ru/politics/articles/2016/11/13/664653-volodin-o-shozhesti-pozitsii-putina-i-trampa; and "V RPTS privetstvovali izbranie Trampa prezidentom SShA," *Interfax.ru*, 9 November 9, 2016, http://www.interfax.ru/russia/536295; and "Opros: uluchsheniia otnoshenii s SShA posle izbraniia Trampa zhdut 46% rossiian," *RIA Novosti*, 18 November 2016, https://ria.ru/us_elections2016/20161118/1481629302.html.
47   Lev Gudkov, "O Trampe, Rossii i krepostnom soznanii," *Levada.ru*, 7 February 2017, https://www.levada.ru/2017/02/07/o-trampe-rossii-i-krepostnom-soznanii/.

most powerful countries led by a woman president."[48] This sexism on the part of Zhirinovsky was of a piece with Trump's sexism, which manifested very clearly during the US presidential debates.[49] It also chimed with Putin's sexism when he criticized Clinton's rhetoric with a reference to her gender: "When people cross the boundary of good manners, this attests to their weakness, not their strength. But for a woman, weakness is not the worst quality."[50]

The American drive to unmask the Kremlin's interference in the US presidential election led to increasing criticism of the Obama administration in Russia and of Hillary Clinton as Obama's political and ideological fellow traveler. From late 2016 to early 2017, both the state-run mass media and the expert and academic community in Russia widely and openly portrayed Obama as a weak president, a failure in office, and a sore loser annoyed by the Democrats' defeat. The racist imaginary was unmissable in the mass media's anti-Obama discourse after Donald Trump's win and Obama's decision to expel thirty-five Russian diplomats from the United States. As Kevin Rothrock has shown, racially tinged productions included, for example, Dmitrii Kiselev's television news and current affairs shows; Mikhail Shakhnazarov's article, "Slamming the Door on the Year of the Monkey," published in the pro-Kremlin tabloid *Life*; and the racist comments on social media by Maria Katasonova, a right-wing youth leader and an aide in the State Duma, and by the Russian journalist Maksim Sokolov.[51] Kiselev later claimed he had never

---

[48]   Andrew Osborn, "Vladimir Putin Ally Threatens Nuclear War If Americans Vote for Hillary Clinton," *Global News*, 12 October 2016, https://globalnews.ca/news/2998588/vladimir-putin-ally-threatens-nuclear-war-if-americans-vote-for-hillary-clinton/.

[49]   Dara Lind, "How Hillary Clinton Lured Donald Trump's Sexism Out into the Open," *Vox*, 27 September 2016, https://www.vox.com/2016/9/27/13067822/debate-clinton-trump-sexism.

[50]   Damien Sharkov, "Where Do Hillary Clinton and Donald Trump Stand on Russia?" *Newsweek*, 5 August 2016, http://www.newsweek.com/where-do-clinton-and-trump-stand-russia-487777.

[51]   Kevin Rothrock, "Russia's Graceless Goodbye to America's First Black President," *Moscow Times*, 30 December 2016, https://themoscowtimes.com/articles/russias-graceless-goodbye-to-americas-first-black-president-56708.

intended to mock Obama's race, but other commentators showed no such inhibitions, indulging their racial prejudices freely.[52]

Thus, both the racial and gender characteristics of Donald Trump correlated with the Russian conservative discourse, a meeting of minds that helped to construct his image as the friendly Other. In general, romanticizing Trump contributed to the demonization of both Hillary Clinton and Barack Obama, and, by extension, to the demonization of the image of Obama's America.

An analysis of the endless pro-Trump, anti-Clinton, and anti-Obama comments on Russia's state-run TV and in the media during the 2016 presidential campaign leaves the impression that Russia was indeed engaged in "electing" its own American president.[53] This seemingly formed the foundation of the report presented by the American intelligence agencies (the CIA, FBI, and NSA), which paid particular attention to the anti-American activities of Russian state-run media in general and *Russia Today,* the prominent English-language news outlet funded by the Kremlin, in particular, citing such activities as proof of the Kremlin's complicity in the cyber-attacks on the Democratic National Committee (DNC).[54] This accusation so far has profited only *RT,* which in 2017 received enviable state financing for furthering the information war against the United States.[55] On the one hand, the romanticized perception of Trump in Russia can be explained by the Russian tendency to divide US presidential candidates into "good" and "evil," depending on their

---

[52]   "Russian Propaganda Edits Out Racist Comment about Obama," *Moscow Times,* 22 November 2016, https://themoscowtimes.com/news/russian-propaganda-edits-out-racist-comment-about-obama-56254.

[53]   David Filipov, "Russia Has Gone Crazy for Trump as Moscow Savors Obama's Departure," *Washington Post,* 19 January 2017, https://www.washingtonpost.com/world/europe/russias-gone-crazy-for-trump-as-moscow-savors-obamas-departure/2017/01/19/e22fab2c-dd78-11e6-b2cf-b67fe3285cbc_story.html?utm_term=.a475341c9c11.

[54]   "Assessing Russian Activities and Intentions in Recent US Elections: The Analytic Process and Cyber Incident Attribution," *Office of the Director of National Intelligence,* 6 January 2017, https://www.dni.gov/files/documents/ICA_2017_01.pdf.

[55]   "RT—amerikanskomu miniustu: my ne znaem, kto daet nam den'gi," *Meduza,* 13 November 2017, https://meduza.io/news/2017/11/13/rt-amerikanskomu-minyustu-my-ne-znaem-kto-daet-nam-dengi-v-rossii.

willingness to be Russia's friend or foe. On the other hand, Putin has been playing his own American card in connection with the national identity construction process.

First, in supporting Trump in his anti-globalism agenda, Putin enhanced the image of Russia as a leader in the struggle against Western dominance. This message was addressed both to the domestic audience and to those abroad who felt they had become victims of America's hegemonist policies. Second, Hillary Clinton had turned the Democratic Party anti-Russian during her presidential campaign and Putin claimed that she planned to continue Obama's policies; the Kremlin expected her to advance democracy everywhere, to use NATO to contain Russia in Europe, and to escalate the US–Russia confrontation in Ukraine and in Syria, whereas Trump was expected to make bilateral relations more pragmatic. For both the Russian political elite and ordinary Russian citizens, Clinton personified America's universal liberalism and the idea of "crusades" for freedom and democracy, while Trump appeared to represent conservative values[56]—he looked like a person who viewed foreign policy as a matter of business, not to be muddied with humanitarian acts. Third, Russian traditionalists took the 2016 US presidential election, with its dynamics, rhetoric, and results, to be additional confirmation of fundamental deficiencies in the US social and political system and thus as a powerful argument in favor of Russian conservative nationalism. In this way the images of Trump and Clinton as respectively the friendly Other and the hostile Other, as well as the image of the US as a dark twin, were used by Putin and the Russian authorities for their own political purposes during the 2016 US presidential election.

In the US, the hue and cry over cyber-attacks on the DNC contributed to the shaping of a solid anti-Russian media and partisan (among Democrats and anti-Trump Republicans) consensus, and led to the growth of anti-Russian sentiment among the American

---

[56]   Aleksandr Goncharov, "Chto oznachaiut dlia Rossii prezident Tramp i prezident Putin," *Carnegie Moscow Center*, 5 May 2016, https://carnegie.ru/commentary/63516; and Michael Crowley, "Poll: Trump Supporters Warm to Russia," *Politico*, 17 October 2016, https://www.politico.com/story/2016/10/poll-trump-supporters-warm-to-russia-229874.

public.[57] Clinton described Trump as a pro-Russia candidate and a threat to America's national security.[58] In his turn, Trump stressed Putin's merits as a political leader as a way to highlight Obama's deficiencies in that capacity. Both Clinton and Trump, then, exploited the image of Russia for their own political goals. As a result, the anti-Trump consensus also became anti-Russian.

At the same time, it is important to remain sensible of the fact that, despite a very high likelihood that the Kremlin was behind the hackers, Trump's 2016 victory was due not to the DNC email leaks but to the deep socio-political crisis currently playing out in the US. That is why the 2016 presidential election became the moment when the "Russian factor" returned to the top of the agenda in the US. For the first time since the end of the Cold War, the Russian Other was so clearly front and center in American socio-political discourse that it could be considered a manifestation of both the crisis in Russian–US relations and the serious identity crisis in the US itself. The history of Russian–US relations yields abundant proof of such a correlation.[59]

At first, Putin was the principal beneficiary of the media-driven story of the cyber-attacks and the promotion of the "Russian president" Trump. He became a sort of "all-powerful person" in Russian interpretation (or a "global supervillain" in Western interpretation), capable of interfering not only in the affairs of Russia's neighboring states but also in the affairs of the US itself.[60] In December

---

57   Eric Bradner, "Poll: 55% of Americans Bothered by Russian Election Hacking," *CNN* website, 18 December 2016, http://edition.cnn.com/2016/12/18/politics/poll-russian-hacking/index.html.

58   See, for example, Team Fix, Abby Ohlheiser, and Caitlin Dewey, "Hillary Clinton's Alt-Right Speech, Annotated," *Washington Post*, 25 August 2016, https://www.washingtonpost.com/news/the-fix/wp/2016/08/25/hillary-clinto ns-alt-right-speech-annotated/.

59   On this, see David Foglesong, *The American Mission and the "Evil Empire": The Crusade for a "Free Russia" since 1881* (Cambridge: Cambridge University Press, 2007); and Zhuravleva, *Ponimanie Rossii v SShA*.

60   "Klip pro 'vsemogushchego Putina' stal khitom v seti," *Vesti FM*, 17 November 2016, https://radiovesti.ru/news/570450/; and Mark Lawrence Schrad, "Vladimir Putin Isn't a Supervillain," *Foreign Policy*, 2 March 2017, https://foreignpolic y.com/2017/03/02/vladimir-putin-isnt-a-supervillain/. See also: Nathan Hodge, "Western Criticism Bolsters Putin at Home," *The Wall Street Journal*, 13

2016, Obama initiated new sanctions in response to the information about Russia's participation in the cyber-attacks, and expelled thirty-five Russian diplomats. This action was interpreted in the US as the start of a retaliation against the cyber-security hack allegedly orchestrated by Russia, but Putin magnanimously left the sanctions unreciprocated. Apparently, Russia's president did not want to create problems for the future Trump administration on which the Kremlin had pinned such great hopes. But it soon became manifestly clear that the Trump–Russia connections and alleged Russian meddling in the 2016 election that was being investigated in Washington were creating a real stumbling block in Trump's policies toward Russia and hampering his ability to score a number of legislative victories.

A "Good President" in the White House: Russian Perceptions of Trump's America, from Hope to Disappointment

During the first two months of 2017, Donald Trump was mentioned in the Russian mass media in a positive manner several times more frequently than Vladimir Putin.[61] But by the end of February, and in the absence of any real positive shifts in Russian–US relations (the two presidents had their much-awaited first face-to-face meeting only on 7 July 2017), references to Donald Trump as a phenomenon practically disappeared from Russia's top TV channels.[62] As the former US ambassador to Russia Michael McFaul wrote on his blog on *Ekho Moskvy*,

> The resignation of Michael Flynn and the appointment of Gen. Herbert Raymond McMaster as the National Security Adviser of the White House should crush all the dreams of the great union between the U.S. and Russia in the Trump-Putin era. Three of the crucial decision makers in the National

---

December 2017, https://www.wsj.com/articles/western-criticism-bolsters-putin-at-home-1513161001.

[61] "Tramp obognal Putina v reitinge samykh upominaemykh person v rossiiskikh SMI," *Interfax*, 1 February 2017, http://www.interfax.ru/russia/547952.

[62] Giorgio Comai, "Russian Media: More Trump than Putin," Giorgio Comai personal website, 3 March 2017, http://www.giorgiocomai.eu/2017/03/03/russian-media-more-trump-than-putin/#more-74681051.

Security Council—McMaster, Secretary of State Tillerson, Secretary of Defense Mattis,—have sober, realistic ideas of Russia and international relations as a whole. They are not dreamers who hope that ideology, a Judeo-Christian union against Islam and China, could unite the two countries. They are realists.[63]

However, according to a Pew Research Center survey conducted among 40,448 respondents in thirty-seven countries outside the US from 16 February to 8 May 2017, Trump got higher marks than Obama in only two countries: Russia (where confidence rose 42 percentage points) and Israel (up 7 percentage points). This poll testified to the fact that since Trump's election the US image has significantly improved in only one country, Russia, where the favorable view of America is up 26 percentage points, from 15 percent in 2015 to 41 percent in 2017.[64] Trump has received a more positive reception in Russia than either of his two predecessors ever did.

Until the end of July 2017, when President Putin announced that the American diplomatic mission in Russia was to reduce its staff by 755 employees in response to new American sanctions, the Kremlin was expecting relations with the US to improve, especially in the context of the first Putin-Trump meeting on the sidelines of the G-20 summit in Hamburg. The Russian media's attention to the events in the US focused on the scandals surrounding Trump's election campaign and his electoral team's ties to Russia, as well as on an anti-Trump political and media consensus in the US, in order to underline the use of the "Trump card" in the US anti-Russia policy and the "Russian card" in internal political games. These optics help explain the subsequent absence of positive changes in Russian–American relations during the administration of a "good president" in the White House.

63`   Michael McFaul, "Prorossiiskie romantiki v administratsii Trampa uzhe proigrali," *Michael McFaul's blog*, 24 February 2017, http://echo.msk.ru/blog/mcfaul/1933886-echo/.

64   Richard Wike, Bruce Stokes, Jacob Poushter, and Janell Fetterolf, "U.S. Image Suffers as Publics around World Question Trump's Leadership: America Still Wins Praise for Its People, Culture and Civil Liberties," *Pew Research Center* website, 26 June 2017, http://www.pewglobal.org/2017/06/26/u-s-image-suffers-as-publics-around-world-question-trumps-leadership/.

Statements made by Russian politicians and media personalities during the first part of 2017 may be provisionally divided into two groups. First, there was the reaction to the comments made in the US concerning the investigation of Russia's alleged meddling in the 2016 presidential election. For instance, Irina Yarovaia, the vice-speaker of the Duma, said in response to a statement made by CIA director Mike Pompeo, "This is primarily another attack on the minds of Americans and Europeans who are being harassed with one goal only: to trap them in their fears and in subjugation to the aggressive arms race and destruction of freedom of thought." She emphasized her hopes that Americans' common sense would win out over "the information and political violence perpetrated by politicians and over the manipulations perpetrated by the bureaucracy."[65] Yarovaya was responding to Pompeo's MSNBC interview, in which he said that "we are decades into the Russians trying to undermine American democracy. So in some ways, there's no news, but it certainly puts a heightened emphasis on our ability to figure out how to stop them."[66]

Second, there was the desire to depict Trump as a realistically minded president who is opposed to forces in his own country that strive to preserve US global hegemony. This idea has been very clearly expressed by, for example, Aleksei Pushkov, chair of the Information Committee of the Federation Council, during the weekly talk show, *Sunday Evening with Vladimir Solov'ev*.[67] Pushkov stressed,

> In the US itself two approaches to the US national interests compete. One approach is more realistic: the US is no longer capable of sustaining the load entailed by the classical global leadership... When Trump said America no longer wants interventions because they are expensive and they backfire, he

---

[65] Irina Mikheeva, "Iarovaia: zaiavlenie glavy TsRU v adres RF 'feikovye i rusofobskie,'" *Izvestiia*, 25 June 2017, http://iz.ru/610760/2017-06-25/iarovaia-zaiavleniia-glavy-tcru-v-adres-rf-feikovye-i-rusofobskie.

[66] "One-On-One with CIA Director Mike Pompeo," *MSNBC* website, 24 June 2017, http://www.msnbc.com/hugh-hewitt/watch/one-on-one-with-cia-director-mike-pompeo-975249475879.

[67] "Vecher c Vladimirom Solov'evym," *Vesti*, 25 February 2017, http://www.vesti.ru/videos/show/vid/721179.

represented the opinion of such people. They understand that common sense prods the US toward a more limited role, and therefore the US needs to deal with Russians, with the Chinese, with North Koreans.... And the other trend is that America is the global overlord and so it must remain. We stand in the way of their creating the Syria they want. This is why there is a campaign against us. And at the same time, [it is] a campaign against Trump.[68]

Pushkov's rhetoric helped create an image of Trump as a realistically minded pro-Russian president opposed to Obama as an idealistically minded anti-Russian president.

Three comments can be made about Pushkov's words. First, Pushkov's vision of political realism is distinct from McFaul's vision, mentioned above. In a sense, this difference has to do with the time-seasoned debate between the champions of a pragmatic versus a values-based approach to US foreign policy regarding Russia.[69] The shift in emphasis from a values-based to a pragmatic approach might indeed soften the climate of Russian–American relations and thus dampen anti-American moods in Russia and diversify American perceptions of events there. Yet for Pushkov and those who think like him, a new American realism must include a rejection of the sanctions regime and elimination of the Crimea question from the bilateral agenda. Second, no one in the US seriously considers the possibility of Russia gaining a leading role that would allow it to really challenge US global leadership. For that, Russia would need not only ambition but also resources. Third, Pushkov's last statement demonstrates that the frank desire to use the Russian card in the US, no matter how justified the US criticism of Russia's domestic and foreign policies, gives Vladimir Putin more ammunition and promotes a high degree of anti-American sentiment in Russia itself.[70]

A four-part series, *The Putin Interviews*, based on conversations between Oliver Stone and Putin from July 2015 to February 2017 and aired by the Showtime channel in the US in June 2017, gave

---

68   *Ibid.*
69   Stent, *The Limits of Partnership*, 274.
70   Margaret Vice, "Russians Remain Confident in Putin's Global Leadership," *Pew Research Center* website, 20 June 2017, http://www.pewglobal.org/2017/06/20/russians-remain-confident-in-putins-global-leadership/.

the Russian president an opportunity to convey his viewpoint to a Western audience. Oliver Stone, three-time Academy Award winner, Vietnam War veteran, and Purple Heart recipient, has made such famous films as *Born on the Fourth of July, JFK, Nixon, Wall Street: Money Never Sleeps, Platoon,* and *Snowden,* and has been criticized for undermining trust in American authorities and for his predilection for conspiracy theories.

The Putin Interviews deserves special attention for several reasons. To begin with, summarizing the most burning issues in Russian–Western relations in general and in Russian–US relations in particular, these interviews elucidate the principal Russian arguments for promoting a demonic image of the US. Putin did not say anything new. Yet his aggregated statements, often unaccompanied by any critical commentary from Stone, can hardly contribute to a better understanding of Putin's Russia in the West. They, however, contribute to strengthening anti-Americanism in that part of the Russian population that is under the influence of state-owned media. This is surely why the film was aired by Russia's Channel 1 in Russian immediately.[71]

Next, the film series demonstrates Oliver Stone's readiness to review Russia's policies by interrogating the policies of the US itself. It is not accidental that Putin, knowing Stone's credo, chose him to convey his thoughts to a Western audience. This is not a new phenomenon in Russian–US relations: in the 1960s and 1970s, for instance, there was a revisionist turn in US historiography, both in American studies and in Russian studies, when left-wing American historians challenged the academic consensus concerning the Cold War and the Russian revolution.[72] It is not accidental that Russian propaganda outlets, including the *Russia Today* channel, actively

---

[71]   "Chetyre vechera podriad na Pervom kanale—dokumental'nyi fil'm Olivera Stouna 'Putin,'" *Pervyi kanal,* 19 June 2017, https://www.1tv.ru/news/2017-06-19/327311-chetyre_vechera_podryad_na_pervom_kanale_dokumental-nyy_film_olivera_stouna_putin.

[72]   Sheila Fitzpatrick, "What's Left?" *London Review of Books* 39, no. 7 (March 2017): 13–15; and Scott W. Palmer, "Scholarship at the Crossroads: The Past, Present, and Possible Future of Russian History in America," *The Journal of the Historical Society* VI (December 2006): 605–609.

invite commentary on the current crisis in bilateral relations from those American political scientists, journalists, and experts who are inclined toward critical revisions of both the US past and its present.[73] Nor is it accidental that during the crisis in bilateral relations the Russian book market was flooded with translations of American books that espoused a critical view of US domestic and foreign policy, such as the new translation of Howard Zinn's *A People's History of the United States* under the title *The American Empire from 1492 till Our Days*, Oliver Stone and Peter Kuznick's *The Untold History of the United States*, and Dinesh D'Souza's *America: Imagine a World without Her.*

Finally, Stone said in an interview with the *Nation* that, to improve Russian–US relations, he intended to explain to the Western audience President Putin's thinking and his arguments, allowing him to speak his mind to the camera.[74] As a result, Stone reproduces Putin's own image of himself: he is a strong leader who has led the country to stability and returned Russia to its national greatness; he is a patriot of his country who opposes the US' nefarious activities; he is physically strong, indeed macho (he plays hockey, he does judo and rides horses); he is a loving father, proud of his daughters; he is a person of the Orthodox confession, for whom faith in God is an organic part of life. Furthermore, with his comments on women's "bad days" and LGBT people, Vladimir Putin showed that he could rival Donald Trump in gender prejudices.

---

73   See, for example, "The American Empire with Allan Nairn (On Contact with Chris Hedges)," *Russia Today*, 28 January 2017, https://www.youtube.com/watch?v=p5X48aRsNSQ; "How Washington Provoked, and Perhaps Lost, A New Nuclear-arms Race—Stephen Cohen," *Russia Today*, 12 March 2018, https://www.rt.com/op-ed/420803-cohen-nuclear-race-washington-moscow/; "Noam Chomsky: NATO became US-run intervention force," *Russia Today*, 7 November 2014, https://www.youtube.com/watch?v=ihff8P6uDbA; and "Noam Chomsky on US–Russia Relations," *Russia Today*, 28 February 2017, https://www.youtube.com/watch?v=lRGLoBTBWW4, etc.

74   Ed Rampell, "Oliver Stone Talks to 'The Nation' about His New Documentary 'The Putin Interviews,'" *The Nation*, 12 June 2017, https://www.thenation.com/article/oliver-stone-talks-to-the-nation-about-his-new-documentary-the-putin-interviews/.

The Putin Interviews could be criticized for factual errors, for Stone's lack of knowledge regarding the real Russian context and his readiness to take Vladimir Putin's lies at face value.[75] But the key feature of this series of interviews is its openly anti-American message. This message boils down to the simple idea that Russia's policies are a reaction against those actions of the US that infringe on Russia's national interests (whether America's withdrawal from the ABM treaty, support for Chechen terrorists, or participation in the "Ukrainian coup d'état"). Putin's anti-American message is received gladly by a significant part of Russian society, especially since Putin's discourse is cleverly interspersed with video snippets selected by Stone himself that present US policies and politicians (chiefly the US presidents) in the most unfavorable light, effectively converting them into "dark twins" of Vladimir Putin.

In the final episode, which is devoted to Russia's attempt to meddle in the US presidential election, Putin emphasizes that "Russian–US relations are merely an instrument of the American domestic political struggle." And this particular argument, alas, sounds convincing enough because of the dual anti-Trump, anti-Russia consensus in the US itself.

Signs of a more realistic approach to the prospects of Trump's policy appeared in the Russian state-controlled mass media and in the statements of Duma deputies and pro-Kremlin experts at the end of February 2017, which could be explained by the changes in Trump's inner circle, by the large-scale anti-Trump political and media consensus in the US, and by the adequacy of the American system of checks and balances.[76] But the real shift in the Kremlin's position happened in response to the new American sanctions against

---

[75]   Masha Gessen, "How Putin Seduced Oliver Stone—and Trump," *New York Times*, 25 June 2017, https://www.nytimes.com/2017/06/25/opinion/oliver-stone-putin-trump.html?_r=0; and Emily Tamkin, "Oliver Stone's 'Putin Interviews' Will Teach You Little about Putin, and Even Less about Russia," *Foreign Policy*, 7 June 2017, http://foreignpolicy.com/2017/06/07/oliver-stones-putin-interviews-will-teach-you-little-about-putin-and-even-less-about-russia/.

[76]   Peter Savodnik, "Why Even Russia is Turning on Trump," *Vanity Fair*, 7 March 2017, https://www.vanityfair.com/news/2017/03/russia-turning-on-trump; and Steve Rosenberg, "Russian Media No Longer Dazzled by Trump," *BBC* website, 17 February 2017, http://www.bbc.com/news/world-europe-39004987.

Russia (along with Iran and North Korea) that were approved by Congress in July and signed by Trump on 2 August 2017. The Russian government, anticipating Trump's approval of new sanctions, retaliated by seizing two American diplomatic properties and ordering the US to reduce its embassy staff in Russia by 755 people. On 31 August 2017, the Trump administration ordered Russia to close its consulate in San Francisco and two diplomatic annexes, in New York City and Washington, DC. These tit-for-tat diplomatic expulsions and seizing of diplomatic properties became the new reality of Russian–American relations, which have reached an all-time low for the post-Cold War period.

On 2 August, Dmitry Medvedev declared the "end to hope for improvement in our relations." He said that "the Trump administration has demonstrated total impotence, handing over executive functions to Congress in the most humiliating way possible" and that "the American establishment has totally outplayed Trump" with the goal "to remove him from power."[77] Thus, Trump has been mocked by the Russian prime minister; and he has also been called "weak" and a "loser" on state media outlets.[78] The Nazi symbolism of the marches in Charlottesville was used to justify Russia's new attitude toward Trump. Veronika Krasheninnikova, a member of Russia's Civic Chamber (an advisory board that answers to President Vladimir Putin) and a vindicator of Russia's law on foreign agents, emphasized, "In Russia, we've had so many illusions about Trump. Now it's clear that he acts with the ideology of hatred, violence, and aggression. The masks can finally come off. Trump alienated America from Russia much more intensively than Barack Obama and the previous US presidents did."[79]

---

77   "'Konets nadezhde na uluchshenie otnoshenii': Medvedev prokommentiroval novye sanktsii SShA," *NTV* website, 2 August 2017, http://www.ntv.ru/novosti/1884338/.
78   Ivan Danilov, "Mezhdunarodnaia izoliatsiia SShA: o pol'ze unizheniia Trampa," *RIA Novosti*, 6 August 2017, https://ria.ru/analytics/20170805/1499810278.html.
79   Amie Ferris-Rotman, "Donald Trump Can Make Friends with Russians or Nazis but Not Both," *Foreign Policy*, 23 August 2017, https://foreignpolicy.com/2017/08/23/donald-trump-can-make-friends-with-russians-or-nazis-but-not-b oth/; and Veronika Krasheninnikova, "Kto takoi mister Tramp i chto nam s nim

Disappointed hopes strengthened the anti-American dis-course in Russia and recalled familiar communicative strategies and dichotomies in the political and public environment. Russian media outlets quickly began voicing outrage over the race-fueled unrest taking place in the US (as they did during racial unrest in Ferguson or in Baltimore) to illustrate the deep racial and social crisis in American society.[80] In its turn, *Russia Today* compared the Char-lottesville events to those taking place in Ukraine and unmasked the hypocrisy of Western media for stigmatizing the American "neo-Na-zis" but not the hooded men in Ukraine carrying torches.[81]

Hoary propagandistic clichés and familiar hostile images were again obvious in the new action series *The Sleepers*, aired on Russia's Channel 1 in October 2017. This spy thriller recounts the struggle between Russian and US intelligence agencies in present-day Russia. The sleepers are foreign agents (politicians and journalists) who must be activated during an international crisis to organize a color revolution in Russia. This "liberal fifth column" is working in coop-eration with an American diplomat, a specialist on color revolutions, to try to destroy Russia. In this black-and-white serial the Russian liberals are the national traitors and the Russian liberal project is the American project. That is why in the office of the "good guys" we see Putin's portrait, symbolizing Russia's national greatness in

---

delat'," *RIA Novosti*, 20 August 2017, https://ria.ru/analytics/20170820/150 0713357.html.

[80]   See, for example, Igor' Dunaevskii, "Amerikanskii Maidan," *Rossiiskaia gazeta*, 15 August 2017, https://rg.ru/2017/08/15/stolknoveniia-v-sharlottsvile-obostrili-rasovye-protivorechiia-v-ssha.html; Victor Marakhovskii, "Amerikanskaia boinia: chemu nas uchit tragediia v Sharlottsville," *RIA Novosti*, 13 August 2017, https://ria.ru/analytics/20170813/1500270834.html; and "Amerikanskie stu-denty trebuiut rasovye kvoty," *Vesti*, 25 August 2017, https://www.vesti-finance.ru/articles/90082. See also, Mikhail Shevchuk, "Nash general: chto poluchit Rossiia ot novykh besporiadkov v SShA," *Delovoi Peterburg*, 15 August 2017, https://www.dp.ru/a/2017/08/14/CHto_poluchit_Rossija_ot_nov; and Julia Ioffe, "The History of Russian Involvement in America's Race Wars," *The Atlantic*, 21 October 2017, https://www.theatlantic.com/international/ar-chive/2017/10/russia-facebook-race/542796/.

[81]   "Far-Right in US & Ukraine—Same Problem, Different Approach among Politi-cians and Media," *Russia Today*, 15 August, 2017, https://www.rt.com/news/399605-far-right-us-ukraine-approach/.

contempt of Western and American intrigues, and in the office of the "bad guys" we see the portrait of Boris Yeltsin, symbolizing the 1990s when Russia had its own destructive "revolution" with the help of the Americans and Russian liberals. This anti-American message in a Cold War style, representing a specific response to the disappointed hopes of Putin's Russia in both Obama's and Trump's America, is directed to that part of the Russian population that takes its bearings from state-owned media. At the same time, this propagandistic film has become an object of criticism in independent mass media outlets and social media.[82] The film's director Yurii Bykov, who was previously known as an open-minded filmmaker and who was not allowed to participate in post-production editing of this film, later apologized publicly for the show to those Russians fighting for the liberalization of their country.[83]

The Other America: Alternative Images of the US in Russia

It should be stressed that Russians have always been and still remain ready to oppose anti-American sentiments; Russian perceptions of the US are by no means limited to the images that the authorities craft and project for their own purposes, and this applies to both the demonic image of Obama and the romantic image of Trump. Even

---

[82]   See, for example, Alia Ponomareva, "'Toshnotvornaia agitka FSB,'" *Radio Svoboda*, 11 October 2017, https://www.svoboda.org/a/28786611.html; Anastasiia Mironova, "'Spiashchie' vmesto aprel'skikh tezisov," *Gazeta.ru*, 13 October 2017, https://www.gazeta.ru/comments/column/mironova/10930460.shtml; Kseniia Larina and Nikolai Svanidze, "Osoboe mnenie," *Ekho Moskvy*, 13 October 2017, https://ruvid.net/video/особое-мнение-николай-сванидзе-13-10-17-hKvov8D 4hec.html; and Yegor Moskvitin, "'Spiashchie': serial o tom, kak Zapad razrushaet Rossiiu," *Meduza*, 12 October 2017, https://meduza.io/feature/ 2017/10/12/spyaschie-serial-o-tom-kak-zapad-razrushaet-rossiyu-ot-rezhissera-bykova-i-stsenarista-minaeva.

[83]   "'Ia predal vse progressivnoe pokolenie, kotoroe chto-to khotelo izmenit'.' Rezhisser Iurii Bykov zaiavil o vozmozhnom ukhode iz kino posle serial 'Spiashchie,'" *Meduza*, 13 October 2017, https://meduza.io/news/2017/10/13/ya-p redal-vse-progressivnoe-pokolenie-kotoroe-chto-to-hotelo-izmenit-rezhisser-yuriy-bykov-zayavil-o-vozmozhnom-uhode-iz-kino-posle-seriala-spyaschie. Bykov, who is also a screenwriter and actor, is best known for directing the films *The Major* and *The Fool*, which received a number of prestigious awards and were highly rated by Western critics.

during the large-scale information war, both the personified and the collective images of the US in Russia were not reduced to a dichotomous vision, although such an imaginary scheme did prevail in the state-run media and became deeply rooted in the minds of ordinary Russians.

Since the beginning of the crisis in Russian–American relations in 2014 anti-Americanism has dominated the journalistic discourse in Russia. At the same time, by contrast, with a few exceptions, there is no "new Cold War" being presented in films or books. Besides, independent and semi-independent media, such as *Vedomosti*, *Novaia Gazeta*, *Republic* (formerly *Slon.ru*), *Dozhd'* TV channel, *Ekho Moskvy* radio station, and the web portals *Polit.ru* and *Meduza* (a Russian language internet-outlet situated in Latvia), still provide opportunities to put forward different opinions and varying assessments of the events in the US and of Russian–US relations. Social media remain platforms for vibrant discussions shaping a marketplace of opinions. The US attracts the attention of people from different social groups who are interested in learning about the multifaceted history and culture of the US and the lessons that can be drawn from American political and economic development.

The tendency to blame America's evil designs for Russia's failures at home and abroad has become the object of a rather broad-based liberal satirical discourse that has been spreading in the Russian segment of the internet. Jokes like "The Russian people have never lived worse than during Obama's administration" or "A bad president can never work well because of the Yankees" demonstrate a critical rejection of the image of the US as the demonic Other, perpetrated by the Kremlin and the Russian state-controlled media for political gain. The cartoons created by Sergei Yelkin, who works for *Radio Svoboda*, *Moscow Times*, and *Polit.ru*, are a vivid illustration of this open-minded alternative discourse. Yelkin mocks the notion that the US should be blamed for all of Russia's problems. For example, he presented Obama's "console for controlling Russia" in one of his cartoons. Obama is shown pushing different rows of buttons—labeled "roads," "prices," "pensions," "education," "oil," "ruble"—to create domestic problems for Russian people.[84] In another cartoon, Yelkin depicted Russia's high-ranking officials thanking Obama for giving them the opportunity to lay the blame for all of Russia's problems at his door.[85]

The real argument against anti-Americanism became the number of Russians trying to emigrate to the US. This figure has never been higher than during the current crisis, according to State Department data.[86] Those leaving for the US are part of a broader exodus of Russians, especially those in academia and in sectors such as high technology, banking, and law. Clearly, images of the US as a land of freedom, democracy, and opportunities retain their place in the Russian consciousness.

Today's information society makes it impossible to cut off Russia with an iron curtain, to cut off the flow of people-to-people, academic, and cultural exchanges, and therefore the space for shaping the repertoire of images of the other country and people will be preserved. Even though many American studies programs in regional universities have been shut down, students demonstrate a stable interest in studying the US academically, something which serves to undermine simplified patterns of mutual perceptions. And as a Pew Research Center survey of June 2017 demonstrates, the appeal of US ideas and customs is strongest among Russia's youth.[87]

Conclusion

The Self–Other opposition remains at the core of the Russian public and political discourse set by texts—commentary, speeches, cartoons, published articles, and opinion pieces—on the US. The image of the American Other, whether the romantic image of the 1990s or the demonic one that came to replace it, has retained its constitutive

---

84   Sergei Yelkin, "Rossiia—pul't upravleniia," *Radio Svoboda*, 17 December 2015, https://www.svoboda.org/z/16979/2015/12/17.

85   Sergei Yelkin's cartoon at *Radio Svoboda*, 24 August 2016, http://www.svoboda.org/a/27943891.html.

86   "Rekordnoe chislo rossiian pozhelali emigrirovat' v SShA," *RBC* website, 16 October 2015, http://www.rbc.ru/politics/16/10/2015/5620d2ef9a79477e79b083c5.

87   Wike *et al.*, "U.S. Image Suffers."

role in the interplay of meanings that defines Russian nationalism and Russia's vision of its place in the world.

The crisis in Russian–American relations that began during Obama's second presidential term and Putin's third was reflected in the Russian official and public anti-American discourse through the opposition of two personified images, Obama's America and Putin's Russia. The "Obama brand" was used to promote the "Putin brand." Within this framework, the hopes that Russia placed in Trump led to a search for similarities between the two personified brands, since both leaders insisted on the "greatness" of their respective countries. At the same time, they pointed to different sources of national greatness—Putin's brand pointed to foreign policy, while Trump's pointed to domestic policy—and this complementarity created a certain space for cooperation. During the first months of Trump's presidency, the image of the US in Russia began to split into two parts: the friendly (pro-Russian) Trump and his supporters; and Trump's hostile (Russophobic) adversaries—the US Congress, the Democratic Party leaders, the press, the Washington bureaucracy, the Americans who voted for Hillary Clinton, and so on. Yet the same stable verbal and visual communicative strategies that were historically integrated into the Russian discourse about America were mobilized both to create the hostile Other image of Obama's America and the bipolar image of Trump's America.

One of these stable strategies of the Russian anti-American discourse is to turn the American presidents into complete opposites (as with Obama) or weak analogues (as with Trump) of the Russian leader (Putin): the American president is conceived as the dark twin of the Russian president. Another popular device is to contrast "fake" American liberal-universalist values (including the oft-mentioned tolerance for gender and sexual diversity) with "genuine" Russian traditional-conservative values. In this sense, Trump with his conservative rhetoric of intolerance accords quite well with the image of a friendly Other. The third typical strategy is to make use of crises, past and present, and thorny issues in US politics and history (from racial disturbances and political scandals to the "double standard" in US foreign policy and its failures) to emphasize that the American desire to school Russia in democracy and international law is ludicrous. This time-honored strategy, baptized as "whataboutism" during the Cold War, was first vividly used to draw parallels between the Jewish pogroms in the Russian Empire and the lynching of African Americans in the US at the turn of the twentieth century. Finally, the imagined reality of international relations can be constructed through references to elements of global popular culture, such as the *Star Wars* characters, that, ironically enough, are primarily of American origin. This device translates the patriotic discourse into the universal language of popular culture and thus makes it potentially attractive to the younger generations, who might otherwise be quite indifferent to it.

In Putin's Russia, the ground for anti-American sentiments remains fertile, while the tacit social contract between the rulers and the ruled is defined as prosperity and freedom in exchange for national greatness. According to a Pew Research Center poll, 87 percent of Russians support Putin precisely for his foreign policy and for the international status Russia has gained through it.[88] In any case, the American Other will hold on to its role in the Russian identity discourse. If the Trump administration has adopted policies that make the US appear less judgmental toward Russia's policies, Russians have seen it as their country's and Putin's personal victory. In the current situation the "fortress under siege" rhetoric continues to draw Russian citizens to rally around their president.

Moving forward, the perception of the US in Russia will be influenced by the situation in the US itself and primarily by the "Russian factor" in the political struggle between Democrats and Republicans. The large-scale foregrounding of the Russian Other in American public and political discourse has blown the discussion about the degree of Russia's influence on the 2016 presidential campaign out of all proportion. Any foreign meddling in the American electoral process undoubtedly merits the most thorough scrutiny and investigation. This is a true cyber-security challenge for that part of Russia connected to US national interests. The problem of

---

88   Margaret Vice, "Russians Remain Confident in Putin's Global Leadership," *Pew Research Center* website, 20 June 2017, http://www.pewglobal.org/2017/06/20/r ussians-remain-confident-in-putins-global-leadership/.

cyber-security has indeed become a crucial one in the bilateral relations, yet it does not cancel out the socio-political crisis in the US that became the principal cause of the unexpected outcome of the presidential elections. The popularity of such candidates as Bernie Sanders and Donald Trump is the best proof of this. The faster Trump's critics realize that he was not imposed on them from the outside, that his election resulted from domestic problems experienced by US society itself, the better the chances will be for an improvement in the situation for Americans, for Russians, and for their bilateral relations. Thus far, the situation in the US only supports the anti-American discourse in Russia.

To change the imagological climate (the current hierarchy of collective and personified images) and to decrease the heat of the information war between the two countries, it is necessary to stabilize Russian–US relations and to expand areas for selective cooperation. Achieving this goal is extremely difficult because of the anti-Trump consensus in the US (which is anti-Russian at the same time), the internal situation in Russia, the current lack of trust, and the loss of the containment culture in Russian–US relations, which is setting the framework for a "new Cold War" on both sides of the Atlantic.

The history of Russian–US relations testifies to the fact that the periods of rapprochement between Russia and the US and, accordingly, the rejection of simplified schemes of mutual understanding have always taken place during those times when Russia and the US have expanded the agenda of their relations out of a need to face a common enemy, address global challenges, and confront threats affecting both (as happened during the two world wars and the large-scale anti-terrorism campaign after the 9/11 terror attack). Such rapprochement has also happened in times of political reform or economic modernization in the Russian Empire, the Soviet Union, or post-Soviet Russia, when the US exported goods, capital, and technologies and Americans taught Russians the lessons of capitalism and reform. Unfortunately, neither of these situations is likely to present itself in the foreseeable future.

New Trends in the Museumification of the Soviet Past in Russia (2008–2018)[1]

Roman Abramov

Abstract: *This article offers a survey of the key tendencies observable in the museumification of the Soviet past in contemporary Russia, based on fieldwork and interviews with museum curators and other staff. The key focus is on aspects of the commodification of and nostalgia for the Soviet era. The article begins by examining repression and the Gulag as objects of museumification in Russia. Special attention is paid to the controversial situation when it comes to museumification of Stalin's repressions in the Russian context. The next part discusses museumification of the "Thaw" era and the growth in the number of exhibitions devoted to the late 1950s–early 1960s in Russian museums and art galleries, especially in 2016–2017. The Thaw era has begun to be re-imagined as an era defined primarily by upbeat interior design, optimism, "Soviet hipsters," and a generally positive mood. Nostalgia for the late Soviet period more broadly is becoming a noteworthy phenomenon in modern Russia. The last thirty years of the existence of the USSR are a key preoccupation unifying and driving the "folk museum" movement. This movement is non-expert in nature. Ordinary people are establishing thematic folk museums, and virtual nostalgic communities are devoted to the material world of the late Soviet period. The article goes on to examine patriotic trends in museumification. Museums and exhibitions played a significant role in military-patriotic education in the Soviet period. The Russian*

---

[1] The article was prepared within the framework of the Academic Fund Program at the National Research University Higher School of Economics (HSE) in 2017–2018 (grant 17-01-0058) and the Russian Academic Excellence Project "5-100." The article is part of a collaboration with Valentyna Kharkhun on the project "Museumification of the Soviet Past in Russia and Ukraine: From Historical Trauma to Nostalgia," conducted at the Kennan Institute, the Woodrow Wilson Center, Washington, D.C., in the spring of 2016.

Ministry of Defense today continues to support the major military museums and is also creating new ones, often with a strong interactive component. In the concluding part, the article analyzes how the growing influx of Chinese tourists in Russia is beginning to influence the forms of museum representation of the Soviet period. This tourism is also breathing new life into Soviet-style museums devoted to the biographies of the leaders of the Russian revolution. The phenomenon of "red tourism" that brings Chinese tourists to Russia forces us to rethink our understanding of the collective memory of communism in the context of global consumption and the mediatized mythologization of the past.

Modern museums function as repositories for the memory of the past. In that function they actively participate in the production of symbolic, ideological, and meaningful forms of collective memory, as well as offering significant resources for the construction of civil and national identities.[2] At the same time, museums are an important component of modernity, with all the contradictions and cultural conflicts that this entails. In this regard, a trip to a museum functions as a "civilizing ritual" for the ordinary visitor, and museum exhibitions are vital tools for influencing their visitors. Researchers have noted that museums can be conceived of as spaces that link the present day with the past. In this sense they function as storage facilities for memory and time that has hardened into concrete form.[3] Museums also work as sites of social memory and help form the common meanings behind perceptions of the past.[4] These meanings are often contested, and thus, museums can, on the one hand, become battlefields in "memory wars." On the other hand, they can be

2   Tony Bennett, *The Birth of the Museum: History, Theory, Politics* (London: Routledge, 1995); and Susan A. Crane (ed.), *Museums and Memory* (Stanford: Stanford University Press, 2000).
3   Andreas Huyssen, *Twilight Memories: Marking Time in a Culture of Amnesia* (New York: Routledge 1995); and Nick Prior, "Speed, Rhythm, and Time-Space: Museums and Cities," *Space and Culture* 14 (2011): 200–01.
4   John Urry, "How Societies Remember the Past," *Sociological Review* 43 (1996): 45–65; and Kirk Denton, *Exhibiting the Past: Historical Memory and the Politics of Museums in Postsocialist China* (Honolulu: University of Hawaii Press, 2014).

sites of historical amnesia, places where the uncomfortable pages of a country's history are "forgotten."

The museumification of the collective memory of the Soviet period in Russia differs markedly from that in other countries of the former USSR.[5] In the latter, we find examples of this part of history being both integrated and rejected. More often than not, historical policy in these countries concentrates on the "invention" of traditions in collective memory,[6] with the aim of serving the goal of nation building. This generally entails presenting the socialist past as a dead-end developmental pathway in the national historical story, one that was imposed on the country from without.[7] This option is not one that is available to Russia, however.

This article offers a survey of the key tendencies observable in the museumification of the Soviet past in Russia today. It is based on an empirical exploration of how the Soviet is represented in Russian museums, including through commodification and nostalgic portrayals of this era. As part of my research, I conducted fifteen interviews with curators and other staff in public and private museums dealing with the Soviet period. These interviews were supported by direct observation of thematic exhibitions in various museums.

In this article, I use the term "museumification" to refer to the process of collecting, categorizing, preserving, and exhibiting material and cultural artefacts, including with the aim of highlighting and characterizing the typical features of a given era that are embodied in the structure of everyday life.

Two arguments lie at the heart of this article. First, it would be a mistake to assume the dominance of any overall official version

---

5   On which see for example Kirsti Jõesalu and Nugin Raili, "Reproducing Identity through Remembering: Cultural Texts on the Late Soviet Period," *Electronic Journal of Folklore* 51 (2012): 15–49; and Paul Williams, "The Afterlife of Communist Statuary: Hungary's Szoborpark and Lithuania's Grutas Park," *Forum for Modern Language Studies* 44, no. 2 (2002): 185–98.

6   Eric Hobsbawm and Terence Ranger (eds.), *The Invention of Tradition* (Cambridge: Cambridge University Press, 1992).

7   Michael Bernhard and Jan Kubik (eds.), *Twenty Years after Communism: The Politics of Memory and Commemoration* (Oxford: Oxford University Press, 2014).

of Soviet history in Russian museums; such a view would be a crude simplification of the real situation. After all, it is not only the state or the Ministry of Culture that is able to construct narratives and organize exhibitions. There are also alternative initiatives that have an important influence on the museumification of the Soviet past, and various mnemonic communities in Russia have proved capable of producing their own visions of the Soviet period. In this article I focus on several cases that illustrate under-studied trends in the presentation of the Soviet in Russian museum exhibitions. These include the memory of the traumatic elements of communist history, the new patriotic wave in the folk museumification of the socialist past, and nostalgic immersion in the material world of the late Soviet period.

Repression and Gulag as Objects of Museumification in Russia

During perestroika and throughout the 1990s, the majority of Russian museum exhibits on the Soviet past served the aims of decommunization. Details of the Stalinist repressions were first included in expositions in the country's two largest historical museums, the Museum of the Contemporary History of Russia (Moscow) and the Museum of the Political History of Russia (St. Petersburg). In this study, I set out to examine how these and other museums have presented the Soviet past in the more recent period, from 2008 to 2018.

My examination of recent exhibits on Soviet history at the Museum of Russian Political History indicates that the curators consistently strive to maintain a balance between the negative and positive aspects of the Soviet past. They do not gloss over the tragic pages of the Soviet period; events such as the famine during collectivization, the Great Terror of the late 1930s, or the persecution of dissidents during the Khrushchev and Brezhnev eras are all presented in this museum. True, some negative events are noticeably absent. There is no mention, for example, of the massacres of Polish officers near Katyn and elsewhere in 1940, and there is little explanation of the Soviet role in crushing the Hungarian Revolution of 1956. However, overall, the authors of these exhibits cannot be

accused of airbrushing the tragedies of the Soviet past out of existence; they provide a relatively complex and balanced account of the
most important pages of Soviet history. One of the museum's employees explained during an interview that the museum actively
seeks to maintain this balance between the positive and the negative, showing the achievements of socialist construction alongside
evidence of the price that had to be paid for this progress in millions
of lives.[8]

Other museums in Russia have followed the example of these
leading museums, adding new displays on previously suppressed aspects of Soviet history over the past two decades.[9] Political repression, dekulakization, famine, and forced collectivization are shown
as the "dark side" of socialist construction; the gloomy underbelly of
Stalin's rule is exposed in many of the large museums of the country.[10] Smaller museums have also opened exhibits that refer to political repression. Many museums, however, have yet to make serious
changes to their Soviet-era exhibitions or to the concepts behind
them. For example, museums such as the Lenin Memorial in

[8] Author's interview with a research fellow at the Museum of the Political History
of Russia (St. Petersburg), June 2016.

[9] For example, exhibitions at the Saratov Regional Museum of Local History and
the National Museum of the Republic of Bashkortostan mainly follow the Soviet
logic of the periodization of the socialist period in the history of these Russian
regions but contain parts about the collectivization tragedy and the deportation
of the German population from the Volga region in the 1930s.

[10] The GULAG History Museum (Moscow), the Museum of the Contemporary
History of Russia (Moscow), the Museum of the Political History of Russia, Memorial Complex Political Repressions "Perm-36" (Perm region). More information about situation with the commemoration on political repressions in
Russian museums see: Valentina Bykova and Dmitrii Kokorin, "'Muzei sovesti'.
Istoriia repressii v muzeinykh ekspozitsiiakh," *Russkii zhurnal* 31 (October 2011),
http://www.russ.ru/pole/Muzei-sovesti-.-Istoriya-repressij-v-muzejnyh-ekspo
ziciyah.

Ul'ianovsk[11] and Lenin's dacha outside Moscow[12] both continue to serve as largely unaltered examples of the Soviet museum style. This inertia is largely the result of a shortage of funds. This is a vicious circle, since those museums which are unable to reinvent themselves as profit-making enterprises are unlikely to attract funding from the Ministry of Culture, at a time when museums are under growing pressure to increase their "efficiency" in neo-liberal terms.

Exhibits in Russia's larger historical museums often offer a long-view survey covering a variety of periods and topics. One typical result of this is that the traumatic experiences of the Soviet period become submerged and lost among the numerous display halls. For example, the dissident movement is often shown through portraits of the poet Aleksandr Galich or the scientist Andrei Sakharov, alongside interiors of kitchens of typical apartments of the 1960s, including a typewriter for samizdat amateur publishing.[13] However, while this symbolism is obvious to educated members of the older generation, it may not have the same resonance with younger people.

In addition to the exhibitions produced by the major museums, various mnemonic communities have made their own efforts to display the dark sides of the communist past in museum exhibits, leading to the founding of specialized museums. A large part of this activity revolves around preserving the memory of the Stalinist repressions and the gulag.[14] Until recently there were four such special museums: the Memory of Kolyma ("Pamyat' Kolymy," founded

---

[11]   At the site of the Lenin Memorial in Ul'ianovsk, there were plans to open a large museum complex dedicated to the whole history of the USSR. These plans, however, were shelved because of the post-2014 economic stagnation in Russia. The idea of creating a State Museum of the USSR on the base of the Lenin Memorial in Ul'ianovsk was discussed in the professional media; see "Proekt 'Muzei SSSR' v Ul'ianovske. Fakty i mneniia," *Muzei* 6 (2013): 26–29; and Mikhail Timofeev, "Muzeefikatsiia," *Labirint* 5 (2014): 25–33.

[12]   Gorki Leninskie, which is still an active museum, was the place of Lenin's last years and eventual death.

[13]   For example, this kind of visual presentation of the Thaw and Stagnation periods is in the Museum of Political History of Russia is available online; see virtual tour: http://tour.polithistory.ru/gallery/#293.

[14]   Ekaterina Postnaia, "Muzei istorii GULAGa kak otrazhenie travmaticheskogo opyta," *Interaktsiia. Interv'iu. Interpretatsiia* 12 (2016): 68–79.

1994);[15] the Memorial Center for the History of Political Repressions at Perm-36 (the largest museum in Russia to be located on the actual site of a former camp, it opened to visitors in 1996); the Gulag Museum in Moscow (established in 2001, in 2015 it was moved to upgraded quarters on 1-yi Samotechnyi pereulok); and the Memorial People's Museum of the History of the Gulag in Yoshkar-Ola (opened 2011).[16] Overall, there are more than 130 museums in Russia in which the theme of the repressions occupies a prominent place.[17]

The fate of the Perm–36 memorial complex is particularly complicated. This museum was created by regional historians and human rights activists who were actively supported by the Memorial society and well-known Russian intellectuals. The Perm regional authorities initially supported the creation and development of the museum, and by 2012 the museum had become world famous, and was regularly selected as a venue for international conferences and seminars. For a long time the museum retained its independent, non-state status and was Russia's only example of a large-scale memorial complex dedicated to Stalin's repressions.[18] The museum was organized according to the principle that certain sites of particularly tragic historical events should be preserved and used for commemorative and educational purposes. This kind of memorial activity is also animated by ethical principles around the notion of a duty to victims, and arguments about the connection between the handling of human rights violations of the past and the risk of repetition of similar events in the future. The creation of the Perm-36 museum thus represented the continuation of a tradition already established in similar museums across Eastern and Central Europe, such as the memorial complexes dedicated to Nazi crimes at the sites of the

---

[15]   http://lagerkolyma.narod.ru/muzey.htm.

[16]   For more detail on Museums of the Gulag, see Vladislav Staf, "Desiat' tezisov s lektsii 'Pamiat' o repressiiakh na postsovetskom prostranstve: muzei GULAGa,'" *Istoricheskaia pamiat': XX vek,* 26 April 2016, http://istpamyat.ru/diskussii-oce nka-novosti/desyat-tezisov-s-lekcii-pamyat-o-repressiyakh-na-postsovetskom-prostranstve-muzei-gulaga/.

[17]   *Ibid.*

[18]   The Katyn memorial complex (opened 2000) is another important example, but Perm-36 was the first large-scale museum complex to include the historical reconstruction of camp buildings and the everyday life of prisoners in Russia.

Auschwitz and Dachau concentration camps. The Perm–36 museum restored camp spaces, such as barracks, prison cells, and outbuildings, that were central to the camp's working. The exhibits contained information about the history of the museum, including information on famous dissidents who were prisoners of the camp in the post-Stalin Soviet era.

In 2012, a power struggle for control of the museum began. The new governor of Perm krai Viktor Basargin initiated a process to move the museum under state control. This offered a pretext to remove the Memorial society and the museum's creators from management positions in the museum. The regional Perm branch of the Communist Party demanded that the museum be closed on the grounds that it "discredited the Soviet past." In 2014 a new autonomous state cultural institution, the Memorial Complex of Political Repression was established at the site, and in this way the museum was placed under state control. The history of Perm-36 is still unfolding, and it is difficult to say whether the pressure on the museum is purely politically motivated or whether there are also commercial interests at play.

Moscow's Gulag Museum was founded in 2001 by Anton Antonov-Ovseyenko, the son of revolutionaries who fell victim to the Stalinist repressions of the 1930s. Having received the status of a state museum (GULAG History State Museum),[19] it reopened in 2004 and in 2015 was moved to a new large building in the center of Moscow. The exhibition area was quadrupled in size, and the museum became an important research and educational center, with its own library and bookstore.[20] The design of the museum inherits the symbolic concept common to museums that commemorate trauma: the visitor is immersed in the gloomy atmosphere of Stalin's terror and receives basic information from photographs, graphs, and exhibit labels describing in detail the terrible routine of Stalin's camps. A special and important place is occupied by testimonies

---

[19]   The Museum was assigned the status of state museum in 2001 by special decree (#702-PP) of the Moscow city government.

[20]   In the museum bookstore one can, for example, buy new academic research on the history of the gulag, such as Galina M. Ivanova, *Istoriia GULAGa: 1918–1958* (Moscow: ROSSPEN, 2015).

from the victims of Stalin's camps; here the dry statistics of mass terror are contrasted with the personal tragedies that shattered the lives of individual people.

It is difficult within the confines of a short article to offer a full characterization of how political repression and the history of the gulag are presented in Russian museums. The scholars Yevgenii Shtorn and Dar'ia Buteiko have provided a more complete picture of this.[21] They underline the contradictory nature of the memory of this history, especially in the mass media, where the accent is on achievements and victory in the Great Patriotic War. The Stalinist repressions, meanwhile, tend to be "normalized"; they are referred to as an ordinary event whose history has been established and does not require additional attention. Much of the history of political repression and the gulag is still in need of further disclosures and more comprehensive museumification.

The contradictions of Russian collective memory have also made their way out onto the streets of cities. On the one hand, we have the initiative led by prominent Russian journalist Sergei Parkhomenko, "The Last Address" project.[22] This project involves affixing modest memorial plaques with the names and biographical information of people who were killed in the course of repressions to the buildings in which they lived prior to their arrest. The key principle behind this project is that remembering past victims can become a civic act in the present and can also help build new communities grounded in a strong sense of place and history. On the other hand, private museums of Stalin have appeared in Russia, and busts of Stalin are being commissioned at the initiative of some local communities.[23] Thus, disputes about Stalin's role in the history of the country are still very much alive today.

---

[21]   Evgenii Shtorn and Dar'ia Buteiko, "Bor'ba za ogranichennoe prostranstvo pamiati na Solovkakh," *Neprikosnovennyi zapas* 4 (2016).

[22]   https://www.poslednyadres.ru.

[23]   For example, a "Stalin Center" was established in Penza city in 2015. The main idea of this center is the development of "Stalin studies" and the positive commemoration of Stalin as the "efficient manager" of the USSR. This center was established at the initiative of the regional branch of the Russian communist party (KPRF); "V Penze otkryli pervyi v mire stalinskii tsentr," *Penzenskoe oblastnoe otdelenie* KPRF website, 21 December 2015, http://kprfpenza.ru/news/

The "Thaw" Exhibit Boom in Russian Museums (2016–2017)

The post-Stalin period of the mid-1950s–early 1960s is commonly referred to as the "Thaw," after the changes in the political, social, and economic life of the country following the relative liberalization occurring in various spheres of life during this period. The period also featured improved living standards and a flowering of the arts against a backdrop of impressive success in scientific and industrial development. This period has always been popular with the Russian intelligentsia and has often been romanticized.[24]

In recent years, a new stage in the media and museum representation of this period has begun that can be described as "hipster" in style, as it is based on the principles of what Simon Reynolds has called "retromania."[25] In this style the design features and external manifestations of an era are viewed as being more important than their political and social content: the young generation enjoys the material and aesthetic spirit of the "Soviet sixties" and is not much interested in the serious events of those times, or even in the global crises of the period such as the "Caribbean crisis" (the Soviet label for the Cuban Missile Crisis) of 1962. The Thaw era has lately begun to be positioned as an era of upbeat interior design, influenced by the optimism of "Soviet hipsters" and the general positive mood of the society. Even the Hungarian revolution of 1956, the shooting of workers in Novocherkassk in 1962, and the continuation of selective political repression have not dulled this positive image of the Thaw era, despite the fact that these events suggest serious limitations in the Soviet ideology and model of governance at the time.

One visible manifestation of this new turn in presenting the Thaw era can be found on Russian television. In recent years, several

---

v_penze_otkryli_pervyj_v_mire_stalinskij_centr/2015-12-21-891. By 2018 around three dozen busts of Stalin had been unveiled in several regions of Russia. All of them have an informal status and they are often located on private land; see "Pamiatnik Stalinu otkryli v Rostovskoi oblasti," *1Rnd.ru*, 21 December 2016, https://www.1rnd.ru/news/1486031.

24   See for example Petr Vail' and Aleksandr Genis, *Mir sovetskogo cheloveka* (Moskva: AST, Corpus, 2013).

25   Simon Reynolds, *Retromania: Pop Culture's Addition to Its Own Past* (London: Faber and Faber, 2011).

programs have appeared that place special emphasis on a nostalgic glamorization of Soviet Thaw-era interiors and fashion design. These include a number of mini-series screened on primetime federal television: *The Thaw* (Pervyi kanal, premiere December 2013); *The Black Marketeer* (Pervyi kanal, premiere March 2015); *The Mysterious Passion* (Pervyi kanal, premiere January 2017); and *The Optimists* (Rossiia-1, premiere Spring 2017). These TV series have altered the way this era is perceived, encouraging the sense of a youthful age saturated with original designer gizmos and fashionable space-age design.

This trend was picked up by Russian museums and galleries in 2016–2017, when the Museum of Moscow and the Tretiakov Gallery on Krymskii Val in particular devoted key exhibits to the Thaw period. In early 2017 the Museum of Moscow hosted an exhibition titled *The Moscow Thaw: 1953–1968*.[26] This was accompanied by a series of public lectures on the history of the Thaw era that shed light on contemporary perceptions of the Thaw as a time when the winds of change blew away the stale air of repression and wiped out the totalitarian idiocy of the Stalin period. The exhibition received wide publicity in printed and online media and attracted many visitors, both old and young. The organizers[27] of the exhibition offered their own vision of this time, expressed in the main spatial metaphor of the exhibition—simple white wooden frames, which separate the various parts of the exhibit.[28] These lightweight, prefabricated wooden structures, and the repeatability and identical dimensions of each cell in the exhibit, symbolize the absence of cultural and symbolic hierarchies in this historical period. The curators explained the reasoning behind the design as follows: "Defining concepts for the Thaw such as 'mobility,' 'structure,' 'capsule,' and 'rhythm' are reflected in the spatial solution—the exposition was divided into the corresponding semantic blocks."[29] The curators set

---

26   See http://mosmuseum.ru/exhibitions/p/moskovskaya-ottepel-1953-1968/.
27   The curators of this exhibition are Yevgeniia Kikodze, Aleksandra Selivanova, Sergei Nevskii, Maksim Semenov, and Ol'ga Rozenblium. See *ibid.*
28   For images of these, see *ibid.*
29   See an official summary of this exhibition, at http://mosmuseum.ru/exhibitions/p/moskovskaya-ottepel-1953-1968/.

out to show that the change of fashion in clothing and apartment interiors was no less important than the temporary lifting of censorship in literature and art. The organization of space, with its wooden rafters, also suggests the metaphor of a construction site, a reference to the massive wave of residential and civil construction, based on the new principles of industrialism, which became symbolic of the era and reshaped people's lives in important ways.

At the entrance, the visitor was greeted by a huge timeline that offered a chronology of the main events of the Thaw period. As my embedded observation on the exhibition showed, this was designed to show the complexity and inconsistency of the period, where the lighter and more tragic pages of this time could coexist at different levels and in different spheres of life. The visual basis of the exhibition was the material and symbolic world of the Thaw, represented by film images, everyday objects, paintings, and fashionable clothing of the time. The exhibition curators and consultants showed their love for the style of the Thaw, which was reflected in bold experimentation in various spheres: in the "new wave" of Soviet cinema, in ceramics of unusual color and shape, in the futuristic design of watches and radios, in the "harsh style" employed by artists of the time, and also in the creative work of scientists in physics and cybernetics. However, behind this bright nostalgia lurk the darker aspects of the period, such as the beginning of the persecution of the dissident movement, economic voluntarism resulting in goods shortages, and increasingly dangerous escalations in the Cold War, when nuclear tests, the shooting down of the American U-2 spyplane, and the Berlin and Cuban crises pushed the world to the brink of a third world war. The organizers of the exhibition do not avoid this other side of the Thaw; they provide references to the Soviet nuclear program, the trial of Brodsky, samizdat, and unofficial art.

A significant motif running through the exposition was the concept of emptiness, interpreted as both a wide-open space for the new architecture and the light of the Thaw era's visual arts. This emptiness can also be understood as the beginning of social and cultural bankruptcy.[30] References of this kind were rather subtle, however, and in general, those aspects of the exhibition suggestive of the shadow sides of the Thaw period would be recognizable only to a trained eye or the particularly well-informed visitor. Perhaps this is fitting, given that this was a period that combined the anticipation of freedom and the enthusiasm of youth with scientific and technological progress, thus opening the pathway to space and allowing the average person to purchase plastic buckets and transistor radios.

In February 2017 the Tretiakov Gallery on Krymskii Val opened its own exhibition titled *Thaw*.[31] Stylistically similar to the Museum of Moscow exhibit, this work also primarily draws attention to the visual side of the Thaw period. The exposition presents textile samples with abstract patterns, the design of household devices of the time, examples of interior design projects for the period's modern housing, and many examples of Thaw-era artwork, much of which reflects the optimism of the period. A notable place is given to the romance of distant travel, the exploration of Siberia and the Far East, and the successes of Soviet science. Again, this does not mean that the curators of the exhibition avoid talking about the Thaw period's difficult moments, such as the mass protests in Georgia and Novocherkassk, renewed persecutions of dissidents, or increasing economic difficulties. Information about all these events is presented on explanatory tablets and stands. Overall, however, it is the visual emphasis that prevails, and thus the main impression produced is one of nostalgic romanticization of the period and enjoyment of the associated objects and images.[32] It seems likely that it is predominantly in this manner, through the prism of television programs and fashion items from the 1950s and '60s, that

---

30   The new wave Soviet film director Marlen Khutsiev detected these symptoms in his famous film *July Rain* (1966), which reflected much of the melancholy and alienation felt by the end of this period, emotions that would become the central mood of the coming stagnation era.

31   See "'Ottepel': novaia vystavka Tret'akovskoi galerei na Krymskom valu," *Elle.ru*, 9 February 2017, http://www.elle.ru/stil-zhizni/events/ottepel-novaya-vyistavk a-tretyakovskoy-galerei-na-kryimskom-valu/.

32   Arnold-de Simine Silke, *Mediating Memory in the Museum: Trauma, Empathy, Nostalgia* (New York: Palgrave Macmillan, 2013).

the image of the Thaw will be offered to visitors in museums. In this way, the era will be presented as a time that, despite its contradictory and transient nature, can be remembered for its achievements and optimism, its success in awakening the country from the dark days of Stalinism.

The Museumification of the "Stagnation" Era: The Vintage Spirit of the Soviet

Over the past seven years, I have been studying nostalgia for the late Soviet period,[33] a phenomenon which has spread throughout Russia among multiple generations, including young people.[34] It is important to note that this is nostalgia not for the "carnivorous" Stalinist regime, but for the "vegetarian" Brezhnev era of the 1960s and 1970s. Furthermore, rather than reflecting any demand for a return to "real socialism," this is a mythological nostalgia for stability and warm, friendly interpersonal relations—a nostalgia for authenticity. We can also interpret this nostalgia as an attempt to heal the trauma of the economic and political chaos experienced in the 1990s.

We know that, in recent decades, the countries of Eastern and Central Europe have been actively dissociating themselves from the communist past, officially presenting it as a traumatic experience caused by external occupation. However, studies have shown that spontaneous nostalgia for the socialist past exists even in countries that suffered from Soviet military intervention, such as the Czech

---

33   In the context of this article I define this period as lasting from the late years of the Khrushchev period to the start of the Gorbachev epoch. A definition of the "late Soviet period" can be found here: Neringa Klumbytė and Gulnaz Sharafutdinova, "Introduction: What Was Late Socialism," in *Soviet Society in the Era of Late Socialism, 1964–1985,* eds. Neringa Klumbytė and Gulnaz Sharafutdinova (Plymouth: Lexington Books, 2015), 1–15.

34   Roman Abramov, "Vremia i prostranstvo nostal'gii," *Sotsiologicheskii zhurnal* 4 (2012): 5–23; "Muzeefikatsiia sovetskogo: mezhdu barakholkoi i vintazhnym salonom," *Muzei (Rossiiskii partner Zhurnala Museum International)* 6 (2013): 4–8; "Reprezentatsii sovetskogo v rossiiskoi blogosfere: Sotsiologicheskii vzgliad," *Vestnik Udmurtskogo Universiteta* 3, no. 1 (2011): 40–48; and "Analiticheskii otchet po sotsiologicheskomu issledovaniiu v ramkakh doklada Vol'nogo istoricheskogo obshchestva 'Kakoe proshloe nuzhno budushchemu Rossii?'" (Moscow: Komitet grazhdanskikh initsiativ, 2017).

Republic, Slovakia, and Hungary. The most famous example of this is "Ostalgie," an ironic nostalgia for the material world of the socialist past that spread in the eastern part of Germany.[35] There is also a version of this in the countries of the former Yugoslavia, called "Yugonostalgia."[36] These types of nostalgia also have their own forms of museumification.[37]

In Russia, the nostalgia for the last thirty years of the existence of the USSR has become a unifying element in the "folk museumification" *(narodnaia muzeefikatsiia)* movement. The folk museumification movement is non-expert in nature. Ordinary people, such as entrepreneurs, designers, or journalists, are at the vanguard as initiators and activists, rather than professional historians or experts in cultural affairs. These enthusiasts are inspired by nostalgic sentiment and, in part, stand in opposition to "official history." Many of them are of the opinion that professional historians neglect and overlook the important details of daily life in the recent past. This is because historians are more concerned with major historical events and politics than with recreating and archiving the "narrative truth" about that time. Thus, folk museumification is an alternative to

---

[35]   Daphne Berdahl, "'(N)Ostalgie' for the Present: Memory, Longing, and East German Things," *Ethnos: Journal of Anthropology* 64, no. 1 (1999): 192–211; Paul Betts, "Remembrance of Things Past: Nostalgia in West and East Germany, 1980–2000," in *Pain and Prosperity: Reconsidering Twentieth-Century German History*, eds. Paul Betts and Greg Eghigian (Stanford: Stanford University Press, 2003), 178–207; Martin Blum, "Club Cola and Co.: Ostalgie, Material Culture and Identity," in *Transformation of the New Germany*, ed. Ruth A. Starkman (New York: Palgrave, 2006).

[36]   Claire Bancroft, "Yugonostalgia: The Pain of the Present," *ISP Collection*, Paper 787 (2009), http://digitalcollections.sit.edu/isp_collection/787); Tanja Petrovic, "Nostalgia for the JNA? Remembering the Army in the Former Yugoslavia," in Todorova and Gille (eds.), *Post-communist Nostalgia*, eds. M. Todorova and Z. Gille (New York: Berghahn Books, 2010), 61–81; Mitja Velikonja, *Titostalgia: A Study of Nostalgia for Josip Broz* (Ljubljana: Mirovni Institut, 2008); and Mitja Velikonja, "Lost in Transition: Nostalgia for Socialism in Post-socialist Countries," *East European Politics and Societies* 4 (2009): 535–51.

[37]   Arnold-de Simine Silke, *Mediating Memory in the Museum: Trauma, Empathy, Nostalgia* (New York: Palgrave Macmillan, 2013); Mitja Velikonja, *Titostalgia: A Study of Nostalgia for Josip Bros* (Ljubljana: Mirovni Institut, 2008); and Mitja Velikonja, "Lost in Transition: Nostalgia for Socialism in Post-socialist Countries," *East European Politics and Societies* 4 (2009): 535–51.

professional "mnemonic communities,"[38] which are based on documents and historical facts. Instead, this folk version of museumification is closely related to the personal memory that members of "the last Soviet generation" still have of their childhood and youth.[39]

Remarkable examples of the folk museumification of the USSR include the Museum of Soviet Arcade Machines in Moscow (which opened in 2009 at Baumanskaia Metro station, later moving to Kuznetskii Most station);[40] the Museum of Socialist Life in Kazan (opened 2011 in a former communal apartment, official slogan "Welcome to the world of positive emotions!");[41] the Museum of the Life of Soviet Scientists in Moscow (opened 2010–2011 in the Metro station of Shchukino);[42] the Museum of the USSR at VDNKh (opened 2012–2014 in the VDNKh Exhibition Center);[43] the Museum of Industrial Culture in Moscow (opened 2010 at Kuzminki Metro station);[44] the Art Commune (opened 2011 in Kolomna, Moscow oblast);[45] the Museum of Soviet Life (opened 2010–2011 in Voronezh);[46] the Museum of the USSR (opened 2009 in Novosibirsk);[47] the Museum-Restaurant "Time Apartment" *(Kvartira Vremeni)* (opened 2015–2016 in Moscow, on the Arbat);[48] the Museum of the Soviet Era (opened 2017 in St. Petersburg);[49] and finally, in a more professional form, the Moscow Design Museum in the Moscow Manege, which

---

38   Eviatar Zerubavel, *Time Maps: Collective Memory and the Social Shape of the Past* (Chicago, IL: University of Chicago Press, 2003).

39   On the connections between remembering childhood and the emotional nostalgic mood, see Maurice Halbwachs, *On Collective Memory* (Chicago, IL: University of Chicago Press, 1992).

40   *Muzei sovetskikh igrovykh avtomatov:* http://www.15kop.ru/.

41   *Muzei sotsialisticheskogo byta:* http://muzeisb.ru/.

42   *Muzei byta sovetskikh uchenykh:* http://moscowwalks.ru/2012/04/13/kurchatnik-museum/.

43   *Muzei SSSR na VDNKh:* http://moscowwalks.ru/2013/01/24/muzei-sssr-vvc-moskva/.

44   *Muzei industrial'noi kul'tury:* https://museum-ic.ru/.

45   *Art kommunalka:* https://artkommunalka.com/ru/content/fotogalereya.

46   *Muzei sovetskogo byta:* http://anechaev.org/2013/12/musei_sovetskogo_bita/.

47   *Muzei SSSR:* http://mesto54.ru/places/muzej-sssr.

48   *Muzei "Kvartira vremeni":* http://www.anothercity.ru/places/museums/9717-flat-of-time.

49   *Muzei sovetskoi epokhi:* https://www.muzeyussr.ru/.

offers exhibits on Soviet design and Soviet packaging styles from 1950 to 1980.[50]

All these museums are active projects that attract the attention of visitors and media. The key intention of the organizers and curators of projects is not the factualization of the past but the achievement of a nostalgic mythologization through the use of what Svetlana Boym has termed "reflexive nostalgia."[51] Reflexive nostalgia realizes its own ephemeral nature, and its historicity speaks about the impossibility of returning to the past. It involves an affective and ethical comprehension of the past and is sometimes associated with a feeling of bitter irony.

These museums target audiences of two kinds. First, they target those who crave immersion in the material surroundings of their childhood and youth, allowing them to share their memories with their children. Second, they target the younger generation, for whom the "Soviet" appears strange and alien, its artefacts attractive precisely because they come from a lost civilization. For example, in Russia a special genre in electronic music, sometimes known as the "Soviet wave," has recently appeared. It uses musical samples and visual images from the late Soviet period and transforms this material under the influence of the new electronic music. The musicians are young people who were born after the collapse of the USSR but who are attracted by the "Soviet" style.[52]

Folk museum curators and staff workers are amateurs who have been seduced by the Soviet material world. Many of them are avid collectors, and they strive to share with the public the wealth of material they have accumulated. Therefore, almost all the folk museums of Soviet everyday life resemble huge junk shops or flea markets filled with various bric-à-brac from the era, from school notebooks and tear-off calendars to full-size automobiles. Critics of the Soviet way of life often accused the material world of the USSR of lacking color and quality items. The exhibits on display in these

---

[50]   *Moskovskii muzei dizaina:* http://moscowdesignmuseum.ru/.
[51]   Svetlana Boym, *The Future of Nostalgia* (New York: Basic Books, 2001).
[52]   Alec Luhn, "Russia's Musical New Wave Embraces Soviet Chic," *The Guardian*, 29 July 2015, https://www.theguardian.com/world/2015/jul/29/russias-musical-new-wave-embraces-soviet-chic.

folk museums, however, directly challenge this thesis. The visitor is both impressed and surprised by the abundance and variety of things on display, both in terms of their originality and in terms of the design and quality of the materials.

In 2017 I interviewed the organizers of most of the museums listed above, and many of them stressed that their nostalgia is not political in nature: what is important for them is to showcase the material world of their childhood and youth, rather than to urge people to return to the social or political order of the Soviet period. As Aleksandr Stakhanov put it in a 2009 media interview:

> With our Museum of Soviet Arcade Machines, we are striving to make a certain kind of museum of childhood. My dream is to have a museum in which various aspects of childhood are collected, such as toys, furniture, clothing, some related items, and food. The site, which acts as a time machine, say for example, a father who has come with his child to our museum will, after a short time, also become a child, if only for an hour or two.[53]

Folk museum activists generally appreciate the impossibility of any such return to the Soviet. Only one of the people I interviewed from these folk museums took the position of favouring such a return, making negative references to the contemporary political system and economic set-up and positively assessing the role of Stalin in Russian history.[54]

The material abundance of these Soviet folk museums, with their non-systematically stored collections of objects and the naïve, one-dimensional interpretation of this period as trouble-free, testify to the subconscious ambiguity behind this "narrative template"[55] regarding the period of the 1960s–'80s. The sacralization and symbolization of the material world of that epoch have not taken place, first, because many of the objects on display are in daily circulation

---

53   Egor Vasil'kov, "'My khotim, chtoby vzroslye liudi igrali...,'" *Chastnyi korrespondent*, 6 August 2009, http://www.chaskor.ru/p.php?id=9091.

54   This interviewee's response was: "I am a Stalinist, I will not let the Stalin era be insulted. Stalin came to a peasant country and turned it into a space country and a country with atomic weapons;" author's interview with a folk museum organizer, 2017.

55   James V. Wertsch, "Collective Memory and Collective Identity," *Social Research* 75, no. 1 (2008): 133–56.

and are not generally considered to be "worthy of a museum," and second, because the creators of state museums do not usually attempt to present these objects as offering evidence of what the period was like. Yet, as one folk museum organizer put it in an interview about the role of material culture in the remembering of the Soviet past:

> There's a trend now where people are trying to remember the Soviet past. Many visitors see the exhibits and tell us: we had a kerosene lamp like that at the dacha, my grandmother owned a sewing machine, my family bought a "Rekord" TV on credit. Visitors remember not political events, but their past everyday life.[56]

Is a school uniform an illustration of the totalitarian nature of the Soviet regime, or a celebration of a model of the "welfare state"? The thematic folk museums and the virtual nostalgia communities discussed here can be viewed as amateur-style attempts to offer a kind of therapy that is designed not only to restore the illusions of the past but also to cope with a present that deviates from the past in many significant ways. This dimension to the new folk museums is encapsulated in a comment by one of my interviewees:

> The entire Soviet world is collected in our museum: from space gadgets to a simple pen. The USSR was such a large country in which all people lived in peace and harmony. Probably there were conflicts between different ethnic groups, but I don't know. My relatives lived in Ukraine. We lost touch in the 1990s. It was so sad. I don't understand what's happening now.[57]

New Patriotism and Interactive Forms in the Museumification of the Soviet

Museums and exhibitions played a significant role in military-patriotic education in the Soviet period. Almost every Soviet museum had a section dedicated to the feats of Red Army soldiers and home front workers during the Great Patriotic War (1941–45). Even in small school museums, exhibiting the work of local schoolchildren

---

[56]   Author's interview with a folk museum organizer, 2017.
[57]   Ibid.

and teachers, we find exhibits and documents related to local war veterans or wartime events that occurred in the area. Today, the Ministry of Defense continues to support those large museum centers which have survived the transition. These include the Central Armed Forces Museum (Moscow)[58] and the Military Historical Museum of Artillery, Engineers, and Signal Corps (St. Petersburg).[59]

In the 1990s the theme of military-patriotic education faded into the background. Consequently, these museums suffered from a lack of funding, and for a long time, no new exhibits were produced. This coincided with a noticeable decline in interest in such museums among the population. The situation began to change under the influence of new state policies in the years 2007–2009, a time when there was a noticeable growth in Russian military power and when the modernization of the Russian army was announced as an important state priority.[60] As the state needed to upgrade the public image of the army and attract active young people into the army service, a new focus on victory in World War II was noticeable. This event was now treated as the central element of a new patriotic ideology, with annual military parades dedicated to this victory returning on a grand scale to demonstrate the revival of the Russian army after the crisis of the 1990s.[61]

[58]   *Tsentral'nyi muzei voennykh sil:* http://www.cmaf.ru/.

[59]   *Voenno-istoricheskii muzei artilerii, inzhenernykh voisk i voisk sviazi:* http://www.artillery-museum.ru/. In the late Soviet period, one long-term construction project was the Victory Park memorial complex on Poklonnaia Hill, which opened only in the 1990s. For details, see Aleksandrina Vanke, "Landshafty pamiati: Park Pobedy na Poklonnoi gore v Moskve," *Neprikosnovennyi zapas* 101, no. 3 (2015): 110–15.

[60]   Aleksandr Gol'ts, "Armiia chetvertogo sroka. Pochemu Putin poshel na reformy Vooruzhennykh sil i pochemu sam ot reform otkazalsia," *The New Times*, 4 May 2018, https://newtimes.ru/articles/detail/161195.

[61]   See Markku Kangaspuro, "The Victory Day in History Politics," in *Between Utopia and Apocalypse: Essays on Social Theory and Russia*, ed. Elina Kahla (Helsinki: Aleksanteri Series, 2011), 292–305; Sergey Oushakine, "Remembering in Public: On the Affective Management of History," *Ab Imperio* 1 (2015): 269–302; and Judy Brown, "Great Patriotic War Memory in Sevastopol: Making Sense of Suffering in the 'City of Military Glory,'" in *War and Memory in Russia, Ukraine and Belarus*. ed. Julie Fedor, Markku Kangaspuro, Jussi Lassila, Tatiana Zhurzhenko (New York: Palgrave MacMillan, 2017), 399–429.

In November 2012, Sergei Shoigu, an experienced politician and an emergency response specialist, took up the post of Minister of Defense. He continued the drive to modernize the army, combining this with work aimed at updating and improving the public image of the Russian armed forces. In 2005 the Ministry of Defense launched its own special TV channel, *Zvezda* (Star).[62] Under Shoigu, this channel has come to play an important role in military patriotic education.

Shoigu also breathed fresh life into two large memorial museum projects. First, construction work was begun on a Federal War Memorial Cemetery, a memorial that will be similar to Arlington Cemetery in Washington, D.C. Located near Moscow, the cemetery is host to the remains of Russia's military heroes. Initially this project was conceived of during the Soviet era, but because of insufficient funding, it was resumed only in 2001. In 2013 the first burial was carried out: the remains of the Unknown Soldier, killed during the Great Patriotic War in Smolensk oblast', were buried at the cemetery.[63]

Second, Shoigu initiated the construction of a large historical and entertainment complex, also in the Moscow suburbs, aimed at the military-patriotic education of youth.[64] This is Patriot Park, a theme park based around the equipment of the Russian army, which officially opened on 16 June 2015. The main thrust of the park is to create a new language and style in transmitting information about the Russian army. The material is related to the history of the Russian army and has been seen in a more positive way by the younger generation. The essence of the park's concept is the intensive use of

---

[62]   https://tvzvezda.ru/.

[63]   See Mischa Gabowitsch, "Russia's Arlington? The Federal Military Memorial Cemetery near Moscow," *Journal of Soviet and Post-Soviet Politics and Society* 2, no. 2 (2016): 89–145.

[64]   Shoigu visits this park regularly. For example, in January 2016 he opened the "Partisan Village" installation in the park; "Sergei Shoigu otkryl 'Partizanskuiu derevniu' v parke 'Patriot'," *360tv.ru*, 13 January 2016, https://360tv.ru/news/obschestvo/sergej-shojgu-otkryl-partizanskuyu-derevnyu-v-parke-patriot-44088/. See also Aleksandr Boiko, "Sergei Shoigu i Andrei Vorob'ev zalozhili park 'Patriot,'" *Komsomol'skaia pravda*, 9 June 2014, https://www.msk.kp.ru/daily/26241.5/3122766/?share.target.id=808824&share.target.class=4.

interactive games to represent history and involve visitors in the events of the past as participants. As Shoigu put it, "We will make a project that will enable young people not only to look at the exhibits, but also to go for a ride, to fly using military equipment, to shoot from combat weapons, to jump with a parachute."[65]

The idea at the heart of this complex was inspired by several circumstances. The project was modeled on a successful project launched in Belarus and dedicated to Stalin-era military fortifications (the open-air complex Stalin Line); it offers reconstructions of various battles of World War II and museum exhibits showcasing military equipment from various periods.[66] The park appears to be a kind of "military-patriotic Disneyland," a format that turns out to be particularly attractive for young people and children. A number of military historical reconstruction clubs have sprung up in Russia, while interest in military equipment and the armaments of the past is growing among young people and the active part of the male population.[67] For these people, the chance to "participate" in the reconstruction of army life and even in combat re-enactment is thus an attractive form of game museumification. This brings us to a third means of updating the image of the Russian army, through interactive computer games on military topics, such as the World of Tanks.[68] Playing these games is a popular pastime for many Russian boys and young men and stimulates an interest in the history of battles, uniforms, weaponry, and military equipment, especially from the World War II period. Computer games build an interest in

---

65   Cited in *ibid.*

66   Sergey Oushakine, "Subalternation: On Postcolonial Histories of Socialism," manuscript, 2017.

67   Take, for example, the large-scale festival run by the "Times and Era" reenactors (June 2017, Moscow). This was attended by no fewer than ten thousand participants. It is characteristic that on the Day of Russia celebrations (12 June) on Tverskaia Street in Moscow, clashes occurred between the police and opposition supporters.

68   Natalia Maslenkova, "Komp'iuternaia igra kak mekhanizm konstruirovaniia kul'turnoi pamiati (na primere 'World of tanks')," *Vestnik Volgogradskogo Gosudarstvennogo Universiteta*, ser. 7, *Filosofiia. Sotsiologiia i Sotsial'nye Tekhnologii* 3 (2014): 116–25.

interactivity, and therefore there is a demand for new innovative forms when presenting military history in museums.[69]

Patriot Park offers solutions to these problems. It offers mock-ups of real military installations, including trenches, aircraft shelters, tents, partisan camps, and even a model of the Reichstag that was stormed by soldiers of the Red Army in 1945. Guides and other staff at the complex are dressed in authentic World War II-era Red Army uniforms. Some of them also wear the new, re-vamped uniform of the Russian army today, which was unveiled to the world during the events in Crimea in 2014.[70] This offers visitors the chance to feel what it would be like to be a Soviet soldier during World War II or a soldier in today's modern army. Visitors can sit in trenches, eat porridge made in the camp kitchen, hold real rifles in their hands, and try on military uniforms from different periods. The aim of creating an interactive history that promotes participation among the general public in museumification is thus achieved. This helps foster pride in military victories and creates a great deal of positive publicity for the modern Russian army.

It should be emphasized that this strategy aimed at the interactive museumification of the military past is not unique to the Russian government or to Defense Minister Shoigu. The US army faced a similar crisis in improving its negative public image in the 1970s, a crisis brought on by a series of defeats and losses during the Vietnam War. In the 1980s the public relations department of the US military developed programs aimed at rehabilitating and improving the image of the US Army, a goal that was partly achieved by increasing interest in the country's military history.[71] In April–July 2016, I visited a number of museums in Washington, DC devoted to US military history, including the National Guard Museum, the Museum of

---

[69] In one well-known computer game, the World of Tanks, over one million players from Russia registered to play.

[70] https://patriotp.ru/obekty/tsentr-voenno-taktich/.

[71] James N. Dertouzos and Steven Garber, "Effectiveness of Advertising in Different Media: The Case of U.S. Army Recruiting," *Journal of Advertising* 35, no. 2 (2006): 111–22; and David C. King and Zachary Karabell, *The Generation of Trust: Public Confidence in the U.S. Military Since Vietnam* (Washington, DC: The AEI Press, 2003).

American History, and the Museum of Aeronautics. The exhibits on display in those museums all feature patriotic content and position the American army as the elite of society, acting in the interests of democracy and the country.[72] Even challenging and contradictory pages of military history, such as the Vietnam War or the 1970 Kent State incident, are presented as tragic but important and even heroic events in the life of the US Army and the National Guard. Ordinary soldiers and officers are portrayed in the exhibits as beyond suspicion of wrongdoing, and visitors are encouraged to focus on the heroic stories of their personal destinies. For example, the Museum of American History details the heavy proportion of American soldiers and pilots who were captured by the Vietcong. In the museumification of US military history, the promotion of patriotism is also actively pursued. The Russian Ministry of Defense under the leadership of Sergei Shoigu would appear to have adopted the "American" approach to the museumification of Russian military history and uses proactive methods of commercial advertising to promote a new image of the Russian army, including a special line of active wear recently launched under the brand of the Russian army.

"Red Tourism" and Cross-Country Hybridization in the Museumification of the Soviet

If you take the night train running between St. Petersburg and Moscow, there is a high chance of being surrounded by groups of Chinese tourists, who fill the cheaper carriages on this route. The growing flood of Chinese tourists into Russia is beginning to influence the forms of museum representation of the Soviet period,[73] as

---

72   See for example the National Guard Memorial Museum (https://www.ngef.org/national-guard-memorial-museum/) and parts of the National Museum of American History devoted to the contemporary history of the US army's participation in international conflicts.

73   "According to the tourist organization World Without Borders, in the first nine months of 2016 almost 320,000 Chinese tourists took advantage of the new visa-free travel rules to visit Moscow and St. Petersburg. This figure is 20 percent higher than results for the same period of 2015"; "Turpotok iz Kitaia v Rossiiu za nedeliu vyros na 100 protsentov," *Lenta.ru*, 11 October 2016, https://lenta.ru/news/2016/10/11/china_russia/. See also Ian Shanskii, "Bespoleznye gosti,"

Chinese tourism has a noticeable "red" connotation: many groups of tourists from the Middle Kingdom visit museums related to the country's revolutionary, military, and socialist past.

The "Red Eastern stream" has resulted in the reformatting of a number of subjects in exhibits on the socialist period in Russian museums. This is also breathing new life into Soviet-style museums focused on the leaders of the Russian revolution. According to the head of the Ministry of Culture's Federal Agency of Tourism (Russiatourism.ru), "The Russian part of the Red Route, which is very popular with Chinese tourists, includes Kazan, Ulyanovsk, Shushenskoe and a number of other settlements linked to the biography of the leader of the October socialist revolution, V. I. Lenin."[74] This interest in Soviet themes is confirmed by Chinese officials in the field of tourism. According to one of the leaders of the Chinese State Administration for Tourism, Zhu Shanzhong, "In China, tens of millions of middle-aged and elderly people grew up on Soviet literature and movies. Each of them wants to visit Russia and see the USSR's heritage with his own eyes."[75] Thus it is mostly elderly Chinese people who come to Russia as they have memories of their own days immersed in communist ideology. Their tourism is nostalgic in nature, even if the routes they take include the main tourist attractions in Moscow and St. Petersburg.

In the course of my conversations with the staff of both private and state-run museums, the role played by Chinese tourism in the development of museum exhibits on the Soviet past was a topic that often came up spontaneously, without prompting. The founder of one of the most successful private museums claimed that Chinese tourism to Russia is highly organized and controlled by a handful of large Chinese and Russian tourist operators. The program of these

---

Lenta.ru, 29 November 2016, https://lenta.ru/articles/2016/11/29/china_down/; and "Golovokruzhenie ot tsifr, 'pokatushki' na bolide, kitaitsy za 60 i drugie vpechatleniia ot Rossiisko-Kitaiskogo turisticheskgo foruma," *ekd.me*, 1 April 2016, http://ekd.me/2016/04/rus-cn-tourism-forum-2016/.

[74]   See "Gosti iz Kitaia: chto interesno turistam iz KNR v Rossiiu i kak tuda dobrat'sia," *TASS.ru*, 21 November 2016, http://tass.ru/turizm-v-rossii/3799857.

[75]   See Aleksandra Vodop'ianova, "'Krasnyi turizm'—eto svoego roda palomnichestvo dlia kitaiskikh grazhdan," *Investitsii v turizm*, 19 March 2015, http://rusturinvest.ru/article/krasnyy-turizm---eto-svoego-roda-palomnichestvo-dl-1400.html.

tourist trips is strictly predetermined. Tours organized by the main commercial operators in Moscow, for example, include visits to the Kremlin museums and the private museum Bunker-42 at Taganka (sometimes called the Cold War Museum),[76] while other equally noteworthy sites are excluded from the program.

The private museum Bunker-42 is located at the site of a Soviet-era nuclear bomb shelter, located in the center of the Russian capital, at a depth of more than sixty meters. For a long time this bunker was the location of a key strategic aviation control post. In 2006 the bunker was purchased by a private organization and a museum was opened at the site, allowing the exposition of installations connected to the Cold War and the history of Soviet-era atomic weapons, including paraphernalia, military equipment, and uniforms. The description of the museum underlines the important role it plays in the patriotic education of Russian youth, even if the museum is more geared toward an "export market"; the exhibits are oriented toward foreign visitors, while the content of the museum's website is available in Russian, English, and Chinese. The museum's English-language webpage notes that: "Our museum is included in the national presidential program 'Routes of Victory.' We are part of this program for thousands of young people of our country and teach the historical understanding of patriotic unity of the people, the country's might and heroism of every citizen to perform heavy daily work for the benefit of the motherland."[77] The entry cost is high compared to the admission price for other Russian museums and galleries, which again suggests the museum is marketed to foreign visitors, among whom Chinese tourists occupy a prominent place.

An employee of the Museum "Presnia"[78] in Moscow told me in an interview that the museum plans to utilize the growing interest of Chinese tourists in the Soviet past overall, and the leaders of the revolution in particular. Chinese tourists are interested, for

---

[76]   http://bunker42.com/.

[77]   http://bunker42.com/eng/patrioticheskoe-vospitanie.php.

[78]   The museum used to be dedicated to the events of the Russian revolution of 1905, but the exhibits now focus on everyday life in the twentieth century.

example, in the figure of the "Russian elder" Mikhail Kalinin, who was a revolutionary and top official in the Stalin period. Kalinin's personal belongings and other artefacts related to his life are in the museum's storage rooms. Because they are of interest to Chinese tourists, in the view of the employee, appropriate Soviet-oriented exhibits should be set up to increase attendance at the museum.

The phenomenon of "red tourism" that brings Chinese tourists to Russia prompts us to revisit the question of the collective memory of communism. This memory is not only a matter of post-Soviet nostalgia or historical trauma; in China, communism is part of a still functioning ideological machine, where extreme market reforms and hard capitalist norms live alongside communist rhetoric and symbolism inherited from the Maoist period. Of course, these ideological conceptions have in many ways become empty signifiers, a form of political advertisement. However, for many Chinese citizens, communist ideology is still important, and therefore the potential for red tourism remains strong in Russia given the continued existence of museum collections and exhibitions focused on the heritage of the communist period. In the Russian context, this Eastern influence on the way the communist period is represented in museums has begun to lead to a hybridization of museum exhibitions or, to put it differently, a tangling of different narrative forms. This hybridization can be viewed as the result of globalized tourist mobility, a series of processes that are still in their infancy.

Conclusion

Russian museum curators and staff face many contradictions in their efforts to represent the communist past in their exhibits. Overall, it is clear that the versions of the Soviet period on offer in Russian museums are far from monolithic; not all museums operate according to the preferences of official memory policy, which seeks to put the Soviet past to work for patriotic purposes. Contrary to the popular view often presented in mainstream Western media, the Soviet part of Russian history is not being excised from the common history of the country. Rather, it is presented as part of a longer and deeper historical chronology: museums show the dark side along with the positive moments of Soviet history. The positive moments emphasized most consistently are the USSR's participation in World War II, the Soviet space program, the Thaw era and the associated consumer boom, and the improved living standards in the postwar era. Museums also include the story of the USSR's collapse and the Soviet republics' battle for independence. The largest Russian museums offer a polyphonic view of the communist past that neither praises the period as a golden age nor stigmatizes it as a trauma or historical failure.[79]

The presentation of the Soviet past in Russian museums has several key features. Perhaps most strikingly, the museumification of the Stalinist era tends to be carried out by counterposing the different aspects, negative and positive, to one another: repressions, famine, and the sufferings of the victims of collectivization are contrasted with the positive features of "building socialism." In exhibits of this kind, it is sometimes hard to distinguish real achievements from the propaganda of the time.

The efforts of both television producers and museum curators have done much to make the Thaw an object of nostalgic romanticization. This new attention has emphasized a number of features, such as modernist furniture, the films of Marlen Khutsiev, Thaw-era poets, and the Spidola record player. It presents young scientists, geologists, and cosmonauts as the heroes of this age. What is noticeable in all this is a certain de-problematization of this period: the internal contradictions and tensions inherent to the Thaw fade away here, relegated to insignificance in comparison with the attractive symbols of consumerism and fashion.

The late Soviet period from the mid 1960s to the mid '80s is still remembered by many of Russia's citizens. As a result, the nostalgia people feel toward the period of their own youth shapes their perceptions—an entirely understandable phenomenon. This period gave rise to a rich world of material objects, such as distinctive styles

---

79   On the incompleteness of the processes of remembering and mourning the traumatic parts of the Soviet past, see Alexander Etkind, *Warped Mourning: Stories of the Undead in the Land of the Unburied* (Palo Alto, CA: Stanford University Press, 2013).

of fashion, household items, electronic gear, posters, and other artefacts of mass culture. Many of these items are still in circulation and familiar to most people; others are attractive to young people precisely because of their "exotic" and "cool" vintage nature.

The rise of the folk museum movement in recent years has coincided with a transformation of attitudes toward the figure of Brezhnev in the mass consciousness: the previous popular view of Brezhnev and his entourage as decrepit, corrupt, and general objects of ridicule, has given way to a new view on the Brezhnev period as the high-water mark of Soviet development. In this connection, as Mikhail Timofeev has argued, we might view the private folk museum representations of the Brezhnev period as "educational-entertainment platforms with a commercial slant. Their appearance is due to a deficit in museum spaces working on the Soviet heritage, on the one hand, and the abundance of no longer in-demand items of this material culture, on the other."[80]

A closer look at representations of the Soviet past in contemporary Russian museums reveals a complex picture. New and distinctive languages of museumification are emerging for each of the various periods of Soviet history, languages that in turn are hybridized by a variety of influences. These influences include the official memory policy of the state, the prevalence of popular media images representing the past, the new interest in the Soviet shown by foreign tourists, and finally, the personal memories of those who actually lived through these periods.

---

[80]   Mikhail Timofeev, "Muzeefikatsia SSSR," *Labirint: Zhurnal sotsial'no-gumanitarnykh issledovanii* 1 (2014): 25–33.

Museumification of the Soviet Past in the Context of Ukrainian Memory Politics[1]

Valentyna Kharkhun

Abstract: This article analyzes how Ukrainian memory policies have affected the presentation of the Soviet past in Ukrainian museums, from the late 1980s through to the post-Euromaidàn period. It includes an examination of specific memory policies created by successive Ukrainian presidents who, as key mnemonic actors, have played an important role in defining the context of how their citizens perceive and remember the Soviet-communist past. The article addresses a set of key questions: Who are the main mnemonic actors/agents creating narratives about the Soviet past in Ukraine? What are the distinctive Ukrainian issues shaping the interpretation and presentation of the Soviet legacy when compared to other Central and Eastern European countries? What narratives are used in museums when it comes to discussing the Soviet past, and do they coexist, overlap, and/or oppose each other? Which mnemonic regimes are dominant in the Ukrainian perception of communism, and what role do museums play in creating these regimes?

The article draws upon a detailed study of approximately fifty cases of museumification of the Soviet era in Ukraine, comprising government museums at the national and regional levels, and independent museums operated by local societies or individuals. It identifies three key narratives employed by museums in presenting the Soviet past: the victimhood narrative; the heroic narrative; and the

---

[1] This article is a part of the project "Museumification of the Soviet Past in Russia and Ukraine: From Historical Trauma to Nostalgia," which I co-led with Roman Abramov at the Kennan Institute, Woodrow Wilson Center, Washington, D.C., in the spring of 2016. The first results of the project were published as an article in the Kennan Institute's journal (https://kennankyiv.org/wp-content/uploads/2016/12/Harhun.pdf) and *Ukraina Moderna* (http://uamoderna.com/demontazh-pamyati/kharkhun-communism).

everyday narrative, in which the emphasis is placed on the lived expe-rience of ordinary people, often through a focus on Soviet material culture. The article further elaborates on how variations in regional and private museumification initiatives affect the political arena in which museums operate, and investigates how these different types of museums reflect, influence, reinforce, or challenge government poli-cies, public opinion, and, ultimately, the national memory regime.

Keywords: *memory politics, memory projects, mnemonic actors, Ukrainian memory of communism, museums about the communist past.*

Introduction and Background

The creation and contestation of memories of the communist past has become a critical component of contemporary European geo-politics. With the break-up of the Soviet Union, the communist ide-ology was stripped away in Central and Eastern Europe. This re-sulted in the creation of new identities for the post-socialist coun-tries as they reevaluated their recent pasts. Over the course of twenty-five years, attempts to construct memories of the com-munist past have become a heated topic in society, media, and scholarly circles. It would not be an overstatement to say that cur-rent discussions of memories of communism have reached the same level of intensity as previous debates over memories of World War II or of the Holocaust. East European memory studies are currently dominated by three different theoretical approaches: Maurice Halbwachs' articulation of "collective memory" and its modern revi-sioning by Jeffrey Olick; the "cultural and communicative memory" approach of Jan and Aleida Assmann; and Pierre Nora's "sites of memory."[2] A number of recent edited volumes have played a major

---

2   Maurice Halbwachs, *The Collective Memory* (New York: Harper & Row, 1980), 182; Jeffrey Olick, *The Politics of Regret: On Collective Memory and Historical Responsibility* (New York: Routledge, 2007), 229; Jan Assmann, *The Mind of Egypt: History and Meaning in the Time of the Pharaohs*, trans. Andrew Jenkins (Cambridge, MA: Harvard University Press, 2003), 513; Aleida Assmann, *Cul-tural Memory and Western Civilization: Functions, Media, Archives* (Cambridge:

role in opening up a larger, panoramic view of memory and identity issues in the region.[3] In these works the East European memory map appears as an arena of memory games, battles, and wars. Even after twenty-five years of building new identities, East European nations find that working with memory issues and overcoming the communist past is still very difficult, and policy and actions in this arena are hotly disputed.

National memory politics in Ukraine since the nation became independent in 1991 have also been the focus of intense debate, both

---

Cambridge University Press, 2011), 406; and Pierre Nora and Lawrence D. Kritzman (eds.), *Realms of Memory: The Construction of the French Past*, trans. Arthur Goldhammer (New York: Columbia University Press, 1997), 642.

[3]   See, for example, Sławomir M. Nowinowski, Jan Pomorski, and Rafał Stobiecki (eds.), *Pamięć i polityka historyczna: Doświadczenia Polski i jej sąsiadów* (Łódź: Instytut Pamięci Narodowej, Komisja Ścigania Zbrodni przeciwko Narodowi Polskiemu, 2008), 398; Nicolas Hayoz, Leszek Jesień, and Daniela Koleva (eds.), *20 Years after the Collapse of Communism: Expectations, Achievements and Disillusions of 1989*, Interdisciplinary Studies on Central and Eastern Europe 9 (Bern: Peter Lang, 2011), 679; Georges Mink and Laure Neumayer (eds.), *History, Memory and Politics in Central and Eastern Europe: Memory Games* (Basingstoke: Palgrave Macmillan, 2013), 270; Michael Bernhard and Jan Kubik (eds.), *Twenty Years after Communism. The Politics of Memory and Commemoration* (New York: Oxford University Press, 2014), 36; Barbara Törnquist-Plewa, Niklas Bernsand, and Eleonora Narvselius (eds.), *Beyond Transition? Memory and Identity Narratives in Eastern and Central Europe*, CFE Conference Papers 7 (Centre for European Studies at Lund University, 2015), 212; and Tea Sindbaeck Andersen and Barbara Törnquist-Plewa (eds.), *Disputed Memory: Emotions and Memory Politics in Central, Eastern and South-Eastern Europe* (Berlin: Walter De Gruyter, 2016), 383.

[4]   The most disputed research includes, but is not limited to, the following: Mykola Riabchuk, "Kul'tura pamiati i politika zabveniia," *Otechestvennye zapiski* 1 (2007), http://www.strana-oz.ru/2007/1/kultura-pamyati-i-politika-zabveniya; *Skhid-Zakhid: Istoryko-kul'turologichnyi zbirnyk*, vols. 13–14, *Istorychna pamiat' i totalitaryzm: Dosvid Tsentral'no-Skhidnoi Ievropy* (Kharkiv, 2009), 428; Andrei Portnov, *Uprazhneniia s istoriei po-Ukrainski* (Moskva: OGI, 2010), 224; Iaroslav Hrytsak, *Strasti za natsionalismom: Stara istoriia na novyi lad. Esei* (Kyiv: Krytyka, 2011), 350; Volodymyr Kulyk, "Natsionalistychne proty radianskogo: Istorychna pamiat' u Nezalezhnii Ukraini," *Historians*, 20 September 2012, http://hi-phi.org.ua/historians.in.ua/index.php/en/istoriya-i-pamyat-vazhki-p itannya/379-volodymyr-kulyk-natsionalistychne-proty-radianskoho-istorychn a-pamiat-u-nezalezhnii-ukraini; Iurii Shapoval (ed.), *Kul'tura istorychnoi pamiati: Ievropeis'kyi ta Ukrains'kyi dosvid* (Kyiv: IPIEND, 2013), 600; and Valerii Soldatenko (ed.), *Viina pamiatei ta polityka prymyrennia: Zbirnyk naukovykh*

domestic[4] and international.[5] Ukrainian scholars are analyzing the crucial points of national memory creation through discussion of primary memory agents and their activities, typically in regard to historical trauma and victimization, and then comparing Ukrainian memory politics with similar experiences of other Central European countries. As in other post-communist countries, domestic discussions reveal that memories of the communist past and memory policies about Soviet times, as well as matters related to memory creation, are highly controversial and disputed issues. Meanwhile, the Ukrainian case has also been integrated into the broader global discussion on memory politics and perceptions of the communist past.[6] This integration opens a new methodological perspective for research and allows a comparative approach that observes the distinctiveness of the Ukrainian experience. Oxana Shevel, for example, who has studied the Ukrainian case in comparison with that of other Central and East European countries, describes the Ukrainian memory regime as "fractured and contentious,"[7] characterized by a

---

prats (Kyiv: Priorytety, 2013), 254. See also chapters of Georgiy Kasyanov's upcoming book titled *Past Continuous: Historical Politics of 1980–2000s (Ukraine and Neighbors)* at http://www.historians.in.ua.

5   Catherine Wanner, *Burden of Dreams: History and Identity in Post-Soviet Ukraine*, Post-Communist Cultural Studies (University Park: Pennsylvania State University Press, 1998), 228; Andrew Wilson, "National History and National Identity in Ukraine and Belarus," in *Nation-building in the Post-Soviet Borderlands: The Politics of National Identities*, ed. Graham Smith (Cambridge: Cambridge University Press, 1998), 23–47; Jilge Wilfried, "Historical Memory and National Identity-Building in Ukraine since 1991," in *European History: Challenge for a Common Future*, eds. Attila Pók, Jörn Rüsen, and Jutta Scherrer (Hamburg: Körber-Stiftung, 2002), 111–34; Taras Kuzio, "National Identity and History Writing in Ukraine," *Nationalities Papers* 34, no. 4 (2006): 407–27; Tomasz Horbowski and Piotr Kosiewski (eds.), *Pamięć i pytania o tożsamość. Polska, Ukraina* (Warszawa: Fundacja im. Stefana Batorego, 2013), 191; and Tomasz Stryjek, *Ukraina przed końcem historii: Szkice o polityce państw wobec pamięci* (Warszawa: Wydawnictwo Naukowe SCHOLAR, Instytut Studiów Politycznych PAN, 2014), 412.

6   All the compilations on memory in Central and Eastern Europe cited in n. 3 above include chapters discussing the Ukrainian case.

7   Oxana Shevel, "Memories of the Past and Vision of the Future: Remembering the Soviet Era and Its End in Ukraine," in *Twenty Years after Communism: The Politics of Memory and Commemoration*, eds. Michael Bernhard and Jan Kubik (Oxford: Oxford University Press, 2014), 152.

variety of regional interpretations of the communist past and by the political elite acting as "mnemonic warriors,"[8] producing their own competing accounts of the Soviet era.

The events of the Euromaidan (2013–2014) and the resulting shifts and developments in memory politics, such as the activities of the renovated Ukrainian Institute of National Remembrance and the implementation of decommunization laws, have made the Ukrainian case a particularly hot topic.[9] A new layer of political, social, and cultural tensions has been introduced by the decommunization process, which has been criticized by many scholars and social activists.

In analyzing Central and East European memory politics, international researchers pay special attention to "sites of memory" or "carriers of memory"[10]—urban landscapes, buildings, monuments,

---

[8]   The phrase "mnemonic warriors" is drawn from the typology devised by Michael Bernhard and Jan Kubik; see their introduction to Bernhard and Kubik (eds), *Twenty Years after Communism*.

[9]   Oxana Shevel, "Decommunization in Post-Euromaidan Ukraine: Law and Practice," *PONARS Eurasia Policy Memo,* January 2016, http://www.ponarseurasia.org/memo/decommunization-post-euromaidan-ukraine-law-and-practice; Ilya Nuzov, "The Dynamics of Collective Memory in the Ukraine Crisis: A Transitional Justice Perspective," *International Journal of Transit Justice* 11, no. 1 (2017): 132–53; and Kateryna Kobchenko, "Dekomunizatsiia v Ukraini: Postkolonial'nyi aspekt," *Ukrainoznavchyi Al'manakh* 19, no. 1 (2016): 66–70. See also a discussion of the decommunization laws: Andriy Portnov, "On Decommunization, Identity, and Legislating History, From a Slightly Different Angle," *Krytyka* (May 2015), https://krytyka.com/en/solutions/opinions/decommunization-identity-and-legislating-history-slightly-different-angle; Mykhaylo Haukhman, "The Case of Decommunization," *Krytyka* (May 2015), https://krytyka.com/en/solutions/opinions/case-decommunization; Serhiy Lunin, "Ukraine's 'Decommunization': Struggle Against the Past and Its Inconsistencies," *Krytyka* (May 2015), https://krytyka.com/en/solutions/opinions/ukraines-decommunization-struggle-against-past-and-its-inconsistencies; David R. Marples "Volodymyr Viatrovych and Ukraine's 'Decommunization' Laws," *Krytyka* (May 2015), https://krytyka.com/en/solutions/opinions/volodymyr-viatrovych-and-ukraines-decommunization-laws; Halya Coynash, "'Decommunization' Laws: Deeply Divisive and Destined for Strasbourg," *Krytyka* (May 2015), https://krytyka.com/en/solutions/opinions/decommunization-laws-deeply-divisive-and-destined-strasbourg; and Volodymyr Viatrovych, "'Decommunization' and Academic Discussion," *Krytyka* (May 2015), https://krytyka.com/en/solutions/opinions/decommunization-and-academic-discussion.

[10] Marcin Kula, *Nośniki pamięci historycznej* (Warszawa: DiS, 2002), 320.

and cemeteries—as well as to different perceptions of communism as portrayed in literature, films, and museums,[11] with a particularly strong focus on the latter.[12] Studies of museum exhibits depicting the communist era have been characterized by two main problems. First, studying a single country's experiences provides a very fragmented view of the museumification of communism.[13] Second, most studies focus on only a few of the most provocative museums, such as the House of Terror and Memento Park in Budapest, the Museum of Communism in Prague, and Grutas Park, the sculpture garden of Soviet statuary in Lithuania.[14] Other museums that also present

---

[11]   Oksana Sarkisova and Péter Apor (eds.), *Past for the Eyes: East European Representations of Communism in Cinema and Museums after 1989* (Budapest: Central European University Press, 2008), 436.

[12]   See, for instance, Volkhard Knigge and Ulrich Mählert (eds.), *Der Kommunismus im Museum: Formen der Auseinandersetzung in Deutschland und Ostmitteleuropa* (Koln: Böhlau, 2005), 312; James Mark, *The Unfinished Revolution: Making Sense of the Communist Past in Central-Eastern Europe* (New Haven, CT: Yale University Press, 2010), 312; A. Bartetzky, "Visualizing the Experience of Dictatorship: Communism in the Museum," *Centropa* 6, no. 3 (2006): 183–93; and Duncan Light, "Gazing on Communism: Heritage Tourism and Post-Communist Identities in Germany, Hungary and Romania," *Tourism Geographies* 2 (2000): 157–76.

[13]   Nikolai Vukov, "The 'Unmemorable' and the 'Unforgettable.' 'Museumizing' the Socialist Past in Post-1989 Bulgaria," in Sarkisova and Apor (eds.), *Past for the Eyes*, 307–34.; James Mark, "Containing Fascism. History in Post-Communist Baltic Occupation and Genocide Museums," in Sarkisova and Apor (eds.), *Past for the Eyes*, 335–69; Izabella Main, "How Is Communism Displayed? Exhibitions and Museums of Communism in Poland," in Sarkisova and Apor (eds.), *Past for the Eyes*, 371–400; Linara Dovydaityte, "Which Communism to Bring to the Museum? A Case of Memory Politics in Lithuania," *Art History & Criticism* 6 (2010): 80–87; and Simina Bădică, "The Black Hole Paradigm. Exhibiting Communism in Post-Communist Romania," *History of Communism in Europe* 1 (2010): 83–101.

[14]   Paul Clements, "The Construction of Post-Communist Ideologies and Rebranding of Budapest: The Case Study of Statue Park Museum," in *Public Art Encounters: Art, Space and Identity*, ed. J. Palmer and M. Zebracki (New York: Routledge, 2017), 51–69; Paul Clements, "The Consumption of Communism: Changing Representations of Statue Park Museum and Budapest," *Art & the Public Sphere* 2, no. 1–3 (2014): 73–86; Beverly James, "Fencing in the past: Budapest's Statue Park Museum," *Media Culture & Society* 21 (1999): 291–311; Julia Creet, "The House of Terror and the Holocaust Memorial Centre," *European Studies: A Journal of European Culture, History & Politics* 30, no. 1 (2012): 29–62; Sara Jones, "Staging Battlefields: Media, Authenticity and Politics in

national versions of perceptions of communism are not usually considered. In Prague, for instance, besides the Museum of Communism, at least five more museums exhibit materials on the communist time period, yet these have received little attention from scholars.[15]

There are several Ukrainian journals[16] and research publications[17] showcasing the European museumification of communism, and they underscore the necessity of examining Ukrainian museum policies. Yet despite this, and despite the growing attention to Ukrainian memory studies and the prominence of current Ukrainian debates over memorialization of the Soviet past, Ukrainian museums and their connections to different mnemonic projects have rarely been the subject of research.

the Museum of Communism (Prague), The House of Terror (Budapest) and Gedenkstätte Hohenschönhausen (Berlin)," *Journal of War & Culture Studies* 4, no. 1 (2011): 97–111; Maya Nadkarni, "The Death of Socialism and the Afterlife of its Monuments: Making and Marketing the Past in Budapest's Statue Park Museum," in *Contested Past: The Politics of Memory*, ed. Katharine Hodgkin and Susannah Radstone (London and New York: Routledge, 2003), 193–206; Paul Williams, "The Afterlife of Communist Statuary: Hungary's Szoborpark and Lithuania's Grutas Park," *Forum for Modern Language Studies* 44, no. 1–2 (2008): 185–98; and Gediminas Lankauskas, "Sensuous (Re)Collections: The Sight and Taste of Socialism at Grutas Statue Park, Lithuania," *Senses & Society* 1, no. 1 (2006): 27–52.

[15]   These five museums are the Museum of the Cold War in Prague's Hotel Jalta; the KGB Museum; the Prague Nuclear Bunker; the National Memorial on Vitkov Hill; and the Military History Museum.

[16]   Ievhen Kostiuk, "Proshchannia z totalitaryzmom," *Istorychna Pravda*, 23 August 2012, http://www.istpravda.com.ua/columns/2012/08/23/91824/; Oksana Khmeliovs'ka, "Ievropeis'ka deradianizatsiia: pro zlochyny komunistychnykh rezhymiv rozpovidaiut' muzei," *Tyzhden'*, 3 March 2013, http://tyzhden.ua/News/73754; and Andrii Kokotiukha, "Muzei natsyzmu ta komunizmu: Vidchuite riznytsu," *Glavred*, 6 March 2015, http://glavred.info/avtorskie_kolonki/muzeyi-nacizmu-ta-komunizmu-vidchuyte-riznicyu-244860.html.

[17]   See my articles "Retseptsiia komunizmu i suchasnyi ukrain'skyi proekt," in *Identychnist' i pamiat' u postradianskii Ukraini*, ed. Myroslava Antonovych (Kyiv: Dukh i Litera), 57–78; "Viina pamiatei u muzeiakh komunizmu," in *Viina pamiatei ta polityka prymyrennia: Zbirnyk naukovykh prats*, ed. Valerii Soldatenko (Kyiv: Priorytety, 2013), 235–47; and "Muzei komunizmu v konteksti polskoi muzeal'noi polityky," *Agora. Vypusk 14. Muzei ta Kul'turna Dyplomatiia*, eds. Kateryna Smaglii and Nataliia Musienko (Kyiv: Vydavnychyi Dim Kyievo-Mohylian'ska Akademiia, 2015), 16–32.

In this article, I analyze the specifics of the Ukrainian museumification of the Soviet past as it relates to memory policies established since the late 1980s. My methodological approach inte-
grates memory studies and museum studies in a regional case study
by examining museums in their role as memory regime creators.
Following Georgii Kas'ianov, I consider "memory policy" or "historical politics" to be the "purposeful construction and utilitarian usage
for political purposes of 'historical memory' and other forms of collective imaginations about the past and its representations."[18] Thus
I regard museums exhibiting the communist past as places of "pre-
existing" (heritage) or constructed history that on material, symbolic, and functional levels reveal institutional, group, or individual
attempts to create mnemonic projects. These museums offer different versions of remembering and different approaches to determin-
ing a national memory regime.

In developing the methodological framework, I have organized the article into two parts. In the first part I examine the
memory policies established by successive Ukrainian presidents
who, as the main mnemonic actors, define the state-controlled
memory policy and determine the specifics of the national experience in dealing with the communist past.[19] I then turn to the current
processes of memory creation, specifically those occurring after passage of the decommunization laws, to identify the main results and
crucial problems caused by the new mnemonic projects.

In discussing different memory policies during each presidency, I analyze approximately fifty cases of museumification of the

---

[18]   Georgii Kas'ianov, "K desiatiletiiu ukrainskogo Instituta natsional'noi pamiati
(2006–2016)," *Historians.in.ua*, 14 January 2016, http://www.historians.in.ua/in
dex.php/en/index.php/en/dyskusiya/1755-georgij-kas-yanov-k-desyatiletiyu-u
krainskogo-instituta-natsional-noj-pamyati-2006-2016.

[19]   Analyses of Ukrainian memory policy using this method are very common. See,
for example, Iaroslav Hrytsak, "Istoriia v osobakh: Do formuvannia istorychnoi
polityky v Ukraini, 1991–2011," in Shapoval (ed.), *Kul'tura istorychnoi pamiati*,
231–50; Svitlana Nabok, "Derzhava i polityka pamiati: Dosvid chotyr'okh prezydentiv Ukrainy," in Shapoval (ed.), *Kul'tura istorychnoi pamiati*, 251–73; and
Georgii Kas'ianov, "Prezydent," *Historians.in.ua*, 6 July 2017, http://www.histori
ans.in.ua/index.php/en/istoriya-i-pamyat-vazhki-pitannya/2232-past-continuo
us-istorichna-politika-1980-kh-2000-kh-rr-ukrajina-ta-susidi.

Soviet past. The institutions involved include both government museums at national and regional levels and independent museums operated by local societies or individuals. The mnemonic policies can be further defined by secondary mnemonic actors or agents. In the government sector, these mnemonic actors may be governors, city administrators, or community officials. In the private sector, they may be museum boards, business associations, or local societies, clubs, or special-interest groups. I examine how changing memory policies determine the creation and function of museum exhibits, and how such exhibits in turn reflect or challenge government policies and public opinion influencing the national memory regime.

My working hypothesis is that in the museumification of the Soviet past, museum exhibits can serve as important indicators of trends in a given memory regime. Museums reveal the importance not only of dominant state mnemonic actors, but also of mnemonic agents associated with regional societies or acting as local citizens, who create their own museum content and thereby transform the specifics of the national memory regime. To test my hypothesis, I analyze the chronology and typology of Ukrainian museums exhibiting the Soviet past, paying special attention to regional variations of museumification and to private initiatives in the sphere of memory and museum politics.

The Late Soviet Era and Leonid Kravchuk's Presidency (1989–94)

Significant changes in memory policy had been occurring even before Ukraine's independence was proclaimed, during perestroika or the "post-Chornobyl" era, when Ukrainian society felt the need to overcome a national amnesia. The social and cultural situation of the period was shaped by several key events. First were the discoveries that under Stalin's dictatorship, knowledge of the promulgation of totalitarian crimes was repressed by the Soviets; the discoveries of these crimes were followed by remembrance of the victims. Second, facts related to the Chornobyl nuclear power plant accident and the long Soviet-Afghan war were gradually disclosed, which further undermined the Soviet heroic discourse. Third, new mnemonic agents, defenders of a nationalist trend in the memory policy, began to play a significant role in political, social, and cultural life. These included the People's Movement of Ukraine for Perestroika, or Rukh; the Ukrainian branch of the Memorial society; and the All-Ukrainian Taras Shevchenko Society "Prosvita" (Enlightenment).

In the context of such changes, alternative approaches to the museumification of the Soviet era began to be developed. The year 1990 can be considered a turning point in this regard. In that year several new museums appeared, dedicated to the previously suppressed history discussed above. These included the Museum of the Chornobyl Tragedy (Narodychi, Zhytomyr oblast'); the Museum of the Military Glory of Soldiers-Internationalists (Yevpatoria, Crimea); the Museum of Soldiers-Internationalists (Feodosia, Crimea); and the Historical and Memorial Museum of Yevhen Konovalets' (Zashkiv village, L'viv oblast').These museums were the first to attempt presenting exhibits on the Soviet period before it was over; however, the actual exhibits were confined to the regional dimensions of these topics. This emphasis showed that museums were moving away from the accepted state-mandated Soviet heroic ideology and more toward private initiative and local interests. In the process they began offering new information and new heroes for remembrance and commemoration.

At the beginning of Ukraine's independence movement, during Leonid Kravchuk's presidency, some initial attempts to regulate the memory of the communist past were undertaken at the state level. The political leaders followed the nationalist trend of downplaying the Soviet era, which was associated not only with a significant influence of right-wing political and cultural forces but also with the "ontological security"[20] of the state in general. At first glance, the memory policy of this period was aimed at overcoming the connection with the communist past and publicly criticizing it. Social and cultural life experienced a radical change: state archives were partially opened, historical studies previously banned were published, Ukrainian history as a discipline was introduced into the

---

[20]   Jennifer Mitzen, "Ontological Security in World Politics: State Identity and the Security Dilemma," *European Journal of International Relations* 12, no. 3 (2006): 341–70.

educational system, and the visibility of civic organizations increased. In 1993 Kravchuk issued a decree "On the Commemoration of the 60th Anniversary of the Holodomor in Ukraine," and a memorial to victims of the Holodomor of 1932–33 was placed in Mykhailivsky Square in Kyiv.

Despite being characterized by a decidedly critical attitude toward the Soviet past, Kravchuk's memory policy was ambivalent as it simultaneously sought to implement nationally oriented values while preserving Soviet models of commemoration. This duality is particularly evident when it comes to the state's interpretation of different periods in Soviet history. Starting with Kravchuk's presidency (and continuing into the present), the Stalinist period has been evaluated quite negatively in Ukraine, an orientation that distinguishes the country from Russia, where a pro-Stalinist mentality appears to be gaining more traction in Russian society[21] and among the political leadership.[22] It was likely complicated for the early presidents of Ukraine to disassociate entirely from the late Soviet period because both Leonid Kravchuk and his successor, Leonid Kuchma, had held significant Communist Party and administrative positions, and had thus both contributed to the Soviet history in Ukraine. Perhaps partly for this reason, this period's "disadvantages" and "mistakes" seem to have been judged less critically, and certainly never as harshly as the Stalin era.

The perception of the Soviet era during the early days of Ukraine's independence also differentiates Ukraine from the Baltic countries. In the Baltic states in the early 1990s the former communist rule was characterized as an occupation, and anti-Soviet and anti-Russian attitudes strongly predominated. This sentiment, codified in official policy, greatly influenced developments in the museum sphere, and two state museums located in former Soviet buildings were opened with that idea. The Museum of Genocide Victims opened in Vilnius in 1992 and the Museum of the Occupation

---

[21]   "Stalin stal liderom v oprose rossiian o samykh vydaiushchikhsia lichnostiakh v istorii: Putin i Pushkin—na vtorom meste," *Interfax*, 26 June 2017, http://www.interfax.ru/russia/568025.

[22]   "Stalin—eto Putin vchera?" *Radio Svoboda*, 5 March 2018, https://www.svoboda.org/a/29079289.html.

opened in Latvia in 1993. Later, in 2003, Tallinn's Museum of Occupations began operating in a newly constructed building. By contrast, the Ukrainian Museum of the Soviet Occupation opened only in 2007. Unlike the Baltic museums, which were state-run, this Ukrainian museum, located in the Kyiv office of the Memorial society, was mostly a private initiative and did not attain a high public profile (though this would change later, when there was a proposal to expand the museum exhibits after the Euromaidan).

During Leonid Kravchuk's presidency, museum exhibits and displays on the Stalinist repressions, the Chornobyl disaster, and the war in Afghanistan were approved at the state level. In 1994 the National Historic Memorial Bykivnia Graves, an important center for the remembrance of victims of the Stalinist repressions, opened, becoming a site for state commemoration events and a destination for visiting foreign delegations.[23] In 1992 the National Museum Chornobyl was opened as the main center for the exhibition of a state-created narrative about the Chornobyl disaster.[24] A state narrative about the Afghan war is presented in an exhibition titled *At the Foreign Wars and the Tragedy and Valor of Afghanistan* (1992); it functions as a separate unit of the National Museum of the History of Ukraine in the Second World War, which is located in Kyiv.[25] Another museum dedicated to the Afghan war created during this period is the Museum of Vinnytsia Region's Soldiers Who Died in Afghanistan (Vinnytsia, 1993). Museums dedicated to the history of the Organization of Ukrainian Nationalists-Ukrainian Insurgent Army (OUN-UPA) dominate the regional non-governmental initiatives.[26]

Transforming existing Soviet-era museums into new ones with a different narrative also became a new trend in museumification. The Museum of Partisan Glory, founded in 1963 at Yaremche,

---

23   http://ua.bykivnya.org/.
24   http://chornobylmuseum.kiev.ua/.
25   http://www.warmuseum.kiev.ua/_eng/expositions/relic_expo/index.html.
26   Some examples are the Open Air Museum UPA Camp Volyn'-South (a museum complex located in Shumsky raion of Ternopil oblast', 1992); the Museum of the UPA History (Pidhaitsi, Ternopil oblast', 1993); and the Museum of the Liberation Struggle (Kavske village, Lviv oblast', 1993).

detailed the Soviet partisan movement. After independence, it was transformed into the Carpathian Regional Museum of the Liberation Movement. Today, it offers exhibits on all stages of the liberation struggle in the region—the Opryshky movement, the history of the Ukrainian Sich Riflemen, the creation of the OUN and the UPA, as well as the history of the SS Galicia Division. At the same time, this museum does still retain information on Soviet partisans led by Sydir Kovpak and Semen Rudnev in the Carpathians.

Overall, in the early years of Ukrainian independence, the plight of victims, a theme employed in the memorialization of the Stalinist repressions, Chornobyl, and the Afghan war, became a defining national narrative. It was produced mostly at the state level of museumification of the Soviet past. At the regional level, primarily in western Ukraine, in addition to the plight of victims there was an active foregrounding of heroism in exhibits dedicated to the OUN-UPA's history, and this continues today. This region is leading the way in transforming Soviet museums into a more diverse experience for visitors by inserting the complementary Ukrainian history which was previously prohibited from being told.

Leonid Kuchma: Between the National and the Soviet (1994–2004)

The decade of Leonid Kuchma's presidency has been described as a period of "consciously practiced ambivalence."[27] The period was characterized by an attempt to combine nationalist and Soviet narratives. Metaphorically, the state memory policy during this time can be seen as oscillating between the nationalist narrative as embodied in Mykhailo Hrushevsky, historian and head of the Central Rada during the Ukrainian Revolution (1917–21), and the communist era, when the outstanding figure was Volodymyr Shcherbytsky, a member of the Soviet Politburo and leader of the Communist Party of Ukraine (1972–89). In 1998 a monument to Hrushevsky was opened in Kyiv, and in 2003 the eighty-fifth anniversary of Shcherbytsky's birth was celebrated at the state level.

---

[27] Hrytsak, "Istoriia v osobakh," 235.

The nationalist trend was aimed at memorializing the traumatic experience of the communist past with a distinct anti-Soviet tone. At the beginning of his term, in 1994, President Kuchma signed an order "On Measures to Commemorate the Victims of Political Repressions Buried in the Village of Bykivnia." That same year a monument to Ukrainian soldiers who had served in the war in Afghanistan was erected. In 1997, the Cabinet of Ministers established a working group to study and evaluate the OUN-UPA. In 1998, Kuchma signed a decree "On the Establishment of the Day of Remembrance for Victims of the Holodomor" and erected monuments to the victims of totalitarianism and the Holodomor throughout Ukraine. In 1999, a memorial complex dedicated to the memory of Chornobyl victims, the Circle of Memory, was opened. In 2003, in accordance with an order signed by President Kuchma, a symbolic image of the Kruty Heroes, who died defending Kyiv against the Bolsheviks in 1918, appeared on legal and regulatory documents.[28]

At the same time, a neo-Soviet narrative also emerged in Kuchma's policy, associated with the renewed commemoration of events and persons who occupied prominent places in Soviet historiography. These included, for example, Bohdan Khmelnytsky, the seventeenth-century Cossack leader who was held up during the Soviet period as having created a "brotherhood" between Ukraine and Russia through the conclusion of the 1654 Treaty of Pereyaslav. In 1995, his birthday, and in 1998, the 350th anniversary of the beginning of the liberation struggle led by Khmelnytsky were officially celebrated in Ukraine. The Pereyaslav Council, an official meeting initiated by Khmelnytsky that convened for a ceremonial pledge of allegiance by the Cossacks to the Tsar of Muscovy, one of the most honored events in the Soviet historiography, retains its importance in Ukrainian memory politics. There are also other examples of the adaptation, continuation and/or revival of Soviet commemorative practices during this period. In 1999, by presidential decree, Ukraine commemorated the "60th Anniversary of the Reunification of

---

[28]   According to the official version, 300 young defenders of Ukrainian independence selflessly fought the 5,000-man Bolshevik army advancing on Kyiv in January 1918.

Ukrainian Lands in a Single Ukrainian State," which in the context of Western historiography can be understood as a celebration of the invasion of Poland by Soviet and German troops in 1939. Also in 1999, in another borrowing from Soviet tradition, a presidential decree established 23 February as the Defender of the Fatherland Day.

In the context of the ambivalent state memory policy during the Kuchma presidency, regional museum practices became more evident: during that time, thirteen of the twenty-six museums existing today that are devoted to the history of the OUN-UPA and its leaders were established. Thus this decade with its oscillating memory policy and growing pro-Russian sympathies can be considered fundamental to strengthening the regional commemoration of the national liberation struggle. This fact points to a difference between state policy and regional/local interests, primarily among the populations of the three regions of Ivano-Frankivsk, L'viv, and Ternopil, which, contrary to the political elites in Kyiv, exhibited the liberation movement in numerous museums, and continued to present strongly anti-Soviet topics and views.

Viktor Yushchenko: Strengthening the National Canon (2005–2010)

In evaluating the commemorative activities of President Viktor Yushchenko, historian Yaroslav Hrytsak noted that Yushchenko was "obsessed with the past and provoked historical discussions both necessary and unnecessary." The historian further stated, "If before the Orange Revolution, historians complained about the lack of a serious discussion regarding Ukraine's historical past, after 2004, there was a great fatigue from discussions of historical themes."[29] In 2006, President Yushchenko followed the example set by the Polish government with the establishment of the Polish Institute of National Remembrance in 1998, and created the Ukrainian Institute of National Remembrance, which continues to be an active and prominent memory agent today. According to the 2009 presidential

---

[29]   Iaroslav Hrytsak, *Strasti za natsionalizmom: Stara istoriia na novyi lad* (Kyiv: Krytyka, 2011), 261–62.

decree "On Certain Measures to Celebrate the Outstanding Events of National Military History," the Institute was to develop proposals for a list of days to be recognized as honoring Ukrainian military victories and establish a register of objects and places related to outstanding events connected to the nation's military history.

Overcoming the mnemonic ambivalence of the previous period, President Yushchenko's memory policy had a distinct nationalist and anti-Soviet character. Three historical events were at the core of his memory politics. The first was the Battle of Kruty. Despite numerous gaps in the historical knowledge of the Battle of Kruty and ongoing factual and interpretive debates, this episode was taken up by Yushchenko and used to craft a heroic narrative of the Ukrainian struggle against the Bolshevik intervention and the Ukrainian liberation movement in general. Besides Askold's Grave, a historical park in Kyiv that has a Memorial to Heroes of the Battle of Kruty, the Memorial Complex to the Heroes of Kruty near Pamiatne village in Chernihiv Oblast is today a principal center for the commemoration of these events. Rukh initially intended to commemorate this event in 1990, but the main part of the Memorial Complex was erected and officially dedicated by Yushchenko in 2006. During his presidency, Yushchenko attended commemorative events here annually, emphasizing the importance of the Kruty Heroes in the newly created historical canon.

The second key element of Yushchenko's memory policy was the commemoration of the Holodomor victims. The Memorial in Commemoration of Victims of Famine in Ukraine (currently known as the National Museum Memorial to Holodomor Victims)[30] was opened on the seventy-fifth anniversary of the Holodomor in 2008. This memorial, along with other memory activities, such as the annual remembrance of the Holodomor victims, is generally regarded as the most successful in Yushchenko's memory policy, mostly because it helped consolidate Ukrainian society around its historical past.[31]

---

[30]   http://memorialholodomors.org.ua.
[31]   The situation with the political games around commemoration of the Holodomor during Yushchenko's presidency, however, reveals many problematic

The same cannot be said of the third element of Yushchenko's policy, honoring the OUN-UPA. As stated previously, the Kuchma presidency had actively commissioned research into the Ukrainian liberation movement of OUN-UPA in 1997; however, when the findings were announced, they were not reflected in the state memory policy. In the face of an obvious lack of support from the public, Yushchenko tried to incorporate this research into the state narrative about the past. In 2007, he signed a decree "On the Celebration of the 65th Anniversary of the Creation of the Ukrainian Insurgent Army" and then honored the soldiers of the UPA during the Victory Day celebrations and many other state events which followed. At the end of his presidency, Yushchenko bestowed on Stepan Bandera and Roman Shukhevych, the main representatives of the Ukrainian liberation movement, the titles of Heroes of Ukraine, which caused an uproar in Ukrainian society and abroad and was recognized as a very politically insensitive decision.

During Yushchenko's presidency, favorable conditions for the creation and operation of museums existed. In particular, in 2007 the exhibition rooms at the Kyiv branch of Memorial were developed into a Museum of the Soviet Occupation. During the next few years, several important museums were opened, including the Memorial in Commemoration of Victims of Famine in Ukraine (Kyiv); the Memorial Museum Dedicated to Victims of Occupational Regimes the Prison on Lonts'koho Street in L'viv;[32] and the Memorial Complex Demianiv Laz in Ivano-Frankivsk, a branch of the Stepan Bandera Museum of the Liberation Movement. It is noteworthy that all these museums except the Museum of the Soviet Occupation received national museum status, which emphasizes their defining role in the state memory policy.

Private initiatives in museumification of the Soviet past were also strengthened during Yushchenko's presidency. Two examples are the Soviet School Museum, in Kolochava village, Zakarpattia

---

points. For more detail, see Georgii Kas'ianov, "Istoricheskaia politika i 'memorial'nye' zakony v Ukraine: nachalo XXI veka," *Istoricheskaia ekspertiza* 2 (2016): 28–57.

[32] http://www.lonckoho.lviv.ua/.

oblast, which opened in 2006, and the Museum of the Totalitarian Period or the Amateur Museum of Management Tools and Economic Literature of the Totalitarian Period, which opened in Ternopil in 2009. These museums do not highlight any specific issue such as victims, heroes, or tragic events but offer exhibits on everyday Soviet life.

The nationalist narrative of Yushchenko's memory policy did not contribute to the consolidation of Ukrainian society. On the contrary, it caused greater regionalization and led to a fragmentation of citizens' ideas about the historical past, accompanied by an increased desire on the part of certain groups and individuals to defend their own versions. This was clearly expressed in the commemorative activities of museums in particular. For example, in Luhansk, the Museum to the Victims of the Orange Revolution was opened in 2007,[33] monuments to the victims of the UPA appeared in Simferopol in 2007 and in Luhansk in 2008, and a monument To Those who Died at the Hands of the OUN-UPA Bandits in western Ukraine was erected in Ulanove village, Sumy oblast, in 2008.

Viktor Yanukovych: Revising the Nationalist Narrative (2010–2013)

Viktor Yanukovych's memory policy was the opposite to that of his predecessor. He replaced the director of the Ukrainian Institute of National Remembrance, downgraded the status of the institute from an executive-level policy office to that of a research center, and in different ways attacked the main points of Yushchenko's historical policy. Official rhetoric about the Kruty Heroes changed year by year under Yanukovych. For example, in 2012 the events at Kruty were interpreted as a military mistake and a failure of responsibility on the part of Ukrainian commanders.[34] Yanukovych even changed the assessment of the Holodomor in a direction more compatible

---

33   Iaroslav Hrebeniuk, "U Luhans'ku vidkryly peresuvnii 'Muzei zhertv Pomaranchevoi revolutsii' u desiatiokh 'prymirnykakh,'" *Radio Svoboda*, 20 August 2007, http://www.radiosvoboda.mobi/a/968356.html.
34   See further Svitlana Nabok, "Derzhava i polityka pamiati: Dosvid chotyr'okh prezydentiv Ukrainy," in Shapoval (ed.), *Kul'tura istorychnoi pamiati*, 251–73.

with Russian interests. Speaking before the European Parliament in 2010, he pointed out that he did not consider the Holodomor to be a genocide of Ukrainian people. The Holodomor section on the official presidential website was removed immediately after Yanukovych became president. Before his visit to the United States in 2011, the website section was restored, but without the official assessment of the event as a genocide. The policy with respect to commemorating the OUN-UPA and their leaders came under the most radical revision. The Donetsk regional court declared illegal Yushchenko's decrees bestowing the titles of Heroes of Ukraine on Bandera and Shukhevych, on the grounds that in both cases the awards were made posthumously and that neither recipient was a citizen of Ukraine.

An affinity with the Soviet period became one of the distinctive features of Yanukovych's policy, as described by Yurii Lukanov:

> Speaking on the occasion of the anniversary of the Declaration of State Sovereignty, the president did not mention either Kievan Rus', the Cossack state, or the Ukrainian People's Republic. He noted only one root of independence: the Ukrainian SSR, which is close to him spiritually. On a daily basis the TV shows Yanukovych meeting with subordinates and giving instructions, in picturesque and unsurpassed depth. A kind of modernized Leonid Brezhnev, who wisely pointed out to the people that "the economy should be economical."[35]

Surprisingly, and most likely due to public outcry about earlier policies which did not promote a diverse memory, during Yanukovych's presidency, a number of significant trends started taking shape in the museum sphere. First, several museums dedicated to the liberation movement were opened, both in Kyiv and in other regions. They included the Museum of the Sixties-Generation Dissident Movement, a branch of the Museum of the History of the City of Kyiv, which opened in 2012;[36] the Museum of the Liberation Struggle of Ukraine, a branch of the L'viv Historical Museum, which also

---

[35]   Iurii Lukanov, "Ianukovych pochav nahaduvaty Brezhnieva," *Gazeta.ua*, 17 August 2010, https://gazeta.ua/articles/comments-newspaper/_anukovich-pocha v-nagaduvati-brezhnyeva/350959?mobile=true.

[36]   http://www.kyivhistorymuseum.org/uk/filiyi-muzeyu/muzey-shistedisyatnitstva.

opened in 2012;[37] and the Drohobych Museum Prison at Stryiska, which opened in 2012–2013. Second, museums that detailed Soviet glories underwent renovation, such as the Museum of the History of the Central-Irmino Mine and the Stakhanov Movement in the town of Irmino, Luhansk oblast (created in 1962, it was renovated in 2011).

Third, beginning in the 2010s, the number of private museums dedicated to the Soviet past noticeably increased, consistent with practices associated with the museumification of communism elsewhere in Eastern Europe. In the 1990s–2000s, perceptions of communism were critical and condemnatory, but in the 2010s people began taking greater interest in Soviet everyday life, resulting in more "people's" or "amateur" museums.[38] Among the most striking examples of this turn are the following Ukrainian museums: the Park of the Soviet Period (Frumushika-Nova village, Odesa oblast, 2011); the Military and Patriotic Museum Shampan (Shampan village, Cherkasy oblast, 2011); the Museum of the History of Ukraine of the Soviet Era on a Private Basis (Budyshche village, Cherkasy oblast, 2011); and Time Machines (Dnipro, 2013). Analysis of these private museums shows that they do not operate in relation to Yanukovych's or his predecessor Yushchenko's policies. Rather, they represent the desire of ordinary citizens to remember Soviet history not as a tragedy or a glorious epoch, but in terms of their experience of everyday life.

Petro Poroshenko: Displacement of the Soviet (2014–)

The post-Euromaidan period and Petro Poroshenko's presidency have been marked by the activation of memory policy in a predominantly moderate version of the nationalist narrative, which augurs a displacement of the Soviet legacy. This policy was determined by the annexation of Crimea and the war in eastern Ukraine, as well as by public and institutional initiatives that made the mobilization

---

[37]   http://www.lhm.lviv.ua/ekspozyciyi/muzey_vyzvolnoyi_borotby_ukrayiny.html.

[38]   On the Polish experience of "amateur" museumification, see my article, "Muzei komunizmu." The Russian case is described in Roman Abramov's article in this issue.

principle one of the most prominent in developing mnemonic projects. The Euromaidan, with the toppling of Lenin monuments throughout Ukraine,[39] intensified the problematic perception of the Soviet past and mobilized all mnemonic actors in regulating memory policy. The year 2015 became a turning point in this regard.

Through the passage of crucial reforms, the Ukrainian Institute of National Remembrance enacted changes to its status, policies and staffing, and became the most visible of state mnemonic actors.[40] The institute drafted decommunization laws that were passed by the Ukrainian parliament in April 2015 without public discussion. President Poroshenko then signed these laws into effect on 15 May 2015. They comprise four acts: "On the Condemnation of Communist and National-Socialist (Nazi) totalitarian regimes in Ukraine and a Ban on Propaganda of Their Symbols"; "On Access to Archives of Repressive Agencies of the Communist Totalitarian Regime 1917–1991"; "On the Perpetuation of Victory over Nazism in World War II"; and "On the Legal Status and Honoring the Memory of Fighters for the Independence of Ukraine in the 20th Century." The nature of this legislation, and the fact that it was rushed through without debate prompted criticism in Ukraine and abroad. Among other points, the laws prohibited the use of Soviet symbols and required changes to Soviet-era place names, which amounted to an irreversible decision to bid farewell to the communist past. At the same time, there was no clear indication in the laws of how they were to be implemented, which led to diverse interpretations and misunderstandings. The most disputed issue was the fourth act, which anticipates the honoring of the OUN-UPA, whose ideology during its initial period was influenced by the Nazis. That particular act also complicated relations with Poland and various Jewish communities.

Beginning in 2015, crucial changes were brought into the Ukrainian calendar, commemorative rituals, and toponymy. The

---

[39] See the recent book on the "Leninopad" (the demolition of Lenin monuments): Niels Ackermann, *Looking for Lenin* (London: FUEL Publishing, 2017).
[40] More about the Institute's history can be found in Kas'ianov, "K desiatiletiiu Ukrainskogo instituta natsiona'noi pamiati."

most important of these changes related to Victory Day and the Day of the Defender of the Fatherland. Controversy regarding the perception of World War II and the circumstances of the current war in the Donbas resulted in the decision to institute a hybrid version of World War II commemorations in 2015: henceforth, Ukraine commemorates the end of World War II on 8 May, along with Europe, spurning the crucial Soviet myth of the war as a victorious campaign and the Soviet people as the main winners in the war. On 9 May, the Soviet and post-Soviet holiday, Ukraine now remembers only the soldiers who fought against the Nazi invaders. This is not a celebration of the Soviet victory but a remembrance of the Ukrainian contribution to that victory by soldiers in various military detachments of different countries who fought against Nazi Germany. In 2015, for the first time, the word "Soviet" was pushed aside by the word "Ukrainian" in Ukrainian Victory Day celebrations. This represented a crucial symbolic victory over the Soviet-Russian version of the war and an important step toward constructing a modern Ukrainian identity.

If Victory Day celebrations were marked by an attempt to find a "moderate" national version of commemoration, the Day of the Defender of the Fatherland was radically changed. Petro Poroshenko, speaking on Ukrainian Independence Day in 2014, announced that Ukraine would no longer celebrate the "Soviet" Day of the Defender on 23 February. In its place, he instituted 14 October as the new date for the Day of the Defender of the Fatherland. This date has a symbolic meaning, as it is also the Orthodox day of celebration of the Protection of the Blessed Virgin, as well as the Day of Ukrainian Cossacks. The Verkhovna Rada subsequently made 14 October a national holiday, a move that further highlights the extraordinary status of this day. These changes in the national calendar indicate a break with the Russian militaristic paradigm and are aimed at establishing a continuity in Ukrainian military history.

Reform of the Ukrainian commemorative calendar continued in early 2017, when the Ukrainian Institute of National

Remembrance presented a draft list of new public holidays.[41] This initiative proposes reducing the number of holidays from work while increasing the number of commemorative days. It is aimed at eliminating the Soviet holidays and introducing new principles of commemoration in which the experience of victims takes precedence over valorizing the heroic. The new calendar project has engendered much discussion,[42] especially when it comes to its proposed abolition of two holidays in particular: International Women's Day (8 March), and Labor Day (1 May). Social activists protested this move, pointing out that both holidays had an international history. Later, after heated debate, the Institute presented a new version of the calendar of public holidays, in response to societal demands.[43]

The debate over the new calendar reveals problems of form and content in new mnemonic projects, problems that become even more striking when it comes to changing place names and dealing with Soviet legacy material. Formally changing the names of cities and streets does not necessarily mean bidding farewell to the Soviet legacy if it does not also involve a public discussion: that appears to be the main lesson from the decommunization occurring in Ukraine over the past two years. It is still too early to summarize the long-term results of the decommunization effort, but several observations seem pertinent.

First, the implementation of the laws to change the toponyms was met with little interest from the people, something which may be attributable to delays in this process and the desire of the people to focus on what they considered more important: economic and social problems. Second, it became clear how difficult it was to distinguish the ideologically dangerous meaning of the Soviet from its

---

[41] "Instytut zaproshuye obhovoryty propozytsiyi do novogo kalendaria derzhavnykh sviat," *Ukraiins'kyi Instytut Natsional'noii Pamiati* website, http://www.memory.gov.ua/news/institut-zaproshue-obgovoriti-propozitsii-d o-novogo-kalendarya-derzhavnikh-svyat.

[42] See for example: Roman Mel'nyk, "Novyi kalendar. Pro kil'kist' vykhidnykh, dekomunizatsiyu ta polityku pamiati," *Zaxid.net*, 7 March 2017, https://zaxid. net/noviy_kalendar_n1419860.

[43] http://www.memory.gov.ua/news/institut-pidgotuvav-novu-redaktsiyu-zakon oproektu-pro-svyata.

"historical" value and the artistic content of its artefacts. The most striking example of this problem emerged in a discussion about dismantling a bas-relief in front of the centrally located former Lenin Museum in Kyiv, which currently serves as Ukrainian House, a business and cultural cooperation center.[44] The bas-relief was a monumental piece of embodied Soviet myth in the socialist realism style, supposedly referencing extraordinary Soviet history made by ordinary people. It depicted a hammer and sickle, a five-pointed star, a famous quotation from Lenin ("Study, study, study some more"), the inscription "Aurora," and other symbols related to the Soviet era. On 18 August 2016, in the lead-up to the twenty-fifth anniversary of independence, the director of Ukrainian House decided to dismantle the bas-relief, guided by the decommunization laws which ruled that after the Revolution of Dignity (Euromaidan), Soviet symbols were to disappear from the capital of Ukraine. Many architects and activists fought the decision, arguing that the bas-relief did not pose an ideological threat and that therefore there were no grounds for dismantling it.

Third, current memory games recall the problem of the heroes' canon. Among the sharpest criticisms of the Ukrainian Institute of National Remembrance is the accusation that it disseminates propaganda about the OUN-UPA. This controversy reached its peak with the renaming of two of Kyiv's avenues: Moscow Avenue was renamed Bandera Avenue in 2016 and General Vatutin Avenue was renamed Shukhevych Avenue in 2017. The current year in the Institute's calendar is full of events commemorating seventy-five years of the UPA, as well as the 110th anniversary of Shukhevych's birth. Institute representatives whose research interests primarily focus on the nationalist movement have energetically refuted criticism that they glorify the OUN-UPA. According to Volodymyr Viatrovych, the director of the Institute, among the most commonly used toponyms during decommunization are the names of heroes of the Euromaidan, the Heavenly Hundred, not names associated with the

---

44   "Chomu spyliuiut' barel'efy na ukrains'komu domi?" *Hromadske Radio*, 20 August 2016, https://hromadskeradio.org/programs/rankova-hvylya/chomu-spyly uyut-barelyefy-na-ukrayinskomu-domi.

OUN-UPA.[45] Oleksandr Zinchenko, responding to the critical statements about Ukraine's policy toward the OUN-UPA by Jarosław Kaczyński, leader of the Polish ruling right-wing party, has likewise cited statistics on commemoration events that debunk the allegation that the country is being "Banderized."[46]

The Ukrainian Institute of National Remembrance supports projects related to memorials and museums, and participates in the restructuring of the National Museum of the History of Ukraine in the Second World War and the National Museum Memorial to Holodomor Victims. The institute has also initiated two ambitious projects, the Ukrainian Pantheon of Heroes, which is still under consideration, and the Euromaidan Museum, dedicated to remembrance of the Revolution of Dignity and the Heroes of the Heavenly Hundred, which is currently under construction.

The Institute's museum initiatives are taking place in the context of a significant energization of Ukrainian state museum policy. Almost simultaneously with the approval of the decommunization laws, the Minister of Culture announced plans to create a new museum of communism. On 1 July 2015, Kyiv's city administration also announced the decision to create a new museum of the Soviet occupation.[47]

In 2015, two strategically important museums for collective memory were reframed in significant ways. The Memorial in Commemoration of Victims of Famine was renamed the National Museum Memorial to Holodomor Victims, emphasizing the singular place of the 1932–33 Holodomor in the national narrative as well as launching a renewed attempt to legitimize the Holodomor as genocide. The National Museum of the History of the Great Patriotic War was renamed the National Museum of the History of Ukraine in the

---

[45] Mykhaylo Drapak, Mykyta Pechenyk, Nataliia Ulynets, "Bandera na p'iedestali: Skil'ky naspravdi v Ukraini pamiatnykiv providnyku OUN," *Dyvys.Info*, 15 October 2015, http://dyvys.info/2016/10/15/bandera-na-pyedestali-skilky-naspravdi/.

[46] Oleksandr Zinchenko, "Liknep dlia Kachyns'koho: 'Kul't Bandery' u tsyfrakh. Iak vidmovliatysia vid togo, chogo nema (Infografika)?" *Texty.Org.UA*, 22 February 2017, http://texty.org.ua/pg/article/textynewseditor/read/74638/Liknep_dla_Kac hynskogo_kult_Bandery_u_cyfrah.

[47] The Museum of the Soviet Occupation will be situated in Kyiv; see http://kmr.gov. ua/uk/content/v-kyyevi-zyavytsya-muzey-radyanskoyi-okupaciyi.

Second World War. Such renaming indicates a decisive attempt to separate Ukraine from any notion of a "common" Soviet and post-Soviet history or vision.

More recently, there have been several important developments on the museum front. On 25 January 2017, at a meeting of the Kyiv city administration's Commission on Culture, the National Museum of Russian Art was renamed the National Museum Kyiv Gallery.[48] In June 2017 the Territory of Terror Memorial Museum in L'viv,[49] depicting Nazi and Soviet occupations, opened its doors to the public.[50] Work is underway on a Museum of Monumental Propaganda of the USSR in Kyiv.[51] On 20 March 2017, the Tkuma Institute and the Holocaust Museum convened a meeting of historians, musicologists, multimedia specialists, artists, and designers to discuss ways to renew the diorama *Battle for the Dnieper* and the hall dedicated to World War II in Dmytro Yavornytsky Dnipropetrovsk National Historical Museum. All of these activities exemplify significant shifts in the museum sphere: first, an elimination of the Russian colonial trace in museums' names; second, the creation of museums codifying the Soviet period as one of occupation; and third, a rethinking of the colonial heritage in interpreting the key events of Soviet history, World War II in particular.

In light of the newest trends in constructing the memory of communism, important questions arise about the participation of regional elites and the creation of alternative narratives. On 9 December 2015, at the peak of the decommunization process, an

---

48   http://www.kmrm.com.ua/.
49   http://territoryterror.org.ua/.
50   Kostiantyn Yanchenko, "Newly Opened Lviv Museum of Totalitarian Regimes Welcomes Visitors and Researchers from Abroad," *Euromaidan Express,* 28 June 2017, http://euromaidanpress.com/2017/06/28/lviv-museum-of-totalitarian-regimes-communism-nazism/#arvlbdata. Some of the museum's exhibits are still under construction.
51   The museum was scheduled to open in November 2017, but the project has been delayed. See Volodymyr Kadygrob, "Dekil'ka sliv pro muzei monumental'noi propagandy," *Ukrains'ka Pravda,* 28 June 2017, https://life.pravda.com.ua/columns/2017/06/27/224996/; and "Viatrovich rasskazal, chto na muzei 'monumental'noi propagandy SSSR' net deneg," *strana.ua,* 12 July 2018, https://strana.ua/news/151011-vjatrovich-rasskazal-chto-strojku-muzej-monumentalnoj-propahandy-sssr-ne-finansirujut.html.

exhibition on Soviet everyday life opened at Zaporizhzhia State University. This was a joint initiative of university staff and students with an educational aim. Unexpectedly, some of the mass media reacted critically, accusing the museum creators of engaging in political propaganda. Vladyslav Moroko, director of the Department of Culture, Tourism, Nationalities and Religions of the Zaporizhzhia Regional State Administration and a professional historian, spoke out in support of the exhibition, and also announced plans to hold an exhibition on the Soviet nomenklatura at the Zaporizhzhia Regional Museum. Moroko's position was that such exhibitions could serve as a valuable negative example. He argued that, "People ought to know that the Soviet times were not ideal... The example of these elementary things should show how shoddy everyday existence and life was in Soviet times, how everyone was dressed the same. To carry out a comparative analysis and compare Soviet people's life of the period of 'developed socialism' and the life of 'decaying capitalism,' these exhibitions are needed."[52]

On 1 April 2018, another example of this trend, the museum "Homo Sovieticus," was opened at Mykola Gogol State University in Nizhyn, Chernihiv Region. This museum tells the Soviet history through a narrative about typical home interiors of four social groups—Ukrainian peasants, workers, intelligentsia, and students. This type of narrative helps to interpret the specifics of everyday life under Soviet ideology and reveals how they intertwined with each other. The appearance of this museum is another indication that public interest in Soviet everyday life continues to grow stronger, and this interest is clearly being reflected through the museumification of the Soviet era.

Two *Facebook* groups also reveal an interest in Soviet daily life, "The Virtual Museum of Everyday Life in the USSR"[53] and the

---

[52]   Vladyslav Moroko, "My pryberemo z Zaporizhzhia vsiu radianshchynu," *Ukrinform*, 23 December 2015, http://www.ukrinform.ua/rubric-society/1935040-vladislav-moroko-direktor-departamentu-kulturi-turizmu-natsionalnostey-ta-religiy-zaporizkoji-oda.html.

[53]   See "Virtual'nyy muzey pobutu v sssr," *Facebook* group, https://www.facebook.com/groups/1675346422747375/.

"Museum of the USSR."[54] Their appearance underscores several points. The first is the increasing role of internet resources in practices of remembering. Second, these *Facebook* pages create a space for dialogue, as they are designed to present and discuss different opinions. Third, there is a certain mobilizing of the community to create mnemonic projects. In a *Facebook* entry of 6 February 2016, Yaroslava Muzychenko, a museum expert and an activist participant in the *Facebook group* "Museum of the USSR," wrote:

> We need a museum of the ussr. Not exclusively [about] terror or totalitarianism, but about the most ordinary everyday life museum. Everyday dishes, food packaging, shops, schools, textbooks.... May Day demonstrations, political information, children's newspapers.... Queues to get washing powder and bags hanging from windows instead of nonexistent refrigerators. Dried bread for a black day. Shops for party apparatchiks, apartments for the nomenklatura. The story about the bank deposits "disappearing" from the ussr savings bank. And lots more. How can somebody understand what kind of bondage we left behind without an exhibition like this, made with creativity, with humor, even if it's a virtual [exhibition]?[55]

While at the state level, victimization and heroism are proclaimed as the main narratives about the communist past, and decommunization has become official policy, the appearance of initiatives aimed at the museumification of Soviet everyday life tells a very different story. Clearly, there is a desire to create a multifaceted image of the Soviet past, instead of one that is homogeneous.

Summary

Ukrainian memory politics during the nation's twenty-five years of independence have been ambivalent and controversial, indicating and reflecting problems surrounding state identity creation. During Kravchuk's presidency, the state memory policy was directed toward overcoming the communist legacy, mostly of the Stalinist period. Under Kuchma, the victimization trend remained predominant in

---

54   See "Muzei sssr – i smikh i hrikh," *Facebook* group, https://www.facebook.com /groups/1006368962735889/.
55   See Yaroslava Muzychenko, *Facebook* post, 5 February 2016, https://www.faceb ook.com/yaroslavam/posts/1191109200916634.

museum exhibits, but the prospect of reconciling with the Soviet past also underwent a revival at the same time. Thus, until the Orange Revolution, the selectivity principle in evaluating the Soviet past prevailed. Yushchenko, being a highly committed memory actor, established new state institutions and symbolic sites of memory that were aimed at radically disconnecting from the Soviet legacy. Yanukovych's presidency saw the adaptation of Soviet schemes of state management. Poroshenko's memory policy has been aimed at decommunization in different spheres of life.

Throughout the period of independence, victimhood has remained a key motif in the Ukrainian national narrative. This motif takes a range of symbolic forms, including references to the Stalinist repressions, the Holodomor, the war in Afghanistan, and the Chornobyl disaster. The Ukrainian case is by no means unique in its focus on victimhood—this is a common motif in many national narratives, especially in post-communist Europe. In the context of the ongoing present-day war in the Donbas, the heroic principle has started to play a more prominent role. Here too there are similarities to other post-communist countries, many of which emphasize heroic narratives when commemorating their anti-Soviet movements. However, the Ukrainian case is much more complicated because of ongoing internal and external ideological tensions in regard to the evaluation of the history of the Ukrainian liberation movement.

Ukrainian state museums have instituted victimization and heroism as the main principles in memorialization of the communist past. But over the past twenty-five years, and especially since the second half of the 2000s, museums based on regional and private initiatives have also started to play an active role, modifying the Ukrainian memory regime. These museums include personal collections, tourist sites, and university memory rooms. Despite the diversity of the genre, these initiatives are united by the intention to create an image of Soviet everyday life—that is, instead of introjecting ideologically opposed clichés, to help form moderate perceptions of communism based on personal, lived experience. Individual museums reveal the interests of different generations, and social media groups are extending the variety of mnemonic projects concerned with the communist past; taken together, all these developments serve to contribute to the emergence of a vibrant and multivocal Ukrainian memory regime.

Ukraine's Civil Society after the Euromaidan: Were Any Lessons Learned from the 2004 Orange Revolution?

Kateryna Smagliy

Abstract: *The Euromaidan revolution achieved significant progress with respect to the sustained mobilization and organization of Ukraine's civil society, as well as the formation of alternative political parties, such as the Democratic Alliance. However, three years after the Revolution of Dignity there is a broad consensus that reforms and the democratic transformation process have slowed, while the role of civil activists has decreased in all spheres. This article compares the role of civil society in Ukraine after the 2004 Orange Revolution and after the 2014 Euromaidan and offers a cautionary tale about the risks of a failed revolution, along with some recommendations regarding pitfalls to avoid.*

The vibrancy of civil society is widely held to be a defining strength of Ukraine's democracy. Civic activists have been the main driving force behind the post-Euromaidan reforms, and their collective energy has brought Ukraine to a new level of societal development.[1] Having catalyzed the work of the most committed citizens and volunteers, the Maidan unleashed the enormous potential of Ukrainians to transform their society. After the 2014 Revolution of Dignity, activists across the country rushed to create advocacy groups,

---

[1]   Iryna Solonenko, "Ukrainian Civil Society from the Orange Revolution to Euromaidan: Striving for a New Social Contract," in *OSCE Yearbook 2014*, ed. Institute for Peace Research and Security Policy at the University of Hamburg/IFSH (Baden-Baden, 2015), 219–35; and Oleksandra Matviychuk, "Civil Society in Ukraine," *Razom for Ukraine* (2016), https://razomforukraine.org/policyrep ort/civil-society-in-ukraine/.

establish reform networks, support the army, and provide humanitarian assistance to internally displaced people and other victims of the illegal annexation of Crimea and the war in the Donbas. To paraphrase Alexis de Tocqueville, after the Revolution of Dignity Ukrainians of all ages, all conditions, and all dispositions got busy forming associations.[2]

However, if Ukrainian society now boasts a new layer of democratic paint, the old oligarchic colors are peeking through in places. Three years after Petro Poroshenko assumed the presidency, the consensus is that a New Ukraine remains out of reach.[3] Numerous experts now warn that a counterrevolution is on the horizon and that Ukraine may slide back into authoritarianism.[4] Anti-corruption activists complain about wiretapping, surveillance, searches, smear campaigns, and even death threats.[5] The state authorities increasingly sideline civil society watchdogs from the reform process, volunteers are fatigued, and public frustration and apathy are on the rise. Ukraine is at serious risk of following in its own footsteps by replicating the failure of the 2004–2005 Orange Revolution, when the civic activism that won the day on the Maidan was not followed by revolutionary political changes.

The main question this analysis addresses is how Ukraine ended up in this situation. What happened to the revolutionary

---

2   "Americans of all ages, all conditions, and all dispositions, constantly form associations"; Alexis de Tocqueville, *Democracy in America* (1835), https://www.m arxists.org/reference/archive/de-tocqueville/democracy-america/ch28.htm.

3   "Tretiy rik prezydenta Petra Poroshenka. Ekspertne opytuvannya" (Third Year of President Poroshenko's Presidency, Expert Opinion), survey by the Ilko Kucheriv Democratic Initiatives Foundation, 24 May 2017, http://dif.org.ua/article/tretiy-rik-prezidenta-petra-poroshenka-ekspertne-opituvannya.

4   "Golovakha: Ukraina ukhodit ot sovka, no ne navernyaka k demokratii" (Golovakha: Ukraine Is Leaving the Soviet Pattern Behind, but It Is Not Necessarily Moving towards Democracy), *Bigmir.net*, 29 May 2017, http://news.bigmir.net/ukraine/1079276-Golovaha-Ykraina-yhodit-ot-sovka-no-ne-navernyaka-k-dem okratii-; and Iaroslav Hrytsak, "Sladkaia kontrrevolutsiia" (Sweet Counter-Revolution), *Novoe vremia*, 5 August 2017, https://nv.ua/opinion/grytsak/sladkaja-kontrrevoljutsija-1607641.html.

5   Halyna Korba, "Travlia bortsov s korruptsiei" (Harassment of Anti-Corruption Activists), *Novoe vremia* 27, 28 July 2017, https://magazine.nv.ua/journal/2554-journal-no-27/travlya.html.

drive of its civil society, and is that civil society strong enough to keep the government in check? Or has its impact proved to be short-lived, just as it was after the Orange Revolution? To answer these questions, we will look at the Orange Revolution, which, though it provides a cautionary tale about the risks of a failed revolution, may also provide us with a map of pitfalls to avoid.

What Went Wrong after the Orange Revolution?

The West hailed the Orange Revolution as a triumph of Ukraine's civil society. In 2007 Freedom House assigned Ukraine, for the first time in its history, a rating of "free" in the categories of political rights and civil liberties.[6] The number of officially registered NGOs grew from 40,000 in 2004 to almost 80,000 by 2014,[7] but this leap in activism did not lead to deeper citizen engagement or political transformation. The impact of civic organizations stayed small—just 8–9 percent of them were active and engaged.[8] An October 2011 survey conducted by the Ilko Kucheriv Democratic Initiatives Foundation found that only 5% of citizens participated in the activities of civil society organizations;[9] only 29.9% of Ukrainians could name a single NGO in their town or village; and 85.2% had never participated in any civic activities. On the eve of the Euromaidan, NGO

---

[6] Freedom House, *Freedom in the World 2007*, https://freedomhouse.org/report-types/freedom-world.

[7] Official statistical data from the National State Registry of Ukrainian Enterprises and Organizations are available at http://www.ukrstat.gov.ua. Data as of 1 August 2014. Crimea and Sevastopol are excluded from the statistics. See also "The 2004 NGO Sustainability Index for Central and Eastern Europe and Eurasia," *USAID*, May 2005, http://pdf.usaid.gov/pdf_docs/Pnadd432.pdf.

[8] Liubov Palyvoda and Sofia Golota, *Stan ta dynamika rozvytku neuryadovykh organizatsii v Ukraini: 2002-2010"* (The State and Dynamics of Development of Non-Governmental Organizations of Ukraine, 2002–2010) (Kyiv, Publishing House "Kupol", 2010), 18.

[9] "Chy zmozhe hromadyanske suspilstvo vplynuty na ukrainsku polityku?" (Can Civil Society Influence Ukraine's Politics?), *Ilko Kucheriv Democratic Initiatives Foundation*, 19 October 2011, http://dif.org.ua/article/chi-zmozhe-gromadyans ke-suspilstvo-vplinuti-na-ukrainsku-polituku.

leaders characterized their organizations as "mostly ineffective" in addressing policy issues.[10]

After the Orange Revolution, Ukraine's civil society mistakenly presumed there would be no backsliding into authoritarianism. Activists spent too much time at international training sessions or conferences and not enough time in town hall or village council meetings. NGOs' effectiveness and impact were mostly monitored by Western donors, not by independent supervisory or public advisory boards.

NGOs were reluctant to involve citizens in public deliberations on state policies. A new "NGO-cracy" phenomenon emerged, whereby professional civic leaders used "access to domestic policymakers and Western donors to influence public policy without having a constituency in society."[11] Other civil society weaknesses included lack of transparency in funding and failure to cooperate with one another to create cross-regional networks.

As a result, the revolution remained unfinished. The lack of vigilance and civil society's inability to hold the Yushchenko-Tymoshenko government accountable to citizens gradually led to deep disappointment in the Orange Revolution leaders and then to the victory of Viktor Yanukovych and his revanchist entourage in the 2010 presidential elections.

Civil Society after the Euromaidan: What Went Right?

The mass mobilization mechanism of the Euromaidan differed from the Orange Revolution protests.[12] Whereas in 2004, political parties

---

[10]   "Hromads'kyi sektor i polityka: vzayemodiya, neytralitet chy borot'ba?" (Civil Society Sector and Politics: Cooperation, Neutrality or Confrontation?) survey by the Ilko Kucheriv Democratic Initiatives Foundation, 13 July 2013, http://dif.org.ua/article/gromadskiy-sektor-i-politika-vzaemodiya-neytralitet-chi-borotba.

[11]   Orysia Lutsevych, "How to Finish a Revolution: Civil Society and Democracy in Georgia, Moldova and Ukraine," Briefing Paper (London: Chatham House, 1 January 2013), 17.

[12]   Svitlana Krasynska and Eric Martin, "The Formality of Informal Civil Society: Ukraine's EuroMaidan," *Voluntas* 28 (2017): 420–49; and Kateryna Pishchikova and Olesia Ogryzko, "Civic Awakening: The Impact of Euromaidan on Ukraine's

and civic platforms (such as that of the youth movement Pora) were the key organizational forces behind the protests, in 2013–2014 they were of secondary importance. Only 3.5% of Euromaidan protesters identified themselves as members of civil society, though this figure grew to 8.4% by the end of the Revolution of Dignity.[13] That ordinary citizens and volunteers spontaneously created horizontal networks despite receiving limited assistance and backing from Western-funded NGOs or political parties is of tremendous importance for understanding the prospects for safeguarding Ukraine's democracy.

The scope of innovation and civic engagement was several times higher during the Euromaidan than during the Orange Revolution. The Revolution of Dignity was a real hub of civic innovation, creativity, and social entrepreneurship. Public opinion surveys show that the Euromaidan provided a strong impetus to the growth of civil society in Ukraine, empowering citizens and helping them develop new skills of self-organization and civic management.[14]

In at least four areas, civil society achieved particularly strong results. First and foremost, the Euromaidan led to an *unprecedented growth of nationwide volunteer groups* providing humanitarian support and social assistance. Volunteers became the most trusted group in Ukrainian society (replacing the Church).[15] Although the percentage of Ukrainians involved in volunteer activities grew only slightly, from 10% in 2012 to 13% in 2015, the total number of their donated volunteer hours increased dramatically, from just a few hours per week to several hours per day. More important, 41% of

Politics and Society," Working Paper 124 (Fride, July 2014), http://fride.org/download/WP_124_Civic_awakening.pdf.

[13] "Vid Maidanu taboru do Maidanu sichy: shcho zminylos'" (From the Maidan—the Camp, To the Maidan—the Sich: A Survey on Changes), *Ilko Kucheriv Democratic Initiatives Foundation*, 16 February 2013, http://dif.org.ua/article/vid-maydanu-taboru-do-maydanu-sichi-shcho-zminilosya.

[14] "Maidan i hromadians'ke suspil'stvo: opytuvannya ekspertiv" (Maidan and Civil Society—Expert Opinion Poll), *Ilko Kucheriv Democratic Initiatives Foundation*, 14 February 2015, http://dif.org.ua/article/maydan-i-gromadyanske-suspilstvo-opituvannya-ekspertiv.

[15] "Komu bil'she doviryayut ukraintsi —vladi, hromads'kosti, zmi?" (Who Do Ukrainians Trust Most: The Government, Civil Society, or the Media?), *Ilko Kucheriv Democratic Initiatives Foundation*, 3 August 2015, http://dif.org.ua/artic le/komu-bilshe-doviryayut-ukraintsi-vladi-gromadskosti-zmi.

Ukrainians donated funds, clothing, and food to charities, with the lion's share of all donations (65%) channeled into support for the Ukrainian army.[16]

At one point, civil society became almost irreplaceable in the humanitarian field and indeed emerged as a kind of "alternative government," fulfilling state functions. It was even argued that by taking over the government's responsibilities in the defense, internal security, counterpropaganda, elections, and lustration sectors, civil society organizations saved the Ukrainian state but breached the limits of advocacy, thus creating new challenges for Ukraine's political order.[17]

Civil society's involvement in the post-Euromaidan reform process represents the second visible difference from the Orange Revolution period. The largest and most visible reform network in Ukraine is the Reanimation Package of Reforms (RPR).[18] In 2016–2017 it has been focusing on judicial and anticorruption reforms, decentralization, reform of public administration and law enforcement agencies, changes to the election law, and key economic changes.

The RPR functions as a coordination center for eighty NGOs and twenty-two expert groups that develop, promote, and control the implementation of reforms in various sectors. The RPR aims to consolidate public efforts to reform Ukraine and turn citizens into active participants in the policy-making process. According to Oleksandr Sushko, research director at Kyiv's Institute for Euro-Atlantic Cooperation, this model requires "a deep and sustained public dialogue and more time for consensus-building" so that reforms are "more grounded and comprehensive."[19]

---

[16]   "Postmaidanna blahodiinist' i volonterstvo - 2015," (Post-Maidan Charity and Volunteerism—2015), *Ukrainian Philanthropists Forum*, 9 December 2015, http://www.ufb.org.ua/aboutus/novini-forumu.htm?id=4468.

[17]   Mikhail Minakov, "Changing Civil Society after Maidan," Danyliw Research Seminar on Contemporary Ukraine, 2014, https://www.danyliwseminar.com/mikhailo-minakov.

[18]   See the website http://rpr.org.ua/en/.

[19]   Oleksandr Sushko, "Reforming Ukraine: Policymaking after the Euromaidan," *PONARS Eurasia Policy Memo* 409, December 2015, http://www.ponarseurasia.org/memo/reforming-ukraine-policymaking-after-euromaidan.

Third, *anti-corruption initiatives became much more systemic and institutionalized after the Euromaidan*. Civil society participated in and continuously monitored the process of constructing two major antic-orruption agencies, the National Anti-Corruption Bureau of Ukraine (NABU) and the National Agency for the Prevention of Corruption. The most active anti-corruption NGO in Ukraine is the Anti-Corruption Action Center, co-led by Vitaliy Shabunin and Darya Kalenyuk.[20] Together with their partner organizations in the RPR network, they pushed the government to launch the electronic system for declaring assets. Not only politicians but also civil servants and judges are now obliged to submit electronic declarations.

Anti-corruption NGOs continue monitoring government actions most closely. They prevented the release of State Fiscal Chief Roman Nasirov, a suspect in a corruption case, and the appointment to NABU of Nigel Brown, a controversial Poroshenko loyalist and auditor whose appointment had been intended to restrict the bureau's independence. The system's resistance is strong, but so is the vigor of anti-corruption groups in eradicating graft and fraud.

And fourth, *Euromaidan led to the development of a new type of ideology- and membership-based political party detached from oligarchic funding*. After the Revolution of Dignity, civil society activists failed to create a new political force or organize a joint campaign to win the pre-term 2015 parliamentary elections. Instead, they let established political forces succeed in breaking their unity and co-opt individual Euromaidan activists into separate parliamentary election campaigns. This was a major mistake on the part of Euromaidan leaders, a sign of their immaturity, lack of responsibility, and inability to unite. Soon after the parliamentary elections, however, young politicians realized their mistake and established the interfactional group the EuroOptimists, which currently has twenty-three members.

As of today, there are two leading civil society–based political forces in Ukraine. An initiative called Syla Ludei (Power of the People)[21] was launched in January 2013 by journalists, lawyers, and civil

---

[20]   See the website for the Anti-Corruption Action Center at https://antac.org.ua.
[21]   See the party's website at http://sylalyudey.org.

activists united around the idea of establishing a party with a strong ideology and real members. The party did not run for the Rada in 2015, but some of its members became deputies of local councils. The party's political council is co-led by Yuriy Bova, a democratically elected mayor of Trostyanets, Sumy oblast, and Oleksandr Solontay, the recipient of the National Democratic Institute's 2014 democracy award.

The second party is the Democratic Alliance.[22] Established in 2010, it is led by Vasyl Gatsko, a prominent Euromaidan leader. In the 2015 elections the Democratic Alliance won two seats on the Kyiv municipal council. On 9 July 2016, MPs Serhii Leshchenko, Svitlana Zalishchuk, and Mustafa Nayyem joined forces with the Democratic Alliance, which currently enjoys only a 3 percent approval rating and relies on crowdfunding instead of financial support from the oligarchs. In conjunction with a series of anti-corruption forums that were held across Ukraine in 2016, the Democratic Alliance raised 2 million hryvnia (about $100,000) in small donations. Additionally, the party already has regional branches that it can build on and is making trips to all twenty-four regions of Ukraine, holding public meetings with the goal of reaching young, college-educated voters, small and medium-sized business owners, and the middle class more broadly.

How Did All the Right Things Go So Terribly Wrong?

The high toll of human sacrifices during the Maidan protests makes it hard to believe that Ukraine's authorities could so cynically restore the old regime and fail to deliver on their promises of reform. "I thought that after the killing of one hundred people at the Maidan, after the deaths of thousands of people in the East, Ukraine would never be the same and that politicians would understand the level of responsibility and importance of the moment. But we still

---

[22]   See the party's website at http://dem-alliance.org/.

witness corruption, the schemes and political deals at the highest level," writes *Novoe Vremya* editor Vitaliy Sych.[23]

In many ways Ukraine's political class appears to be much more Machiavellian and astute. It patiently waited for the Euromaidan revolutionary fervor to pass before starting a gradual but persistent encroachment on civil liberties. The recent political developments in Ukraine clearly demonstrate President Poroshenko neutralizing his political opponents before the 2019 presidential elections. The smear campaign against investigative journalists and former Euromaidan leaders Serhii Leshchenko, who was accused of purchasing a 192-square meter apartment worth Hr 7.5 million ($281,000) in Kyiv in August 2016, followed by the harassment of Vitaliy Shabunin, leader of the Anti-Corruption Action Center, then the "garbage wars" with L'viv mayor Andriy Sadovyi, and, finally, the stripping of Ukrainian citizenship from the ex-Georgian president Mikheil Saakashvili, illustrates the most recent attempts to undermine Ukraine's democracy.[24]

In the new political environment Ukraine's civil society must reconsider its role and resolve some negative features of its post-Maidan developments. The rest of this article identifies seven problems in Ukraine's civil society development after the Euromaidan and makes some recommendations with regard to changes that are necessary for civil society to fulfil its role in promoting reforms.

Seven Problems

The first problem of Ukraine's civil society is the lack of unity among its leaders. Immediately after the Euromaidan, Ukraine's civil society was a potent and vigorous force. Its role increased in all sectors, and authorities were forced to reckon with activists' power. At least

---

[23]   Vitaliy Sych, "Tri goda reform: esli korotko, Ia razocharovan" (Three Years of Reforms: In Short, I Am Disappointed,)" *Novoe vremia*, 7 June 2017, http://m.nv.ua/opinion/sych/tri-goda-reform-esli-korotko-ja-razocharovan-12 54874.html.

[24]   Olena Goncharenko, "Activists, Reformers Say They are Facing More Harassment," *Kyiv Post*, 4 August 2017, https://www.pressreader.com/ukraine/kyiv-po st/20170804/281505046304867.

publicly the authorities proclaimed their intention to cooperate with civil society on reforms. This was a window of opportunity for many Euromaidan leaders to enter politics, and many of them rushed to exchange individual social capital for attractive parliamentary or governmental positions.

In a rather egotistical pursuit of their personal agendas, yesterday's NGO leaders opted for an easy solution: in 2015, instead of forming a united political force to run for the Verkhovna Rada, they allowed the country's rich to divide their ranks and co-opt them into different political projects. As a result, Euromaidan activists lost unity and their distinctive civic identity. Their effectiveness as legislators and reformers was severely undermined by their lack of a common political platform.

The newly elected young reformers did realize their mistake and established a interfactional parliamentary group, the EuroOptimists. Yet internal bickering and political rivalry often stood in the way of their ability to act together. It took almost two and a half years for the EuroOptimists to organize their first (and so far only) public presentation of their legislative agenda.[25]

The lack of unity at the highest level of civil leadership is destructive and not conducive to the sector's growth. It is not sufficient to have a few mission-driven leaders and organizations. To win the revolution, Ukraine needs *a mission-driven sector*, and it is the task of Euromaidan activists to reconsider their leadership role in the process, to unite despite all odds and come up with a new platform of reforms.

The second limitation of Ukraine's post-Maidan civil society leaders is their focus on two key areas, anti-corruption and Ukraine's European integration. This focus is too narrow to engage citizens fully. The platform of reforms needs to be much more comprehensive than the current anti-corruption and EU integration rhetoric. The wave of nationwide anti-corruption forums, organized under the leadership of Mikheil Saakashvili and some Euromaidan activists in 2015, did not result in higher party ratings. The most recent

---

[25]   Forum "Eurooptimists. Coming Out Night," *Ukrains'ka Molod'*, 12 July 2017, http://www.ukrmol.kiev.ua/2017/07/coming-out-night.html?m=1.

opinion poll shows that the Democratic Alliance enjoys only a 0.1 percent popularity rating, while Saakashvili's New Forces Movement is favored by a mere 1.4 percent of voters.[26] The prospects of Saakashvili's party are even poorer after on 27 July 2017 Poroshenko decided to strip the ex-Georgian president of his Ukrainian citizenship.

The people of Ukraine know what civil society activists are *against* but are unaware of what they are *for*. Do the activists have a reform plan and a team to implement it effectively? The signing of the EU–Ukraine Association Agreement and adoption of the EU visa liberalization regime are faits accomplis, and these achievements are largely seen as success stories of Poroshenko's presidency. Civil society should go beyond its Eurointegration mantra and offer specific reform proposals that matter to each citizen in the spheres of health care, education, culture, pension, and social security—all areas where the civilian leadership currently has almost nothing to offer.

Third, civil society activists are not vigorous enough in the area of citizen engagement, and their communication with grassroots activists is not systematic. Polling by the International Republican Institute has demonstrated that even the most active civic leaders remain largely unknown to most Ukrainians. Some 81% of Ukrainians do not know who Svitlana Zalishchuk—a former leader of "Chesno" campaign—is; 58% are unfamiliar with the investigative journalist Serhii Leshchenko; and 30% have never heard of the Euromaidan's hero, Mustafa Nayyem.[27] Many EuroOptimists use Facebook to increase visibility, but in a country with low internet penetration, "Facebook democracy" might not be the most efficient instrument for voter mobilization.

Unfortunately, more often than not citizen engagement efforts prove to be short-term and superficial. The civic movement Switch On!, formed last year by MP Hanna Hopko to "shake up the

---

[26] Opinion Poll, "Citizens Attitudes to Political Situation, Elections and Political Parties," *Ilko Kucheriv Democratic Initiatives Foundation*, 27 July 2017, http://dif.org.ua/uploads/pdf/11837777675979e41751cad8.18422987.pdf.

[27] Melinda Haring, "Can Ukraine's New Liberal Party Succeed?" *Atlantic Council*, 17 October 2016, http://www.atlanticcouncil.org/blogs/ukrainealert/can-ukrai ne-s-new-liberal-party-succeed.

power of the oligarchs and Mafia monopolies," is a case in point.[28] After several regional visits and meetings with local activists, the movement disintegrated and turned into a virtual Facebook community.

Fourth, Ukraine's civil society can be reinvigorated as a result of new approaches to Western donor support. It is time to recognize that nourishing elitist NGO groups is damaging for Ukraine's civil society. The point is best illustrated by the RPR, launched in April 2014 as a voluntary horizontal union of reformers but soon transformed—with Western donor support—into a limited-impact, overly bureaucratized reformist monster.

In 2015–2017 the RPR received lavish, multimillion-dollar funding from Ukraine's key donors—USAID, Pact, the Swedish International Development Cooperation Agency (SIDA), the International Renaissance Foundation, the UNDP, and the Delegation of the European Commission. Although the RPR is officially made up of eighty NGOs, the Western funding was mostly channeled through a limited number of NGOs, such as the Center for Democracy and Rule of Law (cedem.org.ua), Centre UA (centreua.org), the Ukrainian Center for Independent Political Research (ucipr.org.ua), and the Institute of World Policy (iwp.org.ua).[29]

The fact that all of RPR's funding is managed by a limited number of "trusted" organizations creates unnecessary tension among RPR members. They would welcome a more competitive grant-making procedure to ensure support is provided based on specific reform ideas and their effective advocacy. The guaranteed flow of Western grants is like a "warm bath" to RPR key stakeholders. With large-dollar commitments to individual grant recipients, donors lose the ability to wield carrots and sticks in the process of encouraging innovation and monitoring impact.

---

[28] Hanna Hopko, "Vkluchaisia" (Switch On), *The Day*, 10 March 2016, http://day.kyiv.ua/uk/blog/polityka/vklyuchaysya; Hanna Hopko's interview with *Hromadske* radio, 30 June 2016, https://hromadskeradio.org/programs/kyiv-donbas/proekt-vklyuchaysya-ce-ne-charivna-palychka-a-vudka-ganna-gopko.

[29] *RPR Annual Report—2015*, http://rpr.org.ua/wp-content/uploads/2016/03/rpr_zvit2015.pdf; *RPR Annual Report—2016*, http://rpr.org.ua/wp-content/uploads/2017/06/rpr-EN-web-light-1.pdf.

Dependent on Western funding, not the support of private Ukrainian citizens, RPR is more focused on producing reports than on citizen participation. RPR's office, opened in 2014 with zero donor funding, looked like a beehive of civic activism. Today the drive is gone, and bureaucracy prevails over innovation. When asked what made him most proud of the network, Artem Mirhorodkyi, chief of RPR's secretariat, responded that he was particularly glad that RPR's reform bulletins were received and read by all foreign embassies and foreign organizations.[30]

Only three years after the Euromaidan, in February 2017, did the RPR finally launch its regional cooperation project in order to establish closer ties with activists on the ground. After organizing eleven regional meetings, RPR's secretariat observed that in many cities it united people who "would otherwise not have communicated with one another"—a clear testament to the weakness of cross-regional ties between Ukraine's NGO representatives.[31]

It is no coincidence that many results-oriented activists are now leaving the RPR network. As Viktor Griza, a former member of RPR's group on cultural reform, told me, "RPR grew into a club of benefit-seekers [vygodopoluchateli]. Many RPR activists use the RPR 'brand' only to boost their personal capital—to meet foreign diplomats, get media opportunities, be invited to international conferences, or win the most prestigious fellowships in the United States. For some, RPR is a ticket to the corridors of power, where they can make friends with government officials or politicians."[32]

Fifth, the progress of Ukraine's civil society is undermined by the dubious relationship of its leaders with the state authorities. As a result of the illegal annexation of Crimea and the war in the East of Ukraine, many activists and public intellectuals think their criticism of the government can automatically undermine Ukraine's international standing and weaken its position vis-à-vis Russia.

---

[30] Author's interview with Artem Mirhorodkyi, 12 October 2016.
[31] Ivan Omelyan, "Druhyi front reformuvanya krainy: pershi pidsumky rozhortannya" (The Second Front of Reforming the Country: First Results), *Reanimation Package of Reforms*, 13 June 2017, http://rpr.org.ua/news/ivan-omelyan-druhyj-front-reformuvannya-krajiny-pershi-pidsumky-rozhortannya/.
[32] Author's interview with Viktor Griza, 25 February 2017.

However, Ukraine's war in the East cannot serve as political cover for its leaders for assaulting activists, silencing investigative journalists, or harassing reformers. One cannot hail Ukraine for protecting European values against Putin's aggression and at the same time fail to acknowledge that Ukraine's political leaders smash these very values at home. The longer civil society turns a blind eye to the government's encroachment on the civic space, the longer it will take to win this space back. So far, civil society has been giving up this space inch by inch.

The National Reform Council (NRC), which originally had four representatives of civil society, is now made up solely of people loyal to President Poroshenko. The most recent additions to the NRC were MP Iryna Lutsenko (the prosecutor general's wife) and Artur Herasymov (the leader of Poroshenko's parliamentary bloc in the Rada). Similarly, at least twenty-two top reformers resigned from government in 2016. The MPs Svitlana Zalishchuk and Mustafa Nayyem were kicked out of Ukraine's parliamentary delegation to the Council of Europe and replaced by a former ally of ex-president Yanukovych, the Ukrainian oligarch of Russian origin, Vadim Novinsky.

Moreover, civic leaders cannot influence President Poroshenko's Civil Society Coordination Council (tellingly, modeled on a similar body established by Viktor Yanukovych in December 2012), although several prominent figures, among them Yevhen Bystrytskyi, director of George Soros's International Renaissance Foundation, serve as its members.[33] To the surprise of few, the council is not led by a representative of civil society leaders, but by a state official: the deputy chief of presidential administration and vice-prime minister for regional development. So far, the council has held only one meeting, of limited effectiveness: it failed to challenge legislation requiring activists of anti-corruption NGOs to file publicly accessible electronic asset declarations as if they were state

---

[33] "Yanukovych Created a Coordination Council for Civil Society Development" [in Ukrainian], *UNIAN*, 26 January 2012, https://economics.unian.ua/other/600021-yanukovich-utvoriv-koordinatsiynu-radu-z-pitan-rozvitku-gromadyanskogo-suspilstva.html.

officials. It issued no critical assessment of Poroshenko's ban of the Russian social networking sites Vkontakte and Odnoklassniki—a decision Reporters Without Borders described as a "disproportionate measure that seriously undermines the Ukrainian people's right to information and freedom of expression."[34] These blows to the nonprofit sector did not force a single member of Poroshenko's Civil Society Coordination Council to publicly condemn the authorities for cracking down on anti-corruption activities, nor have any resigned from the council in protest.

This timidity in breaking with the pro-presidential forces over principles is worrisome. Instead of preserving their independence and holding the government accountable, many of Ukraine's most trusted civic leaders have opted to preserve their relations with the authorities. In the words of Bohdan Maslych, director of the oldest civil society information and support center, GURT, by participating in the state's game of sham reforms, these leaders "turn into backup dancers in the government's starlight ritual dance with the Civil Society Council to demonstrate its pseudo-engagement in the reform process."[35]

Sixth, the patron-client networks between Ukraine's NGO leaders, Western donors, and oligarchs should be shaken up. In many ways the cultural codes of Ukraine's civil society mirror those of the country's power structures: many Kyiv-based NGOs consist of a rather closed network of people who have been friends for a long time, have a long history of cooperating with one another, and have built patron-client networks either with government representatives, or with international donor organizations, or with the oligarchs.

It has been noted that "in 2014 ... oligarchic groups recognized the functionality of civil society organizations and attempted to use them—sometimes through coercion—either to increase their rent

---

[34] "RSF Urges Ukraine to Scrap Ban on Russian Social Media Sites," *Reporters Without Borders*, 23 May 2017, https://rsf.org/en/news/rsf-urges-ukraine-scrap-ban-russian-social-media-sites.

[35] Author's interview with Bohdan Maslych, 3 February 2017.

or to defend their existing power and property."[36] Ihor Kolomoisky, Viktor Pinchuk, and other oligarchs started employing financial, media, and political resources to promote various activists and NGOs, seeing in them a source of potential support and protection for oligarchs' interests. It was an early first warning sign that certain civil society groups could be corrupted and led astray.

International donors also tend to focus their support on a small and select group of reputable NGOs. In 2010, for example, the International Renaissance Foundation awarded 35 percent of its grant funding to twenty-two Ukrainian NGOs,[37] and its tendency to work with "trusted cadres" continued after Euromaidan. When the IRF's Strategic Advisory Groups (SAG) were established in 2015 to support the government's reform efforts with an additional $3 million donation from George Soros, their "experts" were selected with no open competition to find the most suitable candidates. Instead, management of the groups was assigned to members of IRF's supervisory board or to program managers.[38]

Finally, the most critical issue is the inadequate moral caliber of many of Ukraine's civil society leaders. Even those Euromaidan activists who were elected to the Rada after the Revolution of Dignity have not met the high expectations of society. This brings us to the seventh recommendation: Ukraine's civic leaders should reacquire a sense of individual integrity, morality, and ethics. It is disappointing that many Euromaidan activists who had been elected to parliament on the promise of change regularly miss Verkhovna Rada sessions and committee meetings. The actions of many civil society leaders, such as purchasing luxurious apartments or other forms of prestigious property, cause huge outcries in the media and damage

---

[36]   Mikhail Minakov, "Corrupting Civil Society in Post-Maidan Ukraine?" *Carnegie Moscow Center*, 11 April 2015, http://carnegie.ru/commentary/?fa=59749.

[37]   Orysia Lutsevych, "How to Finish a Revolution," p. 16, *International Renaissance Foundation, Annual Report 2010*, http://www.irf.ua/files/ukr/programs/irf/zvit _2010.pdf.

[38]   "Spryiannia reformam v Ukraini. Rozpochynaiut' robotu strategichni doradchi grupy" (Support of Ukraine's Reforms: Strategic Advisory Groups), *International Renaissance Foundation*, 19 June 2014, http://www.irf.ua/allevents/ news/spriyannya_reformam_v_ukraini_rozpochinayut_robotu_strategichni_d oradchi_grupi/.

the public's trust in civil society. Such shortsighted acts of individual civic leaders cast a shadow on the entire NGO sector and make people think there is no better alternative.

To conclude, unless it draws some lessons from the 2004 Orange Revolution, Ukraine's civil society will not be able to move forward with the reform process. The open question of the current ongoing transformation is whether Ukraine's civil society actors will succeed in reestablishing their leadership role in the course of the post-Euromaidan transformations.

Agency in Russia:
The Case for a Maturing Civil Society

Anna Arutunyan

Abstract: This article argues that after nearly two decades of weakness, culminating in the failure of the Bolotnaia protest movement in 2012, Russian civil society has begun exhibiting signs of increasing efficacy and agency. The article analyzes several vectors of civil society growth: institutional strengthening of opposition movements; increased regional outreach and networking; and growing awareness of agency. Progress made along these vectors in the last five years, this article argues, signals the transition from a civil society exhibiting immature tendencies to one in the process of maturing.

Introduction

Since the breakup of the Soviet Union, Russian civil society has presented researchers and journalists tracking it with nearly insurmountable challenges. Ultimately, these challenges come down to two basic questions: does a Russian civil society actually exist yet? And if so, how is it to be defined? What form can civil society take in a country where the government, whether Soviet or tsarist, has traditionally sought to dominate all spheres of life?

If in the context of Western democracies civil society is more or less taken for granted, the very existence of the concept throughout Russian history has constantly been in question. In part this uncertainty is due to the vague nature of the concept itself and the difficulty of defining, measuring, and assessing its role. What is civil society and what is community, is there a difference between the two in the Russian context, and does Russia really have either in the way these forms of social organization are understood in the West? Did the peasant commune in Russia constitute the beginning of civil society, or was this merely community? Did the destruction of the peasant commune, as well as of fledgling nodes of civil society, by the new Soviet government speak more to the weakness of these beginnings or to the catastrophically repressive role of the government? Is the resilience of Russian authoritarianism the result of a weak or nonexistent civil society or is weak civil society the result of authoritarianism?[1]

In light of the complex character of these questions in the Russian context, it is tempting to question whether civil society even exists in Russia. Nevertheless, this article assumes that it does by definition. If we define civil society as the aggregate manifestation of the voluntary, organized communal activity of citizens independent of the government, then the proliferation of various NGOs and political movements since the breakup of the Soviet Union renders this question moot. The real puzzle, then, is to what degree Russian civil society is effective, and how its efficacy should be measured.

The challenge, once again, lies in defining efficacy. That these groups have existed and have been able to draw in thousands of activists, and that their activities have been able to generate mass gatherings and media attention have not per se given them agency and the ability to effect change or made them less vulnerable in the face of an increasingly authoritarian government. This article explores the efficacy of civil society as a whole in two dimensions. The first is the ability of groups and movements to have a positive impact on policy, that is, to influence the government's implementation of their goals through constructive collaboration and dialogue. The second dimension of analysis is the changing perceptions of agency among those involved in civic action, and how those changes spread through the population as a whole. Agency in this case is defined in terms of perception, or the awareness that one's actions can produce political change (though change is not guaranteed).

---

[1]   See Dorothy Atkinson, *The End of the Russian Land Commune 1905–1930* (Stanford, CA: Stanford University Press, 1983), 3-19; and Mark D. Steinberg and Catherine Wanner (eds), *Religion, Morality and Community in Post-Soviet Societies* (Bloomington, IN: Indiana University Press, Press, 2008), 9–13.

In this article I propose that after nearly two decades of low efficacy, culminating in the failure of the Bolotnaia protest movement in 2012, Russian civil society has begun exhibiting signs of increasing efficacy and agency. These signs, I suggest, reflect a civil society that is entering a certain stage of maturity.

The broad definition of civil society as capable of producing the efficacious organization of citizens poses serious challenges for defining and adhering to a statistical methodology. The task of measuring the activities of millions of people and how exactly those activities influence the actions of government is not easily executed using traditional quantitative and theoretical methods. Many factors—political, economic, and psychological, each multiplied by the large number of individuals involved and their varied economic and political interests and motivations—would have to be assessed to formulate a measurement that did justice to the phenomenon. This article does not attempt to develop such a measure. Instead, I outline in broad strokes the changes that are taking place and try to identify emerging signs of efficacy and agency in Russian civil society. The article thus draws on my own reporting over the past decade, which has involved interviews with hundreds of activists, NGO members, and politicians, to explore the paired dimensions of efficacy and agency among contemporary Russian civil society.

Assessments of the Efficacy of Civil Society in Post-Soviet Russia

In the nearly three decades since the fall of the Soviet Union, there have been challenges to defining and assessing the efficacy of Russian civil society. The problems are largely attributable to objective factors rather than to problems in approach: Russian civil society since the fall of the Soviet Union has proven weak at best, nonexistent at worst. Bluntly, there is simply little to assess if civil society is considered to be a community of citizens whose collective activity produces an impact on the social and political environment by serving as a means to effect political change.

The 1990s saw the emergence and proliferation of a great number of NGOs and interest groups, but even then, in the relative political freedom of that period, their effect was limited owing to a number of objective factors. Even in the environment of political freedom, absence of the rule of law, as Peter Rutland has noted, created a "contradiction ... between the rapid appearance of civil society actors and their limited power in practice."[2] This inability to foster and grow agency was common to all the major sectors of civil society: the media, the business community, NGOs, and non-systemic political parties.[3] Although in each case the reasons were slightly different, a common denominator was resurgent vulnerability in the face of either state power or moneyed interests in the absence of the rule of law.

With respect to the media, after the mid-1990s, as the journalist Sarah Oates has observed, "despite initial optimism on the part of Western and some Russian analysts, the Russian mass media ... failed to develop as a tool for the masses. Rather, after a brief period of plurality, they [became] firmly entrenched as a tool for the elites, as in Soviet times."[4] Rather than evolving into a conduit between business, the government, and a budding civil society, the media became an instrument of an oligarchy increasingly finding itself conflated with the state.[5]

The incestuous relationship between the business elite and the power elite has hampered the development of an independent business community that could cohesively lobby for political change. During Vladimir Putin's tenure, political persecution of businessmen has nurtured a culture in which political loyalty and

---

2   Peter Rutland, "Business and Civil Society in Russia," in *Russian Civil Society: A Critical Assessment,* eds. Alfred B. Evans, Jr., Laura A. Henry, and Lisa McIntosh Sundstrom (London: M. E. Sharpe, 2006), 75.

3   The terms systemic and non-systemic opposition usually refer to the symbolic or token nature of the democratic process in Putin's Russia. While Russia has three opposition parties that have a presence in parliament, despite their rhetoric they normally back Putin and the party of power, United Russia. For this reason, they are widely regarded as a systemic, or token, opposition. The non-systemic opposition usually refers to parties or movements that are kept out of the political establishment either through various legal restraints, failure to register them, or a refusal to allow them access to national media.

4   Sarah Oates, "Media, Civil Society, and the Failure of the Fourth Estate in Russia," in *Russian Civil Society,* eds. Evans, Henry, and Sundstrom, 69.

5   Anna Arutunyan, *The Media in Russia* (London: Open University Press, 2009).

personal ties to government figures are paramount to financial success, and those who wish to survive must curb their political views or aspirations.[6]

In the case of NGOs and labor unions, the absence of diversified sources of funding created a vulnerability to government control, on the one hand, and, in the case of over-reliance on foreign funding, separation from local interests on the other. This problem of lack of diverse income sources has been noted by Valerie Sperling in the context of women's organizations in Russia.[7] Much as with the media, and despite sporadic clusters of success, plurality did not necessarily translate into cohesive agency and efficacy, and, on the whole, aside from the most prominent groups, such as the Committee of Soldiers' Mothers, the impact of NGOs and labor groups has been limited.

As a result of these inherent weaknesses, which were already present in the 1990s, the gradual authoritarian pull of Vladimir Putin's regime, in the words of Sperling, "restricted the potential for the institutionalization of civil society, at least in the terms traditionally accepted in political science, namely, as established intermediary organizations that serve as channels to the state but remain uncontrolled by the state."[8]

During Vladimir Putin's incumbency, the problem of evaluating the efficacy and agency of civil society has come up against another difficulty: the only major evidence of its development beyond the proliferation of major civil society categories (whose limitations were evident during the 1990s) was protest activity. The evidence suggests that, paradoxically, protest activity had already increased in Putin's Russia and was continuing to steadily increase before and after the protest wave of 2011–2012. Studies on collective action based on these trends suggested a strengthening of civil society, but in the restrictive environment of Putin's Russia they were actually

---

[6]   David E. Hoffman, *The Oligarchs. Wealth and Power in the New Russia* (New York: Public Affairs, 2003).

[7]   Valerie Sperling, "Women's Organizations: Institutionalized Interest Groups or Vulnerable Dissidents?" in *Russian Civil Society*, eds. Evans, Henry, and Sundstrom, 164–65.

[8]   *Ibid.*, 171.

the opposite: a symptom of a deficit of civil society rather than an indication that one was necessarily emerging.

Both the strengths and the failings of this protest wave have been suggestive of the relative maturity of Russian civil society. One of the most detailed and notable studies of the efficacy of the 2011–2012 protest wave, and specifically its impact on and significance to Russian civil society, is Samuel Greene's 2014 *Moscow in Movement*.[9]

According to Greene's analysis, the very stirrings of civil society in Russia that are the subject of his study were provoked[10] and caused by the increasing interference of the government in the lives of its citizens. At first glance, this is a counterintuitive perspective, for it defies the general assumption that civil society in Russia is weak because it has been repressed by a totalitarian, then authoritarian, state. Greene counters this common understanding with the argument that civil society has in fact been provoked into being and action by the increasingly authoritarian actions of a government and elite alienated from the populace. "The core argument of this book," he writes, "is that political elites, by structuring the political arena, exert a decisive influence on the patterns of collective behavior that make up civil society."[11]

Greene's analysis concedes the impossibility of measuring civil society through the use of traditional methods such as vote counts or the number of NGOs in any given field, focusing instead on close examination of specific movements and what they have been able to achieve. This approach moves away from quantitative assessments of the efficacy of civil society as whole, but it also allows better measurement of agency. This is particularly important in the Russian case, where the study of civil society in general has been constrained by the assumption that civil society exists in the Western sense, as voluntary organizations that have agency. By asking ourselves the meaning of "civil" and "society" and whether these concepts apply to Russia at all, we stumble over not just a

---

9   Samuel A. Greene, *Moscow in Movement* (Palo Alto, CA: Stanford University Press, 2014).
10   *Ibid.*
11   *Ibid.*, 20–21.

definitional problem but the divide in Russia between formal institutions that are measured in the West as civil society—NGOs, state institutions, protest movements—and the "society" on the ground with which they are supposed to interact. In other words, civil society in Russia exists, but there is not much it is capable of achieving. To measure its development, there is little that can be done other than looking, case by case, at the few movements and what they have achieved.

Another approach, focusing on protest movements as the chief way to assess the efficacy of civil society, exposes a paradox. Do the proliferation and the frequency of public protests in Putin's Russia suggest the beginnings of a vibrant civil society, or do they simply expose the absence of more efficient mechanisms for resolving disputes and solving problems independently of the state? Greene brushes up against this question: his extensive interviews with activists and protesters suggest that protests happen because a threshold of despair has been reached.[12] This sense of despair, of a permanent emergency situation and of the protest as a last resort, has been corroborated by my own interviews of activists. When asked why they are doing what they are doing and what they hope to achieve, ·frequent answers are "This is the last straw" and "We don't have any other options"—responses that are also characterized notably by resignation and the belief that their actions will not likely have any result whatsoever. When such protests do have a result—such as the 2009 demonstrations in Pikalyovo, when Putin flew in and ensured that factory workers received their salaries—the success was on the one hand seen as a miracle, but on the other served to reinforce the already internalized belief that only the government, as alienated from society as it is, can solve a community's problems.[13]

Thus the only available methodology forces one to study not the examples of the beginnings of civil society but adaptations to the shortcomings and absence of said society. Serious journalistic

---

[12] *Ibid.*

[13] Anna Arutunyan, *The Putin Mystique: Inside Russia's Power Cult* (Northampton, MA: Olive Branch Press, 2014).

literature is bound by this methodology. And only the emotional, anecdotal approach forces one to throw up one's hands in exasperation and say, "There *is* no Russian society."

These challenges speak not to problems of approach or to the rigor of work such as Greene's but to the peculiarity of the subject matter at hand. If, as Greene demonstrates, political elites have been "decisive" in influencing and driving Russian civil society, then it becomes nearly impossible to evaluate civil society in Russia according to parameters used to evaluate Western civil society: it simply does not conform to widely accepted definitions of civil society, which presume a great degree of independence from the state. While we should avoid slipping into the tempting idea of Russian exceptionalism or path dependency, or, worse, into a dangerously Russophobic notion that Russians are somehow incapable of civil society or democracy, it is worth noting that geographic, historical, cultural, political, and economic proclivities have colluded, over centuries, toward producing atomization, lack of cohesion, and the binary extremes of collectivism and unbridled individualism—all of which, taken together, facilitate a chronic retardation of civil society.[14]

This retardation, however, is not terminal, and does not preclude the development of civil society. Recent developments over the last two years are culminating in what can be termed the maturation of cohesive civil action—the beginnings of collective activity that, as opposed to the pluralism of the 1990s and the desperate, disparate protest activity of the Putin years, are showing, for the first time, signs of real potential institutionalization and leverage. This article focuses on specific examples of groups and movements and what they have been able to achieve in terms of their impact on policy and public perception.

---

[14]   See Anna Arutunyan, "Only Connect: Russia between Individualism and Collectivism," *Wilson Quarterly*, Winter 2016, https://wilsonquarterly.com/quarterly/the-post-obama-world/only-connect-russia-between-individualism-and-collectivism/.

The Decline in Protest Activity after 2012

After a period of some hope during the "regency" of President Dmitry Medvedev and his offers of fledgling liberal reform, and after a robust protest wave in 2011 and 2012 brought out unprecedented demonstrations in Moscow and St. Petersburg, optimism about a developing civil society in modern Russia was dashed with Vladimir Putin's return for a third presidential term. A political reaction, a spate of targeted repressions, and later the isolationism that followed Russia's annexation of Crimea demoralized what was left of the oppositionist "creative" class that had been active during the Bolotnaia movement of 2011–2012.

Activists involved in the protest wave separated into clusters focusing on nonpolitical niche initiatives, from drivers fighting for more transparency on Moscow's roads to charities like those of Dr. Liza Glinka. Commentators mulling over where to channel the activist drive in a politically repressive environment where the opposition had little leverage revived a nineteenth-century movement called "the theory of small action," which focused on promoting local interests rather than fighting the leviathan of the government. Other activists and journalists criticized this approach as useless and even collaborationist.[15]

Others began speaking of "internal emigration,"[16] the Soviet practice of receding into the private sphere in the absence of genuine civic opportunities. Those who had protested on Bolotnaia Square now took to drinking wine in parks refurbished by Moscow mayor Sergei Sobianin and his urbanist culture minister, Sergei Kapkov; collective action became more about street food and concept stores, about book readings in the park rather than about political initiative.[17]

---

[15] Natalia Zotova, "Kats obeshchaet nichego ne delat'," *Novaia gazeta*, 16 March 2012, https://www.novayagazeta.ru/articles/2012/03/16/48826-kats-obeschaet-nichego-ne-delat.

[16] Igor Savel'ev, "Vnutrenniaia emigratsia nachalas'," *Moskovskii komsomolets*, 20 September 2012, http://www.mk.ru/social/2012/09/20/751262-vnutrennyaya-e migratsiya-nachalas.html.

[17] Based on conversations with entrepreneurial protesters, Moscow, 2011–2012.

In sum, however, it is hard to classify this period from 2012 through 2015 as one of civil recession: these clusters of civic initiative that revolved around specific, nonpolitical interests offered opportunity to accumulate and hone civic skills that would be brought to bear in subsequent years. Perhaps a better description for the civic environment that crystallized following Vladimir Putin's return for a third presidential term would be atomized civic activity, representing, on the one hand, an invigoration of activity and on the other, and as has happened before in Russia, the absence of cohesive common goals and the lack of potential to work together to achieve them.

But it is important to note this precursory period in the context of dynamic developments that started roughly in late 2015 and have culminated in recent times in the emergence of the political movement around Alexei Navalny, the beginnings of institutionalized protest activity, and changing opinion polls, all of which suggest that Russian civil society is seeing a dramatic process of maturation that for the first time is happening independently of the government and is showing the potential to bring about cohesive political change.

Protests as Evidence of Immaturity

Past inquiries assessing civil society in Russia focused on two spheres: groups and NGOs, on the one hand, and protest activity on the other. Since the breakup of the Soviet Union, progress in both of these spheres has largely been characterized by pluralism: evidence of a greater number of various NGOs and a greater number of protests was seen as a harbinger of the robust development of civil society. But when the efficacy of these two spheres to wield political agency is analyzed, it seems their pluralism has often hampered their reach. In other words, even as pluralism is a marker of freedom and independence, it can work conversely to hamper cohesion and, in a territory as economically and geographically varied as Russia, to facilitate atomization.

Protest activity in Putin's Russia in terms of numbers of protests and turnout has been on the rise, but this in and of itself has not translated into increased agency for the groups that organize the protests. Their success is still in the hands of a government that alone chooses how to respond to the threat of protests. The persistent organizational limitations of protesters to enact change once they have brought out enough people into the streets thus suggests that while increased protest activity may signal a civil society in flux, it is still, at least in Russia's case, evidence of immaturity in civil society.

The Bolotnaia protests serve as a good example of this immaturity—through no fault, it should be noted, of the organizers and activists, who risked their freedom and their lives to challenge abuses of power by the Kremlin. But the protests did show that, at least as of 2012, a movement in Russia is only as successful as its turnout numbers, and beyond that it has little organizational leverage. A case in point was the short-lived Coordination Council of the Russian Opposition,[18] an elected, nongovernmental body created in the fall of 2012 on the back of the Bolotnaia and Sakharov protests. The council's function was limited to agreeing on demands and organizing demonstrations. It was disbanded just a year later, following a number of internal clashes and failure to agree on policy. Its only instrument of leverage was holding protests and gatherings, according to one of the criticisms against the council.[19] The council was also criticized for being cliquish and insular, representing only the urban creative class.[20] As such, it proved incapable of achieving any constructive change, such as reforms in government policy or helping get several dozen incarcerated political prisoners released after the protests.

Failure to agree on common aims and failure to achieve incremental, constructive goals is in many ways the result of factors beyond the control of the opposition. In the case of the Coordination Council, it is evidence of a crucial pattern in Russian society: atomization, lack of outreach, and, hence, little capability for meaningful

[18]   "Russian Opposition Coordination Council ceases to exist," *TASS*, 21 October 2013, http://tass.com/russianpress/702508.

[19]   *Ibid.*

[20]   Aleksandr Kynev, "Oppozitsiia tusovki," *Gazeta.ru*, 23 October 2012, https://www.gazeta.ru/comments/2012/10/23_x_4821505.shtml.

negotiation with the authorities. This is not surprising: of the forty-five elected members of the council, consisting of opposition leaders and cultural figures, only two, Gennady Gudkov and his son, Dmitry Gudkov, were acting parliamentarians, but even Gennady Gudkov was stripped of his parliamentary mandate[21] on trumped-up fraud charges.

Lack of parliamentary representation and lack of connections to key government officials are among the main limitations of interest groups or opposition movements whose only recourse is street protest. Putin's Kremlin has made consistent efforts to isolate and separate opposition groups to keep them out of parliament. Yet opposition groups themselves have demonstrated tendencies toward isolation, cliquishness, and a distrust of others—a key factor in preventing them from forming coalitions that could help them get into parliament.[22] Echoing similar complaints, one opposition activist close to the council spoke of deep suspicions about collaboration with the authorities, making negotiation or the establishment of any useful rapport with state officials virtually impossible, especially for newer members (opposition members with higher status had the privilege, she said, of dealing with authorities without being labeled Kremlin agents).[23]

This kind of isolation and failure of outreach has hampered both protest movements and NGOs alike in terms of achieving common goals, such as changing policy in a sustainable, institutionalized manner. But the last two years have seen a process by which initiatives have started to combine the old approaches of protesting to force the Kremlin's hand with new approaches more prevalent in the NGO sector: networking, outreach, and the accomplishment of nonpolitical, incremental goals.

---

[21]   Miriam Elder, "Russian Parliament Expels Opposition Deputy on Eve of Rally," *The Guardian* 14 September 2012, https://www.theguardian.com/world/2012/sep/14/russian-parliament-expels-opposition-deputy.

[22]   Anna Arutunyan, "Why More Protests Won't Bring a Russian Colour Revolution," *European Council on Foreign Relations* website, 16 February 2016, http://www.ecfr.eu/article/commentary_why_more_protests_wont_bring_a_russian_colour_revolution5100.

[23]   From a conversation in Moscow in 2012.

To understand the emergence of these new patterns of activism, a distinction needs to be made between civic activism and political activism. While both can coexist, there are important differences between the two in terms of objectives. A labor protest, for instance, seeks specific objectives, such as higher wages; other civic protests seek the implementation or the cancellation of specific laws, such as taxes or reconstruction. Political activism, by contrast, sets as its chief goal either the removal of specific politicians from government or the inclusion of politicians or political parties in government.[24]

In practice, groups that engage in civic activism—that is, groups that aim to avoid politicizing their objectives—have had an easier time achieving their goals, probably because, to a degree, it is often in the local and federal government's interests to appease protestors by giving them wages rather than have mass protests put a dent in political reputation. This has been evident in the post-crisis labor protests, notably in Pikalevo in 2009 and in the protests for better labor laws for miners in Mezhdurechensk following a methane blast there in 2010.[25]

But this appeasement, without institutional agency, that is, the ability to effect change on a direct, local and regional level without the personal intervention of Vladimir Putin, has until recently constituted the limited agency of civic activism. Even less effective has been political activism. The current trends suggest, however, that the combination of political and civic activism is starting to bring about incremental achievements and increased agency.

---

[24] For a discussion on the difference between civic and political activism, see comments by Alexei Kozlov in Polina Aronson, Sergei Tereshenkov, and Alexei Kozlov, "Beyond Bolotnaya: The Future of Russia's Civil Society," *Open Democracy—Russia* website, 22 February 2017, https://www.opendemocracy.net/od-r ussia/aronson-kozlov-tereshenkov/beyond-bolotnaya-future-of-russia-s-civil-s ociety.

[25] While there is still no institutional agency, Putin's government has tended to respond to strikes with a mix of repression and concessions, signaling growing agency for strikers. For the Mezhdurechensk case, see Vladimir Shlapentokh and Anna Arutunyan, *Freedom, Repression and Private Property in Russia* (Cambridge: Cambridge University Press, 2013), 148–55.

New Patterns of Protest and Civic Action

In late 2015, observers reported an uptick in protest activity in terms of the number of protests being held, despite growing government repression, which had started in 2012 as a response to the Bolotnaia protests. But this time the type of protest was different. Rather than anti-government protests with often vague or unattainable political demands, such as the removal of the party of power from politics, these demonstrations focused on labor issues, forwarding specific demands that could become a subject of negotiation with authorities. According to the Center for Social and Labor Rights, the annual number of labor protests has been rising steadily since 2010, despite growing repression and new laws requiring harsher punishment for unsanctioned protest.[26]

While this increase in labor-related protests did not signal, despite some alarm by authorities and observers, any real threat of a successful, Maidan-style popular revolt, it did display evidence of new, more effective patterns of organization. One of the best examples of this new type of protest, which combined wider outreach with the demands for simpler, incremental goals that did not necessarily imply an existential threat to Kremlin rule, was the long-haul truckers' strike in late 2015. Drivers organized to protest a road tax imposed as part of Platon, an electronic toll collection system created in fall 2015 and owned by the son of a Putin-connected oligarch Igor Rotenberg.[27] Beginning in Dagestan, the truckers' protests spread to other regions, reaching Moscow with a road block that

---

[26]   See Stephen Crowley and Irina Olimpieva, "Is Putin about to Face a 'Colored Revolution'?" *Washington Post*, 10 February 2016, https://www.washington post.com/news/monkey-cage/wp/2016/02/10/is-putin-about-to-face-a-colored -revolution/?utm_term=.72176e056a30.

[27]   "Kremlin Claims There Was No String Pulling in Platon System Operator choice," *TASS*, 3 December 2015, http://tass.com/politics/841197

alarmed federal authorities.[28] Within a few months, the strike had spread to forty-three Russian regions[29] and continues to this day.

Two characteristics of the truckers' protest distinguish it from protests and civic action in the past: its nationwide scope and its potential to achieve limited but important results. The Communist Party spoke out in support of the protestors,[30] one of the rare times that any opposition party included in parliament in Putin's Russia has done so, while the government reduced the fines levied on the truckers and offered dialogue. Soon after the protests began in late 2015, the Kremlin lowered the penalties from 450,000 rubles to 5,000 rubles.[31]

This second aspect has been underestimated because most coverage of the protest has focused on repression and the gap between the protestors' demands and the government's concessions: the government never gives protestors everything they want. Yet we can better gauge the protest's effectiveness in achieving its goals by considering the government's constructive response rather than the size of the protest. Government repression—a negative response—is an important indicator of how seriously the Kremlin views the threat of a protest and, by association, how concerned it is about its own hold on power. But that says more about the government than it does about civil society. By contrast, the ability to elicit a positive response, however minimal, speaks to the strength and potential of the civic action itself and the capacity of a community to effectively organize.

---

[28] Roland Oliphant, "Russian Truckers 'March on Moscow' in Biggest Outbreak of Industrial Unrest in Years," *Telegraph*, 30 November 2015, http://www.telegraph.co.uk/news/worldnews/europe/russia/12024221/Russian-truckers-march-on-Moscow-in-biggest-outbreak-of-industrial-unrest-in-years.html.

[29] "Russian Truck Drivers Strike for 10 Days against Platon Tax System," *Moscow Times*, 22 February 2016, https://themoscowtimes.com/articles/russian-truck-drivers-strike-for-10-days-against-platon-tax-system-51905.

[30] "Dal'noboishchiki i KPRF prodolzhaiut protestovat' vmeste," KPRF press release, 12 November 2016, https://kprf.ru/actions/kprf/160127.html.

[31] "Putin snizil shtraf dlia dal'noboishchikov v 90 raz," *Forbes.ru*, 15 December 2015, http://www.forbes.ru/news/308359-putin-snizil-shtrafy-dlya-dalnoboishchikov-v-90-raz.

The Navalny Protests and Emerging Agency

The grassroots presidential campaign of opposition leader Alexei Navalny and the nationwide anti-corruption protests sparked by the work of his Anti-Corruption Foundation (FBK) have emerged as a culmination of previous patterns and trends toward greater independence, outreach, scope, recognition, and, ultimately, agency of civic initiative. Navalny represents one movement and one campaign, but the success of the movement in recent months, against the backdrop of mounting changes in agency, is enough to demonstrate that its existence alone is evidence of a dramatic maturation of Russian civil society in terms of its impact on agency and especially how activists perceive their own agency.

In March 2017, Navalny's FBK released a well-made, widely watched film that exposed thoroughly investigated corruption allegations against Prime Minister Dmitry Medvedev.[32] Weeks later, Navalny's supporters organized a nationwide protest that spanned ninety-nine cities across the country, including major protests in Moscow and St. Petersburg. Then in June his campaign repeated and exceeded the success with another nationwide protest, this time spanning 160 cities and bringing tens of thousands of people into the streets.

In the past, the success of a protest movement or civic initiative was gauged in terms of numbers; this was the leading factor that put the Bolotnaia protests on the map of history. But the numbers of people protesting as part of Navalny's campaign, while significant, are the least important factor in terms of his success and his increasingly dominant role in the development of Russian civil society. His latest efforts signal an important milestone in the development of Russian civil society: the start of institutionalization.

Five aspects of Navalny's campaign demonstrate the beginnings of this institutionalization and the ways in which civic initiative in Russia is breaking with the past.

---

[32]   Anna Arutunyan, "Why Navalny Should Stop Protesting," *Raam op Rusland* website, 17 June 2017, https://www.raamoprusland.nl/dossiers/civil-society/614 -why-navalny-should-stop-protesting.

1. *Scope.* The protests departed from a long tradition of social and regional atomization among the opposition that plagued even Bolotnaia. Up until 2011, anti-Kremlin protests were common but were largely confined to Moscow and St. Petersburg. Regional protests were focused more frequently on specific issues such as labor conditions or wage arrears rather than more broadly on the regime's legitimacy. A spate of Bolotnaia-like protests occurred across Russian cities, but there was a clear sense that it was Moscow's cosmopolitan class leading the day, with all the social and regional divides that implied.

2. *Outreach.* The protests demonstrated a level of organization and networking unprecedented for the Russian opposition. Liberal parties such as PARNAS have attempted regional campaigning in the past, but their latest efforts during the primaries in the spring of 2016 were fraught with internal rivalries and low turnout and support, often because their platforms, still largely attempting to articulate vague ideas about democracy and human rights, failed to resonate with voters in the regions.[33] More important, Navalny's efforts rallied supporters proactively rather than reactively. Earlier demonstrations had responded to an injustice by the regime—Bolotnaia, for instance, was sparked by Putin's decision to return for a third presidential term and more specifically by rigged parliamentary elections. Navalny's FBK managed to rally efforts around something they, rather than the authorities, had done themselves: their video about Medvedev's extravagant assets and its investigation into high-level corruption in Russia. This was not just about abstract ideals, however inspiring, but about a central, structural problem in Russian society that affects each and every citizen in tangible ways, corruption. The main impact of Navalny's film lay in its helping to introduce a new narrative about corruption, namely, that corruption should

---

[33] "Proval praimeriz Parnasa. Tsepochka sobytii," *Meduza* website, 30 May 2016, https://meduza.io/feature/2016/05/30/proval-praymeriz-parnasa-tsepochka-sobytiy.

not be normalized and that something can and should be done about it. This is no small feat in a country where traditionally, opinion polls have pointed up a fatalistic attitude toward corruption as simply a "normal" part of life. Navalny explodes this concept in the video, first by showing Medvedev himself saying that corruption "should not only be illegal, it should be indecent," then by contrasting the poverty of residents in villages near one of Medvedev's secret dachas.

3. *Prioritizing civic objectives* over political ones. By demanding answers on corruption and an investigation into Medvedev's apparently ill-gotten gains, the Navalny protests had a more realistic focus than previous protests demanding Putin's removal, since both the prime minister and the president have vowed to fight corruption.[34] In that respect, these rallies were more like regional demonstrations in which locals demand specific concessions, and sometimes get them. While it is clear that Navalny's aspirations are political, he has also demonstrated a realistic view of the sheer improbability that he can achieve political office in 2018. As a result, while not denying his political objectives, he has shifted his strategy away from protesting and toward focusing on civic goals, such as fighting corruption and building up an institutional base by expanding campaign offices.[35]

Of course, no one expects Putin's Kremlin to hold such an investigation, but there is an understanding among some members of the elites and society, fed by years of speculation that Medvedev is on his way out, that an investigation is at least within the realm of the

---

[34]   "Kremlin Vows Tough Steps to Fight Graft in Russia," *Reuters*, 30 September 2008, https://www.reuters.com/article/us-russia-corruption/kremlin-vows-tough-steps-to-fight-graft-in-russia-idUSTRE48T5X020080930.

[35]   From comments made to the author by Navalny and his campaign manager, Leonid Volkov. In 2012, Navalny told the author he was not focusing on running for a political seat because Russia did not have a legitimate election system. In the spring of 2017, Volkov told the author that Navalny and the Anti-Corruption Foundation were focusing on expanding campaign offices rather than on protesting. Though this constitutes political activity, the focus on bolstering the institutional base—that is, on creating actual campaign offices—speaks as much, if not more, of civic activity.

possible. By contrast, the Bolotnaia protests tried to focus their agenda on free and fair elections, though it was implicit that they were really about preventing Putin's return as president—something that, realistically, was never going to be stopped. By focusing on corruption and not on Putin, Navalny deftly avoided the trap of pitting the 14 percent of the population that does not approve of Putin against the 86 percent that does. While there were chants of "Russia without Putin!" and "Putin is a thief!" at the demonstrations, and though Navalny's anti-Putin stance is well known, that was not what the demonstrations were primarily about. If anything, they targeted Medvedev, who for years now has been touted as being on his way out, a sacrificial lamb for Russia's floundering economy. As such, the protests accomplished something that had not really happened before in Russia's polarized political culture: they opened the door to expressions of dissent by a large cross section of the Russian population that is increasingly concerned with corruption and income inequality but prefers, for now, to remain loyal to Putin's government.[36]

4. *A focus on fundraising and the establishment of campaign offices.* Beginning with his mayoral campaign in 2013, in which Navalny managed to win a surprising 27 percent of the vote despite having no TV coverage, Navalny has rallied thousands of volunteers, raised millions of rubles, and put together a professional, modern, Western-style election campaign practically from scratch. Soon after announcing in late 2016 his bid to run for president in 2018, Navalny managed to raise 15 million rubles in campaign funds and drew pledges from 25,000 people willing to work as volunteers.[37] By August 2017 he had opened seventy-five campaign offices across the country and attracted nearly 150,000 volunteers to his campaign.[38]

---

[36]   Anna Arutunyan, "Russia Protests: This Time It Is Different," *European Council on Foreign Relations* website, 29 March 2017, http://www.ecfr.eu/article/commentary_four_ways_navalnys_protests_go_beyond_bolotnaya_7259.

[37]   Kathrin Hille and Max Seddon, "Putin Opponent Navalny Determined to Run for Presidency of Russia," *Financial Times*, 12 February 2017, https://www.ft.com/content/dc19f9a4-f105-11e6-95ee-f14e55513608.

[38]   According to Navalny's own figures. See https://2018.navalny.com/.

5. *Prioritizing institutions over ideology,* manifested by a focus on institutions and the ability to reach out to political competition. One of the problems that has plagued Russia's non-systemic liberal opposition, whose movements are forced to operate outside the political establishment, is its political atomization and the inability, or in some cases the outright refusal, to cooperate with other non-systemic opposition groups. Part of this, of course, is fueled by ideology, but even where ideological differences are small or nonexistent the opposition is divided by rivalry and ambition. Navalny, by contrast, has taken a big political gamble by holding a debate in July 2017 with Igor Strelkov,[39] the former FSB officer who was one of the leaders of the pro-Russian separatist insurgency in Ukraine and has since returned to Moscow to head a nationalist opposition movement. Navalny's nationalism, while far more moderate than Strelkov's, has drawn criticism from all political spheres. But the points at which his nationalism overlaps with Strelkov's movement are noteworthy: both groups have made judicial independence, rule of law, and free elections prominent in their political manifestos. The merging of nationalist ideology with calls for the rule of law, though sometimes alarming, is also illustrative of the readiness of Russia's political opposition to focus more on institutions than on ideology.[40]

Navalny's movement is currently the most prominent political challenger to the Kremlin, but its significance in terms of civil society should be seen in its ability to combine both civic and political activism. While it may be the largest and most visible movement, it embodies trends of organizing that are visible elsewhere, specifically in civic activism.

---

[39] "Navalny Debates Nationalist Girkin in Attempt to Broaden Appeal," *Financial Times,* 21 July 2017, https://www.ft.com/content/92146b74-6d96-11e7-b9c7-15af748b60d0.

[40] See Anna Arutunyan and Mark Galeotti, "Kovarnye deti Kremlia," *Svoboda.org,* 29 October 2016, https://www.svoboda.org/a/28081207.html.

Increasingly successful protest and organization movement activities have included demonstrations against Moscow's renovation project, which would see about five thousand apartment blocks demolished. Thousands of Moscow residents organized against the measure, culminating in a protest in May 2017. Activists recognized that their efforts made city authorities change the law on renovation and take a number of buildings out of the program, creating an important precedent for civic engagement whereby activists and government negotiate and reach compromises. As one activist characterized the relationship between her initiative and local authorities, "They give us ultimatums, we give them ultimatums."[41] While this by no means reflects the establishment of normal, equal dialogue, the incremental steps achieved should be seen as important milestones in the maturing of Russian civil society.

In this regard, the protests against the demolition program and the truckers' strike share a common denominator: the introduction of a narrative in which a group of people affected by government policy can articulate coherent, cohesive demands and achieve a constructive response from the government to those demands. Not all of the demands can be met, but the very fact that the government is demonstrating an awareness of the interests of these groups speaks to their agency and creates a narrative that they can achieve their goals.

Beyond Putin

Where protest is concerned, one of the key aspects that has emerged both in recent demonstrations such as the truckers' strike and in the movement Navalny has spearheaded is the diminishing role of Putin's government as a focal point, both positive and negative. This tendency, as evidenced by the testimonies of activists, correlates with a growing sense of agency among activists and supporters.

As noted earlier, protests in the past focused on the government in the hope of either forcing concessions (such as labor protests directed at Putin personally) or to demonstrate opposition. In

---

[41] Comment given to the author in July 2017.

other words, agency and power were still placed in the hands of the Kremlin, which was either to concede defeat or to give protestors something. By focusing instead on specific achievable goals rather than on regime change, activists today have opened the way for dialogue and compromise. More important, even opposition movements like Navalny's and Strelkov's concede that the goal is not to overthrow Putin, which is not realistic in the immediate future, but to accumulate structural and organizational know-how to be applied once Putin has left office.[42]

Finally, one of the most prominent indicators of agency in civil society is reflected in opinion polls that demonstrate growing awareness of corruption and the need for non-political, interest-based protest. The share of respondents who named corruption as their top concern went from 24 percent in 2009 to 39 percent in 2013;[43] more important, 58 percent of respondents said they supported anti-corruption protests.[44] This increasing engagement is largely connected to Navalny's efforts, but it also draws on shifting moods that began earlier, with widespread volunteer efforts for a variety of causes from combating forest fires, to supporting the pro-Russian separatist movement in Ukraine.[45]

Informal conversations with activists engaged in Navalny's campaign and protest activities reveal a marked tendency toward greater perceptions of agency. If during the protest movement in 2011–2012 activists, including Navalny himself, spoke of the impossibility of running for president because the election was a

---

[42]   See Arutunyan and Galeotti, "Kovarnye deti Kremlia."

[43]   Opinion poll, *Levada Center*, 3 September 2013, http://www.levada.ru/2013/09/03/problemy-i-trevogi-rossiyan/.

[44]   Opinion poll, *Levada Center*, 13 June 2017, http://www.levada.ru/2017/06/13/akt sii-protesta-12-iyunya/.

[45]   It might sound perverse to mention volunteers fighting beside and aiding separatists in the context of the development of Russian civil society, but for better or worse it is an example of successful organization, even if this organization is ultimately co-opted and weaponized by the Kremlin. On volunteers in Ukraine, see Anna Arutunyan, "Russian Agitators Infiltrate Eastern Ukraine," *USA Today*, 7 April 2014, https://www.usatoday.com/story/news/world/2014/04/07/russia-ukraine/7418719/.

"Coronation,"[46] activists who took part in the protest movement during the summer of 2017 spoke with greater confidence about the possibility of achieving tangible results. In the case of Navalny, who decided to try to run for president in the 2018 election, this increase in confidence can be linked to the cumulative impact his movement's activities have had on the government: in 2013, an investigation by the FBK into Duma deputy Vladimir Pekhtin's undisclosed real estate holdings in Miami led to Pekhtin's resignation.[47] In another incident, one involving Navalny's trial on embezzlement charges in the summer of 2013, a mass protest in Moscow's streets was followed by Navalny's release from prison, while the expected five-year jail sentence was replaced by a suspended sentence in a move widely interpreted as evidence that the Kremlin felt threatened by the protest.[48] Finally, the March 2017 release of an FBK investigation into corruption allegations against Dmitry Medvedev, the protests that ensued, and the relatively harsh government response galvanized Navalny supporters, who increasingly felt that the government was beginning to take them seriously.[49]

Other small but incremental successes have fed a growing sense of agency among the citizens involved. Muscovites, for example, including activists and members of preservationist NGOs who rallied against demolition plans by city authorities in the summer of 2017, spoke of improvements in constructive dialogue with city authorities.[50]

Aside from the precedent of successes, which have the cumulative effect of strengthening the idea that civic actions can have

---

[46] Based on a conversation with Navalny in the winter of 2012.

[47] Howard Amos, "United Russia MP Resigns over Florida Property Allegations," *The Guardian*, 20 February 2013, https://www.theguardian.com/world/2013/feb/20/russia-mp-resigns-florida-property.

[48] See Masha Gessen, "Alexey Navalny's Very Strange Form of Freedom," *New Yorker*, 15 January 2016, https://www.newyorker.com/news/news-desk/alexey-navalnys-very-strange-form-of-freedom.

[49] Based on conversations with Navalny's supporters and demonstrators in the spring and summer of 2017.

[50] Based on conversations with activists and NGO members who pushed back against Moscow city administration moves to demolish and renovate apartment blocks.

positive results, the ever nearer departure of Putin has created a growing awareness among political activists that their current activities are building "know-how" that can be constructively applied in the power vacuum that is likely to emerge in the post-Putin era.[51]

Conclusion

Taken together, these developments paint a picture of a civil society in flux in ways that have not been evident since the breakup of the Soviet Union. While the development of civil society is a continuous process, these latest trends—an increase in scope, rising awareness, the prioritization of civic objectives over political ones, greater outreach and networking, and institutionalization—suggest that important milestones have been reached.

The truckers' protests, preservationists' opposition to the Moscow demolition program, and, most of all, Alexei Navalny's campaign demonstrate the mounting impact of incremental achievements on government policy and Russia's institutional landscape. The protests against the Platon tax and the demolition program won important concessions from both the federal government, in the first case, and the local Moscow government, in the second case, creating an important precedent not just of appeasement, as had been the case before, but of constructive negotiation between civil society and the government. Meanwhile, Navalny's activities have transformed the civic and political space by bringing into being the only grassroots political organization with an institutionalized presence across the country. Most important, as opinion polls have shown, the awareness that this activity can lead to positive change rather than merely repression introduces a new narrative that counters deeply entrenched ideas about passivity and the dangers and uselessness of protest while bolstering positive perceptions of agency.

Though it is not yet possible to speak of a "mature" civil society, it is evident that the events of the last several years signal the

---

[51]   Based on conversations with political activists in nationalist and liberal opposition camps.

transition from a civil society exhibiting immature tendencies to one in the process of maturing. The cumulative impact of civic action and the changing perceptions of agency among activists over the past five years in particular serve as evidence of the dynamic development of civil society.

ABOUT THE CONTRIBUTORS

ANDREY MAKARYCHEV is guest professor at the Johan Skytte Institute of Political Science, University of Tartu. His areas of expertise include EU–Russia studies, the EU–Russia common neighborhood, and regionalism in the post-Soviet space. He teaches courses in "Regime Change in Post-Soviet Countries," "Regionalism and Integration," "International Relations," "Media in Russia," "EU-Russia Relations," and "Critical Approaches to Europe and Russia." He is co-author (with Alexandra Yatsyk) of two books, *Celebrating Borderlands in a Wider Europe: Nations and Identities in Ukraine, Georgia and Estonia* (Nomos, 2016) and *Lotman's Cultural Semiotics and the Political* (Rowman and Littlefield, 2017). His articles have appeared in *Russian Politics, Region: Regional Studies of Russia, Eastern Europe and Central Asia, Ethnopolitics, Geopolitics, Slavic Review, Journal of Contemporary Central and Eastern Europe*, and other academic outlets.

NINA ROZHANOVSKAYA is coordinator and academic liaison in Russia at the Kennan Institute, Wilson Center. She has published on the topic of nuclear nonproliferation and the US–Russian disarmament dialogue, including two chapters in the *Nuclear Nonproliferation Textbook* (in Russian). She holds a Master of Arts degree in Political Science from Central European University and has extensive experience of working on international academic projects.

ROMAN ABRAMOV is Associate Professor, Candidate of Sciences in Theory, History and Methods of Sociology, and Deputy Head of the Department for the Analysis of Social Institutions at the National Research University Higher School of Economics, Moscow; and Senior Researcher at the Institute of Sociology, Russian Academy of Sciences.

ANNA ARUTUNYAN is a Russian–American journalist and writer. She has covered Russian politics and society for over a decade for publications around the world, including *The Moscow News, USA Today, Foreign Policy,* and the *European Council on Foreign Relations.* She is the author of three books on Russia, including *The Putin Mystique* (2014). Most recently she is senior analyst on Russia for International Crisis Group.

MARYNA BESSONOVA (PhD in History) is Associate Professor and Senior Research Fellow at the Institute of World History, National Academy of Sciences of Ukraine (Kyiv). Her fields of scientific interest are anti-Americanism, American Studies, US–Canada relations, and Canadian Studies. Selected articles: *The Mirror Images of the Cold War* (2016); *Anti-Americanism in the Post-Soviet Space: Russian and Ukrainian dimensions* (2015); *The East European Vector of the U.S. Foreign Policy in the Second half of the XX century: The Ukrainian Context* (2013); *The Heritage of the Bipolar System of International Relations: Anti-Americanism in the Post-Soviet Space (Belarus and Russia case)* (2013); *Anti-American Slogans during the Election Campaigns in the Independent Ukraine* (2012).

VALENTYNA KHARKHUN is a Professor with the Ukrainian Literature and Journalism Department, Mykola Gogol State University (Nizhyn, Ukraine). She is the author of 2 books, *Socialist Realist Canon in Ukrainian Literature: Genesis, Evolution, Modification* (2009), and *Volodymyr Vynnychenko's Novel, The Snubnosed Mephisthopheles' Notes: Generics, Semantic Sphere and Imagology* (2011); 6 textbooks; and more than 100 articles. She participated in two Fulbright fellowships (Pennsylvania State University, 2005–2006; Columbia University, 2011–2012); J. Mianovsky and Queen Jadwiga fellowships at Jagellonian University, Poland (2008, 2009); the Ivan Vyhovsky fellowship at Warsaw University, University of Rzeszow and Maria Curie-Skłodowska University (2014–2015); and the George F. Kennan fellowship (Woodrow Wilson Center, Washington, 2016). Her research interests include: the memory of communism in museums; the projection of "sovietness" in the modern world; Soviet-era literature; the socialist realist canon and its reflection in Ukrainian literature; methodologies of literary studies; and Vynnychenko studies. She is currently working on a project entitled *Memory Wars: The Museums of Communism in Central and Eastern Europe*. She lives in Alexandria, Virginia.

OLEKSYI KRYSENKO, PhD (*kandidat nauk*) is Associate Professor at the Department of Political Science, Karazin National University in Kharkiv. From 2003 to 2014 he worked as a researcher of Ukraine–Russia relations in the regional branch of the National Institute for Strategic Studies in Kharkiv. He participated in a series of Regional Seminars for Excellence in Teaching (HESP ReSET) on "European Security and NIS: New Teaching Framework for New Europe" and "The EU as an emerging European security actor: exploring theoretical paradigms," 2006-2013 (Odessa, Ukraine). In 2013 he graduated from the Moscow School for Political Studies. He is the author of more than 50 academic publications on analysis of forms of power and techniques of socio-political control in modern political systems, structures of power and regional political processes in post-Soviet societies, and issues of European security.

NATALIA MOUSSIENKO (PhD) is a Leading Research Fellow at the Modern Art Research Institute of the National Academy of Arts of Ukraine (Kyiv). She is the author of numerous books and articles on art history, cultural diplomacy, cinema, and urbanism, including *Art of Maidan (2016)*, *Kyiv Art Space (2013)*, and *Arts and Politics (2002)*. In 2016 the National Academy of Arts of Ukraine awarded Moussienko a Golden Medal for her achievements in cultural diplomacy. She was also awarded a Fulbright Scholarship to conduct research at the Kennan Institute, Wilson Center, in Washington DC (2011–2012) and a Thesaurus Polonia fellowship to study at the International Cultural Center in Krakow (2017). Moussienko is an initiator and curator of the *Art of Maidan*, a continuing project begun in 2014 to document the explosion of artistic creativity during the Revolution of Dignity in 2013–2014. Central to the project is a book and exhibition that has already been displayed in sixteen locations in Ukraine, the United States, and Europe.

OLEKSANDR V. POTIEKHIN (Dr.Habil, Kyiv National University, 1989) is Principal Research Fellow at the Institute of World History, National Academy of Sciences of Ukraine (Kyiv, Ukraine), project "Non-proliferation of WMD and Nuclear Disarmament of Ukraine," and Professor of International Relations at the Sumy State Pedagogical University. Historian, diplomat and political analyst, he is Advisor to Deputy Secretary of National Security and Defense Council of Ukraine on the US foreign policy and US–Ukrainian relations. His major books and articles are available at nas.academia.edu/oleksandrpotiekhin/papers. His new book, *Chained by One Chain? Military-Political Alliances and European Stability in the 20th-21st Centuries'* (with Yu. Klymenko) is currently in press.

KATERYNA SMAGLIY (Ph.D, CEU Budapest) is a Visiting Fellow at the European Values Think Tank (Prague) and Next Generation Leaders Program Fellow at the McCain Institute (Washington DC). In the past, she served as director of the Kennan Institute's Ukraine office, consultant of the European Endowment for Democracy, program director at the International Renaissance Foundation and political assistant to the U.S. Embassy in Kyiv. Her articles have appeared in *Ukraina Moderna, Kennan Cable, Kyiv Post, Dzerkalo tyzhnia, Agora, Muzeiynyi prostir* and the Atlantic Council blog *Ukraine Alert.*

SERGEY SUKHANKIN is a Fellow at the Jamestown Foundation and an Associate Expert at the International Centre for Policy Studies (Kyiv). His primary areas of scholarly interest comprise Kaliningrad and the Baltic Sea region, Russian information and cyber-security, A2/AD and its interpretation in Russia, and the development of Russian Private Military Companies after the outbreak of the Syrian civil war.

ALEXANDRA YATSYK is Visiting Researcher at the Uppsala Institute for Russian and Eurasian Studies, Sweden. She is an author and editor of works on post-Soviet nation building, sports and cultural mega-events, biopolitics, art, and refugee crisis among those are co-authored books *Lotman's Cultural Semiotics and the Political* (Rowman & Littlefield International, 2017); *Celebrating Borderlands in a Wider Europe: Nation and Identities in Ukraine, Georgia and Estonia* (Nomos, 2016); *Mega-Events in Post-Soviet Eurasia: Shifting Borderlines of Inclusion and Exclusion* (Palgrave Macmillan, 2016); *New and Old Vocabularies of International Relations After the Ukraine Crisis* (Routledge, 2016); and *Boris Nemtsov and Russian Politics: Power and Resistance* (ibidem Verlag, 2018). Her articles have appeared in, among other outlets, *Slavic Military Review, Demokratizatsiya, Problems of Post-Communism, International Spectator, European Urban and Regional Studies, Sport in Society,* and *Nationalities Papers.*

VICTORIA I. ZHURAVLEVA is Professor, Chair of the Department of American Studies at the Russian State University for the Humanities in Moscow. Her field of research interest is American history with a specialization in Russian–American relations and US foreign policy. She is the author *Understanding Russia in the United States: Images and Myths* (2012); and co-author and editor of several volumes on Russian-American relations and American History. She is an Alumna of the Fulbright Program and the Kennan Institute Program.